Mammals of the Great Lakes Region

Mammals
of the Great Lakes Region

WILLIAM HENRY BURT

Ann Arbor Paperbacks
The University of Michigan Press

First edition as an Ann Arbor Paperback 1972
Copyright © by The University of Michigan 1957
All rights reserved
ISBN 0-472-06183-6
Published in the United States of America by
The University of Michigan Press
Manufactured in the United States of America

1991   1990   1989   1988   11   10   9   8

———

Preface

The purpose of the present volume is twofold. First, it summarizes and brings up to date present knowledge of the habits, life histories, economic importance, and distribution of mammals of the Great Lakes region, and makes the information available to the public and to high schools and colleges in their courses in natural history. Second, it is hoped that many of those who use the book will find encouragement for further research on mammals. With these aims in mind, I have tried not only to present what has been learned, but also to indicate many things unknown about the mammalian fauna. The statements throughout are based, insofar as possible, on specimens and field notes in the Museum of Zoology, University of Michigan. When information from this source was lacking, I have utilized the publications of workers outside this institution. The references are assembled at the end of the book.

This volume includes accounts of the Recent mammals now in the wild in the Great Lakes region. Some of these are introductions into the area. The introductions not yet established in the wild, however, are not included. Species formerly found here, but no longer inhabiting any part of the Great Lakes region, although still occurring elsewhere, are listed under Vanished Species.

This is, in fact, a revision of *The Mammals of Michigan,* with species added to include the area surrounding the Great Lakes. In this way, we are treating a natural, not a political, area. Although much of the text and the mammal portraits by Richard Philip Grossenheider appeared in *The Mammals of Michigan,* there has been a rearrangement, and new information has been added. The keys have been rewritten in large part, and the distribution maps are all new. Figures 29, 37, 40, 45, and 48 are new illustrations by staff artist William L. Brudon, Museum of Zoology. Figures 1, 2, 12–28, 30–36, 38, 39, 41–44, 46–47, and 49–54 are by the late staff artist Grace Eager.

The maps with the small mammal sketches were prepared by myself. These sketches have been stylized to help in identification of the group of animals, not of the species. Many of the shrews and voles are similar in appearance. To try to show subtle differences between some of these species with pen drawings would be impossible. If the sketches help the reader to place a mammal as a shrew, a vole, or a member of some other group, they will have served their purpose.

For identification to species, the key should be employed. This necessitates having the mammal in the hand or at very close range. Measurements, except in the keys and formulae, are given both in inches and millimeters; weights in grams and ounces.

On the distribution maps, the shaded land represents the area in which the species shown on a particular map is likely to be found if its proper habitat is present. No kind of mammal is uniformly distributed over the entire area included in its range. Although care has been taken in outlining the geographic ranges, based on present knowledge of each species, some kinds will undoubtedly be found beyond the limits herein designated. These should be reported so that subsequent distribution maps may be more nearly accurate.

In most instances I have not included the subspecies in the scientific Latin name of the animal, which, in our system of classification, normally has three parts: genus, species, and subspecies. The smallest category, the subspecies, is subjective and had best be left to the specialist. For our purposes, then, the species is the unit with which we are concerned. It is well to know that individuals of a population included in a single species may vary in observable characteristics from one geographic area to another. This geographic variation and the variable characteristics are often correlated with environmental differences.

I wish again to express my appreciation to those who helped in one way or other to bring *The Mammals of Michigan*, and thus the present revised volume, to fruition. I am particularly indebted to the late Norman A. Wood and to Lee R. Dice for the many records and notes that they compiled and maintained in the files of the Museum of Zoology. For additional assistance, I should like to express my sincere appreciation to Philip M. Blossom, Richard H. Manville, William P. Harris, Jr., Emmet T. Hooper, Robert T. Hatt, Frederick M. Gaige, Richard P. Grossenheider, the late Miss Grace Eager, members of the Game Division, Michigan Department of Conservation, and many of my graduate students. In the preparation of the present volume my thanks go to Lee D. Beatty, who made a special effort to furnish records from some of the islands in northern Lake Huron, and to William L. Brudon, who prepared some of the illustrations as well as the base map on which the ranges are outlined.

WILLIAM HENRY BURT

Contents

Introduction   3
    Faunal Position of the Great Lakes Region   3
    Changes in the Mammalian Fauna   4
    Economic Importance of Mammals   6
    Adaptive Radiation (Divergence)   9
    Home Ranges and Territories   15
    Populations   18
The Mammals of the Great Lakes Region   22
    Subclass Theria   23
    Infraclass Metatheria   23
    Pouched Mammals (Order Marsupialia)   24
    Opossum *Didelphis marsupialis*   24
    Infraclass Eutheria   26
    Moles and Shrews (Order Insectivora)   26
    Moles (Family Talpidae)   26
    Eastern Mole *Scalopus aquaticus*   26
    Hairytail Mole *Parascalops breweri*   28
    Starnose Mole *Condylura cristata*   30
    Shrews (Family Soricidae)   32

Masked Shrew *Sorex cinereus*   32
Smoky Shrew *Sorex fumeus*   34
Arctic Shrew *Sorex arcticus*   35
Southeastern Shrew *Sorex longirostris*   36
Longtail Shrew *Sorex dispar*   38
Northern Water Shrew *Sorex palustris*   38
Pigmy Shrew *Microsorex hoyi*   39
Least Shrew *Cryptotis parva*   40
Shorttail Shrew *Blarina brevicauda*   42
Bats (Order Chiroptera)   43
Plainnose Bats (Family Vespertilionidae)   44
Little Brown Myotis *Myotis lucifugus*   44
Indiana Myotis *Myotis sodalis*   45
Keen Myotis *Myotis keeni*   46
Small-footed Myotis *Myotis subulatus*   47
Silver-haired Bat *Lasionycteris noctivagans*   48
Eastern Pipistrel *Pipistrellus subflavus*   49
Big Brown Bat *Eptesicus fuscus*   50
Evening Bat *Nycticeius humeralis*   52
Red Bat *Lasiurus borealis*   53
Hoary Bat *Lasiurus cinereus*   55
Flesh Eaters (Order Carnivora)   56
Bears (Family Ursidae)   56
Black Bear *Ursus americanus*   56
Raccoons (Family Procyonidae)   58
Raccoon *Procyon lotor*   58
Weasel-like Mammals (Family Mustelidae)   60
Marten *Martes americana*   60
Fisher *Martes pennanti*   62
Shorttail Weasel *Mustela erminea*   63
Longtail Weasel *Mustela frenata*   65
Least Weasel *Mustela rixosa*   66
Mink *Mustela vison*   68
River Otter *Lutra canadensis*   70
Badger *Taxidea taxus*   71
Spotted Skunk *Spilogale putorius*   73
Striped Skunk *Mephitis mephitis*   74
Dogs, Foxes, and Wolves (Family Canidae)   76
Red Fox *Vulpes fulva*   77
Gray Fox *Urocyon cinereoargenteus*   79
Coyote *Canis latrans*   80

Gray Wolf *Canis lupus*   82
Cats (Family Felidae)   84
Lynx *Lynx canadensis*   84
Bobcat *Lynx rufus*   86
Gnawing Mammals (Order Rodentia)   87
Squirrels (Family Sciuridae)   88
Woodchuck *Marmota monax*   88
Thirteen-lined Ground Squirrel *Citellus tridecemlineatus*   90
Franklin Ground Squirrel *Citellus franklini*   93
Least Chipmunk *Eutamias minimus*   94
Eastern Chipmunk *Tamias striatus*   96
Red Squirrel *Tamiasciurus hudsonicus*   98
Eastern Gray Squirrel (Black Squirrel) *Sciurus carolinensis*   100
Eastern Fox Squirrel *Sciurus niger*   102
Southern Flying Squirrel *Glaucomys volans*   104
Northern Flying Squirrel *Glaucomys sabrinus*   106
Pocket Gophers (Family Geomyidae)   106
Plains Pocket Gopher *Geomys bursarius*   106
Beavers (Family Castoridae)   109
Beaver *Castor canadensis*   109
Mice and Rats (Family Cricetidae)   111
Western Harvest Mouse *Reithrodontomys megalotis*   112
Deer Mouse *Peromyscus maniculatus*   113
White-footed Mouse *Peromyscus leucopus*   117
Eastern Woodrat *Neotoma magister*   119
Southern Bog Lemming *Synaptomys cooperi*   120
Heather Vole *Phenacomys intermedius*   121
Boreal Redback Vole *Clethrionomys gapperi*   123
Meadow Vole *Microtus pennsylvanicus*   124
Yellownose Vole *Microtus chrotorrhinus*   127
Prairie Vole *Pedomys ochrogaster*   128
Pine Vole *Pitymys pinetorum*   130
Muskrat *Ondatra zibethica*   132
Old World Rats and Mice (Family Muridae)   133
Norway Rat *Rattus norvegicus*   134
House Mouse *Mus musculus*   135
Jumping Mice (Family Zapodidae)   136
Meadow Jumping Mouse *Zapus hudsonius*   136
Woodland Jumping Mouse *Napaeozapus insignis*   138
Porcupines (Family Erethizontidae)   139

Porcupine *Erethizon dorsatum* 139
Hares, Rabbits, and Pikas (Order Lagomorpha) 141
Hares and Rabbits (Family Leporidae) 141
Snowshoe Hare *Lepus americanus* 142
European Hare *Lepus europaeus* 144
Eastern Cottontail *Sylvilagus floridanus* 145
New England Cottontail *Sylvilagus transitionalis* 148
Cows, Bison, Deer (Order Artiodactyla) 149
Deer (Family Cervidae) 149
Elk *Cervus canadensis* 149
Whitetail Deer *Odocoileus virginianus* 151
Moose *Alces alces* 153
Woodland Caribou *Rangifer caribou* 155
Vanished Species 156
Collecting and Preparing Specimens 160
Equipment 160
Collecting Mammals 161
Habitats of Representative Species 165
Preparation of Specimens 165
Classification of the Mammals of the World 179
Artificial Key to Mammals of the Great Lakes Region 185
Key to Skins Only or Animals in the Flesh 186
Key to Skulls Only 196
Glossary of Terms Used in Keys 215
Dental Formulae of Mammals of the Great Lakes Region 219
Summary of Measurements (in mm.) and Life History Data 222
References 226
Index 237

Illustrations

Figures in the Text

1. Adaptive radiation in the teeth and in the feet and limbs 13
2. Home ranges, territories, neutral areas, and unoccupied areas in a quadrat for a given species of mammal 15
3. Starnose mole 31
4. Least shrew 41
5. Big brown bat 51
6. Least weasel 66
7. Mink 69
8. Gray wolf 82
9. Least chipmunk 95
10. Prairie vole 129
11. Bison 158
12. Specimen label 167
13. Proper method of measuring mammals 167
14. First stages in skinning a mammal 170
15. Last stages in skinning a mammal 171
16. (*a*) Prepared cotton body and leg and tail wires, ready for insertion, (*b*) wrapping wire for tail 173

17. Inserting: (a) cotton body into skin, (b) leg wire, (c) tail wire ... 174
18. (a) Sewing opening in belly of skin, (b) finished skin pinned to board ... 176
19. Skull with attached label ... 177
20. Front foot of a mole (Scalopus) ... 187
21. Hind foot of the water shrew (Sorex palustris) ... 187
22. Ear of a bat (Myotis) ... 189
23. Interfemoral membrane and calcar of a bat ... 189
24. Ear of an evening bat ... 189
25. Labeled parts of skulls of the gray fox and of the beaver ... 197
26. Open orbit of a wolf skull ... 198
27. Rostrum of an opossum skull, showing expanded nasals ... 198
28. Closed orbit of a deer skull ... 198
29. Rostra of shrews showing unicuspids ... 201
30. Palatal view of the teeth of a bat (Lasiurus) ... 203
31. Rostrum of a marten (Martes) ... 203
32. Rostrum of a river otter (Lutra) ... 203
33. (a) Red fox: lobed upper incisors; (b) gray fox: upper incisors without lobes ... 205
34. (a) Red fox: mandible without notch; (b) gray fox: mandible with notch on lower border ... 205
35. Basicranium of a lynx: separate foramina ... 206
36. Basicranium of a bobcat: confluent foramina ... 206
37. Arrangement of zygomatic plate: (a) vertical plate, deer mouse (Peromyscus); (b) horizontal plate, jumping mouse (Zapus) ... 207
38. The relationships of the zygomatic arch and the molar teeth in the ground squirrel ... 208
39. The relationships of the zygomatic arch and the molar teeth in the flying squirrel ... 208
40. Pocket gopher (Geomys), showing grooved upper incisors and external cheek pouches ... 208
41. Longitudinally grooved upper incisors of a lemming (Synaptomys) ... 208
42. Ungrooved upper incisors of a vole (Microtus) ... 210
43. Redback vole (Clethrionomys): shelflike posterior border of the palate ... 210
44. Vole (Microtus): central support of the posterior border of the palate ... 210
45. Enamel patterns of the upper cheek teeth of microtines ... 210

46. The zygomatic plate and the infraorbital foramen, as seen from the side, in the white-footed mouse (*Peromyscus leucopus*)   211

47. The zygomatic plate and the infraorbital foramen, as seen from the side, in the woodland and deer mouse (*Peromyscus maniculatus gracilis*)   211

48. Top view of skulls of hares and rabbits   212

49. Cervidae: the lachrymal bone not connected with the nasal   213

50. Bovidae: the lachrymal bone connected with the nasal   213

51. Elk (*Cervus*): posterior narial cavity not separated by the median vomer   214

52. Deer (*Odocoileus*): posterior narial cavity separated by the median vomer   214

53. Bison: branch of the premaxillary bone not extended to the nasal   215

54. Cow: branch of the premaxillary bone extended to the nasal   215

Mammals of the Great Lakes Region

Introduction

FAUNAL POSITION OF THE GREAT LAKES REGION

LIMITS OF DISTRIBUTION–Seventy-four endemic species of wild mammals are now living in what is here considered the Great Lakes region. The elk, which has been re-established, the European hare, the Norway rat, and the house mouse are not considered as endemics. Of the complement of full species, as now recognized, twenty-eight range throughout the area. Of the remaining forty-six species, slightly more than one-third (seventeen) are southern forms with the northern limits of their ranges in the area. Sixteen are northern with the southern limits in the area, eight find their eastern limits and five their western limits here. It is, thus, a transition area, especially from north to south. Barriers to distribution seem to be (1) the Great Lakes for some species, and (2) ecological conditions for most of them. Northern (boreal) species do not normally penetrate southward beyond the limits of the coniferous forest nor do the southern species normally extend northward beyond the limits of the deciduous forest area. The northern species are more definitely limited on the south than are the southern species on the north. This may be attributed in part to disturbance of habitats by man (see below).

FAUNAL RELATIONSHIPS–From the point of view of relationships, rather than limits of distribution, the mammalian fauna has a similar, but slightly different aspect from that above: some species range throughout the area, but show relationships with the faunas to the north, south, east, or west. When we break the fauna down into categories we find that fifteen species are so wide ranging that it is impossible to assign regional affinities to them. Of the remaining fifty-nine species, twenty (about one-third) are chiefly northern (boreal). These are primarily mammals of the coniferous forests, swamps, and bogs. About one-fourth (fifteen species) are present only in southeastern North America and are mammals of the deciduous forests and semiopen country. The remaining twenty-four species comprise five small groups (two to seven species in each group) with their affinities to the east, northeast, west, southwest, and south. It is evident that the mammalian fauna of the Great Lakes region, as now constituted, is weighted toward a boreal type with a strong southeastern influence.

CHANGES IN THE MAMMALIAN FAUNA

Changes in nature have been taking place since the beginning of geologic time. Faunas and floras are never static. The mammalian fauna of the Great Lakes region is no exception to this rule. The prehistoric mammals were different from those of today, and the mammal fauna a century hence will differ from that of the present. Through fossil evidence it is known that elephants and mastodons, giant beavers, southern peccaries, and northern musk oxen roamed over parts of the area in the distant past. There is, as yet, little evidence of what the smaller beasts were like, but surely they, too, differed in many respects from the present mammals. Even within historic times a marked change has been witnessed in the composition of the mammalian complex. Much of this change has resulted directly from man's activities. The wholesale cutting of forests, draining of swamps, and plowing of land have destroyed or altered many of the original habitats and created new ones. Some kinds of mammals are restricted to certain types of habitats (marten and fisher to large forests, for example), and when these habitats are removed the mammals go with them. On the other hand, if one type of habitat is destroyed another is created, and animals adapted to the new habitat may be expected to occupy it and flourish. Thus, one complex is replaced by another.

Some of the more obvious changes in the mammalian fauna within historic times may be listed. Certainly, there were many others of which there is no record. Several mammals, mostly large or conspicuous kinds, have disappeared entirely, or in part. The wolverine, cougar, bison, and elk are probably gone. The elk has been introduced and re-established in a few places, but the original herd is no longer here. The gray wolf, lynx, and moose are now restricted to the wilder, northern part of the area. Members of this group of animals, valued for fur or meat, have been the victims not only of changed habitats, but of the trap and gun.

Other mammals still abundant in the northern parts of the area have disappeared from the southern farming districts. Their geographic ranges have been restricted by man's activities. Some were nearly extirpated at one time, but wise conservation methods have brought them nearly to their former numbers. The black bear, river otter, beaver, and bobcat have given ground to agricultural interests, hunting, and trapping. The porcupine and snowshoe hare have been victims chiefly of depleted habitats in the southern part of the area, but the gun also played a part.

With the clearing of the land an open type of habitat was created. Inasmuch as animals usually occupy all of the available habitat suitable to them, unless barriers intervene, it was to be expected that certain species would follow the clearings northward and thereby increase their respective ranges. At least five species, the opossum, eastern mole, striped ground squirrel, prairie deer mouse, and cottontail (possibly a sixth, the fox squirrel), are known to have done this.

Some mammals have maintained approximately their original ranges, but are more or less numerous depending on whether or not their habitats have become more or less favorable. The opossum undoubtedly has increased in abundance. It was considered rare in the area until about 1900; now it is one of the commonest of the larger mammals in the southern section. The gray squirrel and woodchuck, although still present in all parts of the area, are fewer in much of it —the gray squirrel because of the restricted woodland habitat, and the woodchuck because of the constant vigilance of the farmer with his twenty-two-caliber rifle.

Thus, the mammalian fauna is ever changing in its general aspect. Some mammals are increasing their ranges, others are decreasing them—some are becoming more abundant, others are becoming scarce—familiar species disappear entirely, and new elements come in. This has been going on for untold centuries. It is one of the laws of nature, and man can do little except to speed up or slow down the process by his own activities.

ECONOMIC IMPORTANCE OF MAMMALS

Wild mammals played an extremely important role in the history of the area. Before the white man came, the Indian depended to a large extent on mammals for food, clothing, and shelter. Trappers, exploring the wilderness for fur resources, were among the first white men to penetrate the extensive forests. The fur trade was "big business" in the early days. Close on the heels of the trappers were the lumbermen, and with them came the hunters of game for the markets. Men are still living who remember, and possibly participated in, market hunting of deer and other wild animals. Unchecked hunting and trapping by the white man with modern equipment could not last long. Soon the supply of deer and of beaver, the chief fur animal, was nearly exhausted. Few realize that wild animals, like domesticated stock, may be cropped, but that it is essential to leave a supply of breeding animals to maintain the herd. Nature is not inexhaustible. Fortunately, some of the hunted animals escaped destruction, and wise legislation put a stop to the slaughter. The deer herd and the beaver were repopulated under man's protection. Such a good job was done that now there are too many deer for the available browse over much of the area. But, remembering the past, we are reluctant to harvest the crop. The "buck law" is a good thing when deer are scarce, but it can work to the disadvantage of the herd when the population reaches the carrying capacity of the range.

Not all wild animals are considered to be of positive value. It is difficult to determine with accuracy which animal species are beneficial and which are harmful from the human point of view. Not enough is known about any kind of mammal to enable one to make a definite, detailed statement of its economic status. All that can be done is to generalize from small scattered items on specific phases of the animal's activities. There is no general agreement as to the value of some kinds of mammals because the standards of evaluation vary. The beaver may be vigorously defended by the trapper and the recreationist, and it may be condemned with equal vigor by the fisherman and the forester. The coyote may be defended by the grain farmer, who sees the possibility of crop destruction by rodents, or by the nature enthusiast, who wishes to see the native fauna preserved, but a sheep raiser would not be sympathetic to the plight of the coyote after one had destroyed a sheep. The best anyone can do is to make an impartial attempt to balance values. A mammal may be harmful at one time or at one locality and beneficial at another.

In most of the area two predators, the wolf and coyote, have been condemned, with the offer of a bounty. The wolf is decreasing in numbers and without doubt will be exterminated in the near future, except in the wild parts of Canada, unless some action is taken to save it.

The large, conspicuous animals naturally receive more attention than do the small rodents that are seldom seen. One house mouse or meadow vole will eat an insignificant amount of grain, but if that amount is multiplied by tens of thousands it represents a serious loss. The work of these rodents goes on unnoticed in the dark recesses of a granary or inside a shock of unhusked corn. It is estimated that meadow voles, if present, may destroy at least one-half of the corn left in the shock over winter. This loss can be avoided by husking in the autumn. The house mouse does most of its destructive work in and around buildings. The wise farmer will keep these pests at a minimum by the constant use of snap traps. Most of the many estimates of the damage done to crops by small rodents run into astronomical figures and are little more than pure guesses. There is no doubt, however, that many small rodents do considerable damage locally. Inasmuch as they reproduce rapidly under favorable conditions, it is futile, in most instances, to attempt to destroy them with poisoned baits or by mechanical means. The best and simplest control is to destroy their habitat in the immediate area of anticipated destruction. For mice and voles, an orchard with a heavy growth of grass and weeds is an ideal spot in which to winter. Under a protective cover of grass and snow they go about their destructive activities of girdling trees. If the ground cover in and immediately surrounding an orchard is destroyed in the autumn, the danger from these rodents will be eliminated or reduced to a minimum. Except in years of extreme abundance, voles do not customarily live where there is no ground cover.

The Norway rat is probably the most destructive mammal we have. A native of Europe, it "hitchhiked" into this country and has been able to adapt itself to conditions surrounding human habitations, where it flourishes. It is most destructive around farm buildings and warehouses in which foodstuffs are stored. Crops in the field, poultry, and wild game birds all suffer from the depredations of this uncouth creature. It destroys property by gnawing and burrowing about buildings, and it is a potential carrier of disease. It has been estimated that this undesirable pest costs each person about two dollars a year.

The farmer whose premises are harboring rats loses from thirty to eighty dollars a year through their depredations.

The economic importance of wild mammals is fairly obvious from the preceding discussion, but there are also less tangible aspects of wild mammal values. The tourist business is one of the most important sources of income for the residents of the Great Lakes region. The tourist is thrilled to see in the wild a moose, deer, bear, otter, bobcat, beaver, or porcupine. The colorful little chipmunks and graceful tree squirrels playing about camp are continual sources of enjoyment.

I recall driving slowly down the winding road in Wilderness State Park, Michigan, about ten o'clock one night looking for a place to camp. I came upon a group of people with flashlights and stopped to see what was going on. Raccoons had been coming to the camp each evening, and, as on previous nights, the campers had placed food (their last can of beans) and water on the table. An old "coon" was helping himself to the food, and other "coons" were coming from all directions. The beam from a flashlight picked up the eye shine of the animals some distance from the camp site. There were not only raccoons present, but also deer. The campers said that on the previous night a couple of skunks were at their table. As we stood there with flashlights in hand, a shadow silently passed in front of me. I thought it was a bat, but, presently, from the corner of my eye I caught a glimpse of another shadow. Following it with my flashlight I discovered a flying squirrel that had landed on the trunk of a near-by oak. Our attention was diverted from the raccoon feeding on beans to the oak tree. More flying squirrels came to the rendezvous in the oak. One squirrel mistook a tourist for a tree stump and landed just above his belt. These people had never observed flying squirrels before and were thrilled to see them come out of the void, silently land on the tree trunk, and climb nimbly up into the branches, where they sat eating acorns. I left after about two hours, but the campers were still watching the animals. These people would almost surely return to this spot in other years. Moreover, they probably spread the news to their friends, who, in turn, may be drawn to the same spot. This is most effective advertising for tourists. The animals are an asset, but one which cannot readily be translated into dollars and cents.

Small mammals undoubtedly have a profound effect on soils and vegetation. Burrowing animals are nature's tillers of the soil. They continually bring subsoil to the surface, open subterranean passages through which air and water can penetrate, and fertilize the soil with accumulations of vegetation and their own excreta. They also are nature's planters. It has been said that were there no squirrels there would be no hickory trees. This probably is an overstatement, but certainly there would be fewer nut trees if the great army of squirrels was not forever planting the nuts. The beaver was the original "soil conservationist." By damming the streams and impounding the water he kept the water table high and made possible the accumulation of debris and eroded soil behind his dams. Over a period of years meadows were formed where, had it not been for the beaver, there would have been a continuous forest to the stream's edge. These open meadows are feeding grounds for moose, deer, and elk. Mice and shrews, in their small way, help maintain the forests by consuming large quantities of injurious insects. By keeping the forest floor worked into a soft mulch, these little mammals help to check the deleterious erosional effects of the runoff of water.

ADAPTIVE RADIATION (DIVERGENCE)

In any geographic region where topography, soil, climate, and vegetation are sufficiently varied the mammal species also are varied in structure and habits. The larger the region and the more diverse the conditions the greater is the diversity of mammals. Each environmental complex contains its particular kind or kinds of mammal species, the structures and habits of which fit them for life in that particular complex. Each animal is adapted to live under certain conditions—a land animal cannot live long in the water nor can a water animal live on land.

Fossil evidence indicates that all present-day mammals evolved from a single primitive type. In the course of evolution, through geologic time, the primitive mammals gave rise to a great diversity of types. The adaptations were roughly in four general directions: (1) to the surface of the soil (the primitive terrestrial type), (2) to subterranean life (fossorial), (3) to the trees and air (arboreal and aerial), and (4) to an existence in water (aquatic). Some mammals fit nicely as regards adaptations into a single category (the mole into fossorial), whereas others overlap two or more of the above adaptations (the meadow vole combines terrestrial, fossorial, and aquatic), although the adaptations for one kind of condition are usually more pronounced than for others. Some animals retain in recognizable form certain adaptations for a former way of life, although their essential adaptation is quite different; thus, the whale, now wholly aquatic, still retains lungs for air breathing—a land adaptation of its ancestors. Among the fauna of the Great Lakes region there are examples of most of the general adaptations present in mammals; all but the strictly aquatic.

Adaptations in Limbs and Feet

TERRESTRIAL ADAPTATIONS (Fig. 1)

Ambulatory (an ambling gait)

This is the central type of adaptation for land mammals from which the other adaptive specializations have radiated or diverged. Mammals in this category, for example, opossum and shrews, are of a generalized type, probably similar in many respects to the ancestral forms. They are typically five-toed (sometimes four-toed) and plantigrade (walking on the sole of the foot); the metatarsals and metacarpals (foot and hand bones) are separate, not fused, and are longer than the phalanges (toe bones); the ankle and wrist joints permit moderate movement in various directions, but chiefly for locomotion; the claws are narrow; the animals are small to medium-sized.

Cursorial (running)

DIGITIGRADE (walking on the toes). Examples: rabbits, dogs, and cats.

The cursorial digitigrade type is derived from the ambulatory. Instead of walking on the entire sole of the foot (heel to toe) the animal walks on its toes. This enables it to develop speed. The limbs of these animals are used chiefly for locomotion and are usually limited to a fore and aft movement. They are under the body, not out at the sides. Typically, they have no more than four functional toes. The foot joints allow for limited movement, but give additional strength wherever the articulating ends of the bones are keeled. There is a reduction in the fibula and ulna. From the standpoint of numbers of mammals represented, this category is perhaps the most important.

UNGULIGRADE (walking on toenails = hoofs). Examples: deer and horses.

The cursorial unguligrade adaptation represents the extreme of specialization in this direction. The keeled and grooved joints of the lower leg allow only fore-and-aft movement. The femur and humerus assume a nearly horizontal position and are imbedded in the muscles of the body. The lower leg bones (tibia and radius) and the foot bones (metatarsals and metacarpals) are elongated; the phalanges are shortened and fewer. The fibula and ulna are reduced; the ankle and wrist bones are fewer and partly fused. Hoofs are developed on the terminal phalanges.

GRAVIPORTAL (supporting heavy weight). Example: elephant. There are no living representatives of this adaptation among the native Great Lakes fauna. In it the limbs are straight and pillar-like, and the bones of the joints flatten on the articulating ends.

ARBOREAL ADAPTATION

The arboreal adaptation, for example, that of the tree squirrel and the marten, probably developed from a terrestrial ambulatory type. Many modifications in structure are necessary for life among the treetops. Some of the more important of the arboreal specializations are: elongation of limbs and phalanges; long, recurved sharp claws supported by strong phalanges; free movement of limbs in all directions, as a result of the development of ball and socket joints at the girdles; a long tail, either bushy or prehensile; ears and eyes usually well developed. Mobility in the limbs with a sacrifice of strength, except in the phalanges, is important for an arboreal animal.

AERIAL ADAPTATION

The flying adaptation, which among mammals is confined to the bats, probably arose from the arboreal through an intermediate volant (gliding) stage. Mammals possessing the aerial adaptation are characterized by elongated fingers with a connecting membrane (the flying organ), reduced hind limbs with sharp recurved claws (for hanging during nonactive hours), keeled sternum, and the reduction of distal muscles in the wings.

FOSSORIAL ADAPTATION

Several mammals, representing different orders, and developed from the terrestrial ambulatory type, dig into the ground, where they spend a large part of their lives. These subterranean dwellers, for example, the mole and the badger, are known as fossorial animals. Some of the more apparent specializations for this kind of life are: reduction of ears, eyes, and tail; fusiform body; short neck; short powerful limbs with proximal bones reduced in length, developing prominent tuberosities for muscle attachment; phalanges and claws elongated; strong pulley joints in phalanges of front foot; and limbs that project outward from the sides of the body.

SEMIAQUATIC ADAPTATION

Aquatic adaptations, for example, in the otter, are similar in general to those of the fossorial animal. They differ, however, in that the eyes are not reduced, the tail often develops into a swimming organ, and the claws are not elongated, although the toes are webbed. The whale and its relatives represent the maximum of this specialization among mammals. The nearest approach to aquatic adaptation in mammals considered here is in the river otter. The beaver and muskrat combine aquatic and fossorial adaptations.

Adaptations in Teeth

Adaptations in the teeth (Fig. 1) are not necessarily correlated with adaptations in the feet and limbs, but have evolved separately and reflect the various food habits of mammals. The ancestral type of tooth, adapted for a diet of insects, had three simple cusps (tubercles) arranged in the form of a triangle. This is known as a tritubercular tooth. Examination of the teeth of mammals from different geologic levels, including living representatives, reveals that the ancestral type, with slight modifications, has persisted in some kinds and that, in addition, there have been four general divergent lines of development from this central type. Also, some myrmecophagous mammals (ant-eaters)—a degenerative type—show a simplification and eventual loss of teeth.

TRITUBERCULAR (insectivorous). Example: shrews.

The teeth are low-crowned with sharply pointed cusps. In Recent mammals there are slight modifications from the ancestral type, chiefly the addition of accessory cusps, but the three primary cusps (protocone, paracone, and metacone) still persist. The teeth are adapted for a combination of crushing and cutting.

SECTORIAL (cutting-shearing). Examples: cats and weasels, flesh eaters or carnivorous mammals.

The sectorial adaptation is derived indirectly from the tritubercular through an intermediate stage known as tuberculo-sectorial (partly crushing, chiefly cutting, as in the dog). The cat has the purely sectorial adaptation; shearing is accomplished by the functional cheek teeth. In modern carnivores these specialized teeth are the fourth upper premolar and the first lower molar. The crushing heel of the tooth, found in the dog, is absent in the cat.

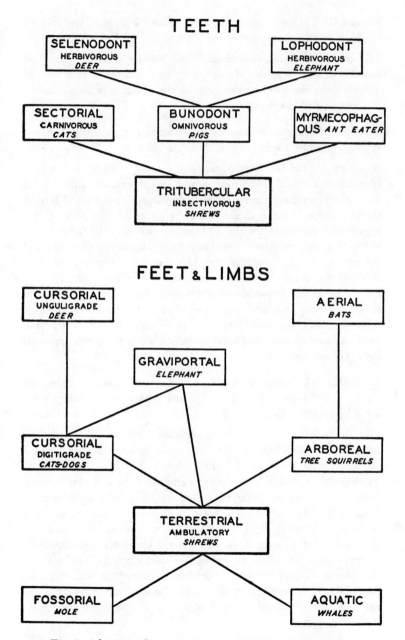

Fig. 1. *Adaptive radiation in the teeth and in the feet and limbs.*

BUNODONT (low, rounded cusps). Examples: man and pig—a crushing tooth for an omnivorous diet.

The bunodont tooth, low-crowned and usually quadrate, has low, rounded cusps (tubercles) for crushing nuts and fruits. It is derived directly from the tritubercular type by the addition of cusps and by the rounding of the points.

SELENODONT (crescentic cusps). Examples: deer, cow, horse—a cutting, grinding tooth for a herbivorous diet.

By converting the low rounded cusps of the bonodont tooth into crescent-shaped cusps that wear down and expose enamel ridges on the flat surface, a grinding mechanism is developed. Simultaneously with the conversion of cusps to crescents, the crown of the tooth became higher to compensate for the additional wear to which it was subjected. The intermediate stages between the bunodont pig tooth and the extreme development of the high-crowned (hypso-selenodont) tooth of the horse are well represented by the deer and cow. The deer tooth is still low-crowned and retains the outer cusps, but has developed inner crescents (buno-selenodont). The cow tooth is higher crowned than is the deer tooth, but not so high-crowned as the horse tooth; it has both inner and outer crescents, but is still a short-crowned tooth (brachy-selenodont).

LOPHODONT (tranverse lophs, or ridges and valleys). Examples: elephant and tapir (also rabbit, but not typical)—a grinding tooth for a herbivorous diet.

Like the selenodont tooth, the lophodont tooth is derived directly from the bunodont type. It serves the same function, that of a grinding mechanism. A series of lophs (ridges) extends across the tooth transversely, exposing, with slight wear, hard enamel ridges, separated by softer cement. As in the selenodont tooth, high crowns are developed to compensate for the wear. In the development of this type from the bunodont (piglike) tooth, the first stage is the buno-lophodont tooth (with outer cusps and inner cross crests, low-crowned), represented in the extinct mastodon. The next stage, the brachy-lophodont tooth (with cross crests, oblique or transverse, but still low-crowned), is represented in the tapir. The final development is the extremely high-crowned (hypso-lophodont), cross-crested tooth of the modern elephant.

MYRMECOPHAGOUS (degenerative teeth). Examples: Anteaters, sloths, and armadillos.

This category is not comparable to the others, but represents a type of degeneration, in which the teeth become simple pegs without enamel covering (sloths) or are entirely lost (anteaters).

HOME RANGES AND TERRITORIES

HOME RANGES–Every individual mammal, after it is old enough to leave its birthplace, must move about to procure food (Fig. 2). The area is usually around a nest site or resting area, which may be

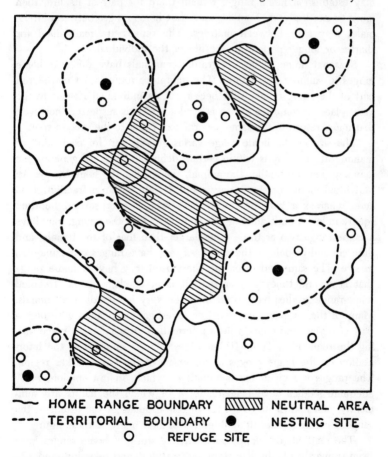

— HOME RANGE BOUNDARY ▨ NEUTRAL AREA
---- TERRITORIAL BOUNDARY ● NESTING SITE
○ REFUGE SITE

Fig. 2. Home ranges, territories, neutral areas, and unoccupied areas in a quadrat for a given species of mammal.

called a home. The space around the home that the animal traverses in its normal activities of food gathering, mating, and caring for young is its home range, of which there are three general types.

Permanent home ranges. Some mammals, especially among the mice and shrews, may establish a home range and remain there throughout their lives. They may wander or move about shortly after they leave the parental nest, but once a home is established they do not move from the home range of their own will.

Semipermanent home ranges. This category probably is characteristic of many of the small and medium-sized mammals. An individual may establish a home range, remain there for part of its life, then move to another area. Females may shift home ranges between litters, males may shift between matings. The ranges are maintained for shorter or longer periods in the life of the individual.

Seasonal home ranges. Migratory mammals have different home ranges in summer and winter. The migratory route is not considered part of the home range. Whether or not an individual returns to the same place season after season is not known. It is suspected, however, that many return to the same general area if not to the precise spot.

The size of the home range varies greatly, but for each kind of mammal it probably is within certain definable limits. In general, one may say that the smaller the animal, the smaller the home range. An individual mouse or shrew may spend its life within a fraction of an acre, whereas a wolf or cougar may wander over several hundred square miles. A male animal, free from caring for the young, may have a home range two or three times larger than that of the female, and different individuals of the same sex may have ranges quite unequal in size. The same individual at one season may have a home range that is several times greater than it is at another season. Detailed home-range studies have been made on very few kinds of mammals. Many of these reports are based on investigations dealing with only a part of a year and contain little information on what takes place during the remainder. Table III on pages 222–25 summarizes the information on the home ranges of mammals of the Great Lakes region. The ranges are given for mammals of which, in my opinion, fairly adequate studies have been made or of which the habits are sufficiently well known to give a reasonable estimate of the extent of the range. Further studies undoubtedly will alter many of these figures.

The methods developed so far in the study of home ranges have been primarily (1) by live trapping, marking, and releasing, and (2) by tracking animals in snow or soft sands. Though mammals have been marked in numerous ways, no perfect method as yet has been discovered. Small mammals may be marked by using various combinations of ear notches made with a poultry punch, by the amputation of toes, by placing numbered metal bands around the legs or metal tags in the ears, and by dyeing or painting various parts of the body. Tattooing has also been used successfully in marking some of the larger mammals. Recently, radioactive materials have been used to "tag" individuals. Their positions may then be determined by the use of a Geiger counter. This method has been tried to advantage with moles.

The object of marking an animal is to find out, by following its movements, the extent of the area over which it ranges. This may be done by direct observation from a blind or, after continued trapping and releasing, by plotting the points of capture on a map of the area. To obtain the best results from trapping at least one hundred traps should be set for small mammals and fifty for large ones. The area trapped should be several times the size of an individual home range, and the traps should be spaced so that at least ten are within the home range of an individual. Some preliminary experimentation is necessary to determine these limits if one does not have previous knowledge of the species. A spacing of about forty-five feet between traps seems to be satisfactory for small mice. One trap to the acre may be sufficient for rabbits and tree squirrels. If traps are used, they should be visited frequently in order to prevent the death of the imprisoned animals from heat, exposure, or hunger. In traps for small mammals, a tuft of cotton for nest material is essential.

TERRITORIALITY–In recent years field biologists have turned their attention to behavior studies of wild animals. These studies are relatively new, and the techniques are not yet perfected, but many possibilities may be explored by the field man who has the interest, ingenuity, and energy to pursue this type of investigation. It is well established that many animals have a sense of ownership. Man is the outstanding example. He considers it one of his prerogatives to own property—property which he will defend against exploitation by others. Some of the wild mammals also defend food stores, nests, or certain areas around their home sites against trespass and exploitation by other mammals, especially of their own kind. This is known as territoriality.

Wild mammals defend two fundamental types of territories. Some, like the red squirrel, protect their food stores. Others, for example the muskrat and beaver, defend nesting sites and homes. Most mammals that store food probably are concerned with protecting it against pillage. If the owner of a food cache is present when an invader appears, he will attempt to chase the interloper not only from the immediate vicinity of the food supply, but for some distance beyond. The area established around the food supply may not have definite boundaries, but within somewhat flexible limits an invader may be chased or attacked if he enters when the "owner" is present. This may also happen in a nesting or home territory, but it may be the young, not necessarily the food supplies, that are being protected. Whatever the motivating factor, whether food, young in a nest, or a combination of the two, if an animal defends any part of its home range it is said to display territorial behavior. This defensive behavior may be limited to the breeding season or to one or the other sex (female chipmunk, male sea lion) and usually is restricted to adult animals. It exists in many kinds of monkeys and apes, squirrels, mice, beaver, muskrat, rabbits, seals and sea lions, and in some artiodactyls. It is strongly developed in domestic dogs and in man.

The wildlife technician should know as much as possible about the behavior of the animals with which he is concerned. If there are too many muskrats in a marsh they fight and the pelts are scarred. If animals have territories and each must have a certain amount of living room, the wildlife manager should know the extent of the area required for optimum conditions.

There are many other behavioristic studies that might be made with profit. We know very little about the courting behavior of mammals or of the relationships of the sexes and of adults to young.

POPULATIONS

Animal populations are never static. As young animals appear and old ones die or are killed by predators and as individuals move from one place to another, the population varies in a given area. One of the most interesting phases of population study concerns the apparent regularity with which certain species of mammals increase to a peak in number of individuals, suddenly decrease to negligible numbers, and then start again to increase. These fluctuations have been termed "cyclic" by many authors and, in some kinds of mammals, apparently occur at rather definite intervals and may represent true cycles. In other kinds the time intervals between the extremes in the populations are very unequal. I prefer to speak of the variations in abundance as fluctuations until there is a better understanding of what actually takes place in the dynamics of populations. It is fairly certain that, starting with a depleted population, there is a gradual increase, which is accelerated as time goes on, until a peak is reached. This process requires about four years in some species of voles and ten or eleven years in snowshoe hares. Something then happens and nearly the entire population may be wiped out within a single season. This is known as the "crash." Elton (1942) stated that in regard to the lemmings: "The three factors that spring at once to mind—food shortage, epidemic, and emigration—probably all play a part . . . ."

The causal agents and biological principles involved in fluctuations in mammal populations are as yet little known. In the meadow vole the breeding activity accelerates as the population grows. The breeding season extends over a longer period (more litters per year) and the number of young per litter increases (Hamilton, 1937). There must, therefore, be some physiological readjustment. External factors that may have some effect on populations are: (1) Climatic conditions —temperature and precipitation may affect directly or indirectly the livelihood of individuals. (2) Food and shelter—if food is abundant and shelter is available the chances of survival should be enhanced. Animals in good condition may produce more young than do underfed individuals. This has been demonstrated in the whitetail deer. (3) Predation—if predators are numerous they keep populations of prey species down, if scarce the prey species has a chance to increase. (4) Disease—epidemics are more likely to occur in dense than in thinly scattered populations and may be among the main causes of diminution in numbers.

The study of population dynamics is in the formative stage. Techniques are still being perfected. We have learned a few of the "whats," but most of the "hows" and "whys" are still mysteries.

Census methods for large mammals.—It might seem fairly simple to select an area and count all mammals of the size of deer and elk on it. On the open prairies, where the animals are exposed to view, a rather accurate estimate of numbers can be made. On such terrain the most satisfactory method is to count the animals from an airplane. By flying along predetermined strips and by having two counters, one for each side of the plane, it is possible to ascertain the number of animals, especially if there is snow on the ground. This method has been employed with success by governmental agencies. In heavily wooded areas, in which deer can hide in dense swamps, other techniques must be used. Deer drives have been fairly successful when sufficient man power has been available. For this method an area of a square mile or more is surrounded by men, spaced so that each man is always in view of the man to his right and to his left. At a signal the men start walking through the area, tallying the deer that pass through the lines. The greatest disadvantage of this type of census is its cost. It is usually prohibitive unless volunteer labor is available. An idea of relative abundance of the animals may be had by counting tracks (after a fresh snow) that cross roads or trails. With this method one does not know how many times the tracks of the same animal are counted, but a rough index to the relative abundance of animals in different areas is provided.

Census methods for small mammals.—The quadrat method has been used rather extensively, and with a moderate amount of success, in attempting to determine populations of small mammals. An area of known size is marked off and trapped until it is thought all mammals have been caught. This must be done in a fairly short time to eliminate animals that will come in from surrounding areas. If the animals are removed from the area as they are caught, in order to catch them as quickly as possible the traps should be closely spaced. Unless an isolated habitat to which the animals are restricted is being trapped, one should include, beyond the outer lines of traps, as part of the area trapped, a strip about one-half as wide as the diameter of an average home range of the species concerned. For live trapping and marking, as indicated for home-range studies (p. 17), it is not necessary to use so many traps nor to trap the area in as short a time. The calculation of the area should be the same. The quadrat system requires much equipment and labor and is not practicable on a large scale. It approaches the absolute census as closely as does any method yet devised.

To speed up the census and to eliminate some of the labor, one may take a census count of a sample area fairly accurately in two nights of live trapping—marking all animals caught the first night. By applying the system developed by Lincoln (1930) to determine numbers of waterfowl one may arrive at a figure fairly close to the actual population. An actual trapping record for individual white-footed mice provides an illustration. Live traps were set for four nights, and a total of thirty-six mice were caught. Twenty-three were taken the first night, and twenty-five the second night. Seventeen of the mice caught on the second night had been taken on the first night. The ratio of previously caught animals to the total catch on the second night should equal the ratio of the first night's catch to the total population, or $17:25: :23:x$, where x equals total population $(= 34)$. The actual catch (thirty-six in four nights) was two more than the calculated catch (thirty-four) based on the first two nights. By first trapping and marking, then hunting cottontails and applying this formula, D. L. Allen (1938) calculated their population in the Kellogg Bird Sanctuary in Michigan.

The relative abundance of small mammals in different areas or in different years in the same area may be determined roughly by counting signs in sample areas selected more or less at random. The indications may be fecal pellets, dens, runways, middens, or other fairly obvious tokens of the presence of mammals. These methods, to date, have not given any indication of actual numbers of animals.

The Mammals
of the Great Lakes Region

As a class, the mammals are distinguished from all other vertebrates by two primary morphological peculiarities: (1) the presence of hair as a body covering (hair always appears in some stage of development, sometimes only as bristles about the snout in adult animals), and (2) the presence of a great variety of integumental glands, some of which are modified into mammary, or milk glands (poorly developed in the Monotremata, highly developed in the Eutheria). Other morphological characters, some of which are present in other vertebrates and not confined to the Mammalia, when used in combination, set off the present-day mammals as a distinct group. In the soft anatomy there are additional characters: (1) viviparity (young are developed in the uterus), except the egg-laying monotremes, (2) the four-chambered heart with closed circulation, (3) a nearly constant body temperature (homoiothermal), and (4) separation of the pulmonary (thoracic) and abdominal cavities by a diaphragm. In the skeleton are the following characters: (1) the vertebrae are differentiated into cervicals, thoracics, lumbars, sacrals, and caudals, (2) there are usually seven cervical vertebrae (except in the tree sloth and the manatee), (3) epiphyses are present on the ends of the long bones, (4) there are two occipital condyles on the skull, (5) the lower jaw is in two parts (usually fused in old age) and articulates directly with the cranium, (6) the palate is roofed over between the upper tooth rows, (7) the quadrate group is reduced and modified into the bones of the middle ear, (8) the teeth are heterodont, differentiated into incisors, canines, premolars, and molars, (9) replacement of the teeth is limited to a second series of incisors, canines, and premolars, (10) the shoulder girdle is reduced and partly or wholly freed from the sternum, (11) the pelvic girdle is consolidated into a pair of innominate bones, usually sutured to the transverse processes of the sacrals, (12) there are three proximal and four distal carpals, except as consolidated or reduced by loss of lateral digits, and one centrale is sometimes present, (13) two proximal and four distal tarsal elements are present, except as reduced or consolidated, (14) each foot has primarily five digits, the lateral digits may be reduced or lost, (15) two phalanges are present on digit one, three on each of the other digits, (16) the tympanic bulla is usually formed partly or entirely from the tympanic bone, but is sometimes absent.

Generally speaking, mammals are distributed over the entire earth surface. Every continent and nearly every island of any size has a mammal fauna. There are mammals in the arctic and antarctic regions, on the lowest plains, and on the highest mountains. Many kinds inhabit the humid tropics, the arid deserts, and the oceans. Mammals have reached many of the islands near continents, and some of the smaller kinds, such as rats and mice, are on islands five hundred miles or more offshore. The size of the range of a given kind may be a few square miles (for some mice) or nearly world-wide (for man).

The scientific names in this volume are those in current usage as of 1956.

SUBCLASS THERIA

The subclass Theria includes all living mammals except the egg-laying Monotremata, which with some extinct forms comprises the subclass Prototheria. The characters given above for the class Mammalia, with the exceptions for the Monotremata, may be applied to this subclass.

INFRACLASS METATHERIA

The most important characters of the Metatheria are: (1) an external marsupium or pouch, enclosing the teats, is present on the abdomen of the female (absent in a few forms), (2) there are often more than forty-four teeth, (3) there are never more than three premolars, (4) the angle of the mandible is nearly always inflected (also true of some rodents), (5) the nasals are broadly expanded on the face in front of the orbits, (6) the jugal is large, reaching posteriorly to the glenoid fossa and often forming part of the fossa, (7) the brain is small, with a smooth cerebrum not covering the optic and olfactory lobes in front or the cerebellum behind, (8) the tympanum never forms a bulla (sometimes a false bulla is formed by expansion of the alisphenoid), (9) epipubic bones are present (absent in some forms), (10) there is no true placenta.

POUCHED MAMMALS (ORDER MARSUPIALIA)

There is only one order in the Metatheria. Its characters are the same as those for the infraclass.

OPOSSUMS (FAMILY DIDELPHIIDAE)

OPOSSUM *Didelphis marsupialis* Linnaeus

SIZE–Total length, 730–800 mm. (28–32 in.); weight, 4–12 lbs.

DESCRIPTION–The adult opossum is about the size of a large house cat. The general coloration of grayish white results from the white underfur and the black-tipped overhair on the body. The **tail** is long, **naked,** scaly, and **prehensile,** and the **leaflike ears** are thin and naked. Old individuals often have the edges of the ears and the tip of the tail frozen back. The legs are short, and the feet are **five-toed.** The opposable inside toe of the hind foot is the only one that does not have a claw. The position of this toe, which is set at an angle to the others, and the fanlike spread of the toes on the front foot give to this animal a characteristic track. The female has an abdominal pouch lined with soft fur.

The skull of the opossum is set with the greatest number of teeth present in any Great Lakes mammal. The brain case is small for the size of the skull, and the nasal bones are greatly expanded posteriorly over the face in front of the orbits. The angle of the lower jaw is inflected.

HABITAT–The opossum is fairly confined to wooded areas along streams, around lakes, and in swamps.

HABITS–This mammal is almost entirely nocturnal in its habits and, therefore, is seldom seen, unless it is caught in a trap or is treed by a dog. It is slow-moving and has a sort of ambling gait. When pursued it rarely turns upon its adversary, but seeks safety up a tree, in a brush heap, or, if a retreat cannot be reached, by playing "possum."

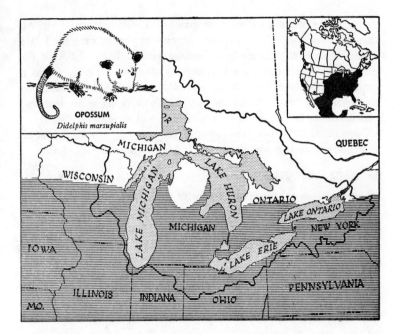

OPOSSUM
Didelphis marsupialis

An opportunist among wild mammals, the opossum makes its home in almost any shelter in which it can be dry and safe from enemies. Deserted dens of other mammals may be taken over, or it may find a home under an old building, in a brush pile, or in a hole in a tree. Its food is as varied as are its home sites. It will eat almost anything—carrion, spoiled fruits, fresh fruits, nuts, and choice poultry. Insects probably form a substantial part of its diet.

The gestation period of the opossum is thirteen days. The young (three to fourteen or more in number), when first born, are naked and grublike in appearance. The front limbs are sufficiently developed for the newly born opossum to crawl into the pouch of its mother, where it attaches itself to a slender teat. Further development of the embryo takes place in the pouch. At the age of four or five weeks the young are ready to leave the pouch for short periods. They remain ninety to one hundred days with the mother, and thereafter they are able to take care of themselves. The male parent is not tolerated by the female after mating has been accomplished. The home range, as determined in Texas, is eleven and one-half to thirty-eight and one-half acres (Lay, 1942).

REMARKS—Formerly, the opossum was rather rare in this area, but now it is one of the more common mammals in the southern parts. Although considered to be deficient in mentality, it has succeeded as a species where other forms have become extinct. It has followed the progress of civilization even into regions of severe winters, where it remains active throughout the year. An animal without distinctly specialized structures, it differs but slightly from its early ancestors and is able to live under diverse environmental conditions.

ECONOMIC STATUS–The status of the opossum is nearly neutral. It sometimes raids the poultry yard, but otherwise does little harm.

INFRACLASS EUTHERIA

The true placental mammals comprise the Eutheria. They are characterized in part by (1) the presence of a true placenta, (2) never more than forty-four teeth, (3) all but molar teeth successional (some exceptions in insectivores), (4) a usually vertical angle of the mandible (except in some rodents), (5) a large cerebrum, usually convoluted, (6) the tympanum forming a bulla (except in some insectivores).

MOLES AND SHREWS (ORDER INSECTIVORA)

The insectivores constitute a diverse group of mammals, widely distributed over the earth's surface and difficult to define as an order. Many of their characteristics are present in other groups, and no one characteristic is confined to the group as a whole. It is, therefore, the combination of several characters that seems to set them apart from the other orders of mammals. They are, in general, small, more or less plantigrade, and the snout is usually long and often developed into a short proboscis. Their eyes are small, and the brain simple for the Eutheria. The teeth, usually, are of a generalized type with low, sharp cusps. As a rule, there are five toes on each foot.

MOLES (FAMILY TALPIDAE)

Members of this family are the extreme in specialization for subterranean life. The front feet and limbs are broad and powerful, for digging. The fur is short and dense, the eyes are reduced, and the external ear conch is absent. The sternum has a well-developed crest to support the powerful pectoral muscles. The zygomatic arches of the skull are present, but weak.

EASTERN MOLE *Scalopus aquaticus* Linnaeus

SIZE–Total length, 148–96 mm. (6–7.8 in.); weight, 66–143 gms. (2.4–5 oz.).

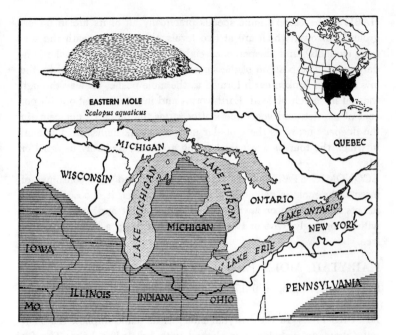

EASTERN MOLE
Scalopus aquaticus

DESCRIPTION–The body of the adult eastern mole is thickly covered with short velvety fur, which has a silky silver sheen. The **tail** is short and **scantily haired**. The external ear is evident only as a small opening beneath the fur. The eyes, covered by thin membranes, the fused eyelids, are so small that they cannot be seen without parting the hair around them. The nose is long, naked, and pointed, with the nostrils opening upward; it lacks the fringe of fleshy projections present in the starnose mole. The greatly enlarged, spadelike front feet are broader than long, and the palms face outward. This character alone distinguishes the moles from all other mammals of this area. The six mammae are in three pairs, one pectoral, one abdominal, and one inguinal.

The skull of the eastern mole is triangular in outline, pointed in front, and broadest near the back. The bones of the brain case, which appears to be inflated, are thin, dense, and smooth. The zygomatic arches are weak but present in a properly prepared skull. The combination of teeth, twenty in the upper jaw and sixteen in the lower jaw, is present in no other mammal of the Great Lakes region. The cheek teeth have sharp pointed cusps adapted for crushing insects.

HABITAT–Formerly, this mole was probably restricted to the grassy prairie and oak openings. With the clearing of land it has followed man into farming districts. It prefers sandy soils and loams.

HABITS–The eastern mole spends practically all of its life in underground burrows, which are at two levels, those just beneath the surface (tunnels) and deeper ones eighteen to twenty-four inches underground. The position of the surface tunnel may be detected by the low ridges of broken earth formed as the mole pushes its way through the soil in search of food. Earthworms and insects form about 85 per cent of its diet, and vegetable matter forms the other 15 per cent. In the deeper burrow is the globular nest, about six inches in diameter, in which the four or five naked young are born, probably in April or May.

ECONOMIC STATUS–As a tiller of the soil and as a consumer of insects, the mole is definitely beneficial, but when it chooses to hunt insects in a garden or lawn it can become a pest and must be dealt with accordingly. One or two mole traps will keep a lawn or garden free.

HAIRYTAIL MOLE *Parascalops breweri* Bachman

SIZE–Total length, 150–170 mm. (6–7 in.); weight, 40–64 gms. (1.5–2.3 oz.).

DESCRIPTION–In the hairytail mole, as its name implies, the short **tail** (about an inch long) is clothed **with bristle-like hairs.** The fur on the body is velvet-like, dark slate to blackish, often stained with yellowish on snout and belly. The eyes are small and inconspicuous. The broad, front feet have the palms facing outward and slightly downward. The nose is naked and pointed. There are eight mammae.

The triangular skull, broadest at the back, is similar in outline to that of the eastern mole. Its surface is smooth, with the sutures closing early in life. Zygomatic arches are present, but weak. The skull is smaller (less than 35 mm.) than that of the eastern mole and contains forty-four teeth instead of thirty-six.

HABITAT–The hairytail mole prefers sandy loams with good surface cover of vegetation. It is not likely to be found in extremely wet or dry soils or in heavy clays.

HABITS–Like all moles, individuals of this species spend most of their lives underground. Surface tunnels are used during spring, summer, and fall for food getting. During the cold of winter these moles retreat to deeper tunnels, which may be eighteen inches below the surface. In one of these is the nest of dry leaves and grass (about six inches in diameter), in which the four naked young are born in early May. Breeding occurs in late March and early April. The gestation period is probably four to six weeks, but is not definitely known. Young

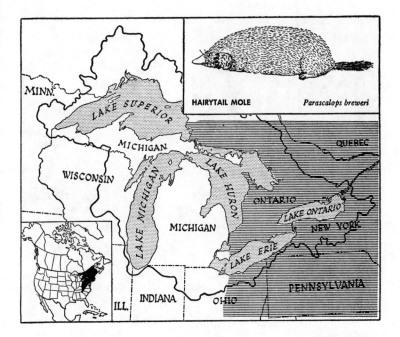

HAIRYTAIL MOLE   *Parascalops breweri*

remain in the nest about a month before venturing out. They become sexually mature at about ten months of age.

The winter home range may be confined to an area no more than eighty feet in diameter. In the summer this is probably increased. An average of two adult moles per acre is a high population. Eleven were taken from a one-acre plot in New Hampshire in two weeks time by Dr. W. Robert Eadie (1939). Most individuals live no longer than three years, a few may reach four or more years of age in the wild.

Food consists primarily of insects (45–50 per cent by bulk) and earthworms (30–35 per cent). In captivity, these moles have been known to consume earthworms in excess of 300 per cent of their own body weight in twenty-four hours. This probably rarely happens in nature.

ECONOMIC STATUS–Away from gardens, lawns, and golf courses, these moles are wholly beneficial. Many of the insects they consume are harmful to crops. Where they are a nuisance locally, they may be eliminated temporarily by trapping. They will re-invade the area when trapping ceases.

REMARKS–The small mounds that these moles push up, especially in the fall, are usually no more than six inches in diameter and three inches in height. The surface tunnels are less conspicuous than are

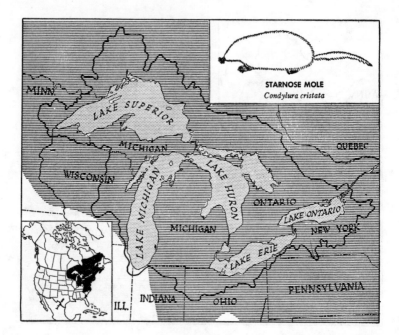

STARNOSE MOLE
Condylura cristata

those of the eastern mole. Many other animals, including mice and shrews, use their tunnel systems as highways or retreats. One tunnel was known to have been used by these moles over a period of eight years.

STARNOSE MOLE *Condylura cristata* Linnaeus

SIZE—Total length, 169–205 mm. (6.7–8 in.); weight, 35–77 gms. (1.2–2.7 oz.).

DESCRIPTION—The character that distinguishes the starnose mole from all other mammals is the presence of twenty-two fleshy, **finger-like feelers** distributed around the **tip of** the **nose** (Fig 3). It is from this peculiar structure that the animal gets its name. Although of about the same total length as the other moles, the starnose mole is smaller in body than its close relatives. The front feet are wide and spadelike, but not so large as those of other moles. The **tail** is relatively long, about one-half as long as the head and body, is **constricted near** the **base**, and is swollen with stored fat near the middle. The dense fur is **black** or **dark brown**. There are eight mammae, two pairs pectoral, one pair abdominal, and one pair inguinal.

The slender and delicately built skull of the starnose mole tapers gradually from back to front and terminates in a long slender rostrum. The total number of teeth, forty-four (the minute second upper incisor is often lost in cleaning the skull), is exceeded in North America only in the opossum.

Fig. 3. Starnose mole.

HABITAT—For its home the starnose mole prefers swamps, bogs, and low, wet meadows.

HABITS—This mole often emerges from the monotony of its dark underground burrow to spend part of its time above ground or in the water. It is, perhaps, as proficient at swimming as it is at burrowing through the saturated soil, and it even comes out in the winter to swim beneath the ice of small ponds. Its food, as far as is known, consists chiefly of aquatic worms and insects. The burrows are usually deeper than those made by the eastern mole and about the only telltale evidences of their presence are large mounds of black soil pushed up from below. On occasions the tunnels are sufficiently near the surface to form the low ridges characteristic of the other moles.

Three to seven young are born in each litter, and one litter a year probably is all that is raised by each breeding female. Mating apparently takes place sometime during late winter, and the naked young are born from April to June in the spherical nest (about five inches in diameter) of dry leaves and grasses, situated above high water level. Our knowledge of the life history of the starnose mole is far from complete. It is supposed, on the basis of indirect evidence, to be a sociable animal that lives in colonies. Any direct observations on the life history of this mole are worthy of record. According to Hamilton (1931), a population of five pairs to the acre is not uncommon in parts of New York state.

ECONOMIC STATUS—The starnose mole rarely interferes with man's activities, for it lives chiefly in what may be termed nontillable land. The few mounds of earth it throws up in low meadows suffocate some grass, but the good that the mole does in eating insects and aerating the subsoil undoubtedly more than compensates for any damage done to grass on the surface. It can and does at times damage well-watered greens on golf courses.

SHREWS (FAMILY SORICIDAE)

The family Soricidae includes the smallest mammals. Although the teeth are specialized in some respects, the skeleton as a whole is probably little changed from that of the earliest mammals. The front teeth are modified into grasping pincers. Just back of the median incisors is a series of three to five simple pointed teeth, the unicuspids, by the arrangement and relative size of which, in addition to certain other characters, the species of long-tailed shrews are to be distinguished. Farther back are the molars, which are tritubercular or quadrituber-cular, with sharp, crescentic cusps. There is no zygomatic arch. Audital bullae are absent. The eyes are small, and the nose is long, pointed, and proboscis-like. There are five toes on both front and hind feet of all forms considered here.

MASKED SHREW *Sorex cinereus* Kerr

SIZE–Total length, 80–109 mm. (3–4 in.); weight, 3.5–5.5 gms. (.1–.2 oz.).

DESCRIPTION–This sprite of a mammal looks like a small, long-nosed mouse, but in reality is a quite different creature. Of its total length one and one-half inches is tail. The eyes are small, inconspic-uous black beads, and the ears are nearly concealed in its thick, soft, brown fur. Shrews may be distinguished from mice most easily by the teeth. Mice have two large chisel-like teeth (incisors) in the front of the upper and lower jaws, then a considerable gap between these and the grinding teeth. Shrews have a continuous row of small sharp-pointed teeth from front to back. These teeth are usually deep chest-nut on the tips. The feet, both front and back, have five distinct toes. Without recourse to the skull this shrew might be confused with the pigmy shrew, *Microsorex*. There are six mammae, one pair ab-dominal, two pairs inguinal.

The skull is delicate, almost jewel-like, and fragile. There are no zygomatic arches. The first incisors are notched on the back side. In the masked shrew the upper third unicuspid is about the same size as the fourth, and both of these are slightly smaller than the first and second (Fig. 29a).

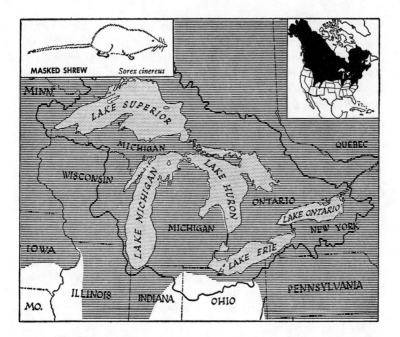

MASKED SHREW *Sorex cinereus*

HABITAT–The masked shrew inhabits brushy and grassy areas near water, also woodlands with logs and litter on the forest floor.

HABITS–These little mammals are abroad throughout the year, always searching for sufficient food to keep their active bodies supplied with energy. They probably eat more than their own weight in food every twenty-four hours. A captive female ate three and three-tenths times her own weight every twenty-four hours (Blossom, 1932). The food, as far as is known, consists chiefly of insects, with perhaps small mice, other shrews, and some vegetable matter. The animals usually follow small runways made by themselves or by other shrews or mice, but they may at times cross open spaces where no runways are apparent. Their small globular nests of dry leaves or grasses may be in or under old logs, in hollow stumps, or under small piles of grass or brush. There is little definite information on the breeding season, but this probably continues from March to September. Embryo counts indicate that four to ten young may be born in each litter. A newly born shrew weighs about one tenth of a gram. The number of litters that one female will bring forth in a season is not known. These shrews are chiefly terrestrial in habit and probably burrow only occasionally They are as active in the daytime as at night.

ECONOMIC STATUS–No one rightfully can accuse this shrew of being in any way detrimental to the interests of man. Although it undoubtedly is common throughout its range, it is seen so seldom that few know of its presence. Its food consists almost entirely of small animals which would be injurious to cultivated crops if not checked by shrews and other predaceous animals.

REMARKS–Two races of this species occur in the Great Lakes region, *S. c. cinereus* Kerr in the northern part and *S. c. lesueuri* Duvernoy in the southernmost section.

SMOKY SHREW *Sorex fumeus* Miller

SIZE–Total length, 110–25 mm. (4.3–5 in.); weight, 6–11 gms. (.2–.36 oz.).

DESCRIPTION–This is one of the **largest** (except *S. palustris*) of the shrews of the genus *Sorex*. In winter it is **dark gray** above, with slightly paler underparts. In summer it is **dull brown**, slightly yellowish below, with bicolored tail and pale feet. There are six mammae, all inguinal.

The greatest length of the cranium is usually between 18 and 19 mm., and its greatest width between 8.4 and 9.1 mm. Without recourse

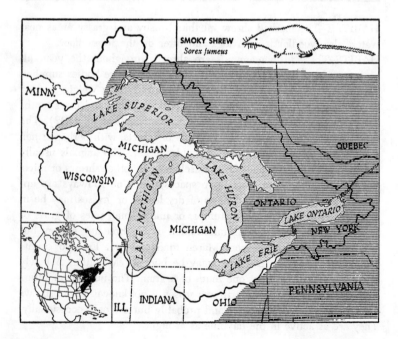

to known comparative material, it may be impossible for a student to identify the skull with certainty.

HABITAT–The smoky shrew is fairly confined to typical northern forests in which there is a deep leaf-mold cover. It prefers birch and hemlock.

HABITS–These shrews make use of the burrows of other small mammals and perhaps make some of their own, through the damp leaf mold where they search for insects and other small invertebrates. Their nests of dry leaves and herbaceous plants may be found beneath old stumps, logs, and rocks. Four to seven naked, blind young are born in late April. Another litter may be born in July or early August. The gestation period is not known (probably less than three weeks), nor is it certain how many litters one female may bear in a year. Other unknowns are: home-range size, population density, and longevity. It is suspected that few live more than a year in the wild (Hamilton, 1940).

ECONOMIC STATUS–Inasmuch as most of the food of the smoky shrew consists of arthropods, it is probably wholly beneficial.

REMARKS–Apparently these shrews are not distributed evenly over their range. Their abundance locally at times is suggestive of colonial habits.

ARCTIC SHREW *Sorex arcticus* Kerr

SIZE–Total length, 104–25 mm. (4–5 in.); weight, 7–11 gms. (.25–.36 oz.).

DESCRIPTION–The arctic shrew differs from the other shrews of the Great Lakes region in its tricolor pattern. The back, from head to base of tail, is dark brown, nearly black in winter. The sides are considerably lighter brown and sharply contrasted with the color of the back. The underparts are paler than the sides. The tricolor pattern is less distinct in summer than in winter. This shrew is larger than the masked and pigmy shrews. The mammae are in three pairs, one abdominal and two inguinal. In the skull, the fourth unicuspid is smaller than the third (Fig. 29f).

HABITAT–The arctic shrew lives in tamarack and spruce swamps.

HABITS–Little is known of the habits of this seclusive and seldom-seen shrew, but from inference one may say that they are similar, in general, to those of other shrews. Its food consists chiefly of insects, which it obtains from its moist surroundings. Jackson (1928) recorded one female of this species that contained six embryos.

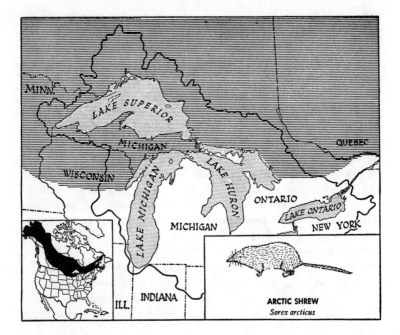

ARCTIC SHREW
Sorex arcticus

ECONOMIC STATUS–As little is known about the habits of this shrew it is difficult to evaluate its status. One is safe in saying that it is wholly beneficial. It interferes in no way with man's activities, and it destroys many harmful insects.

SOUTHEASTERN SHREW *Sorex longirostris* Bachman

SIZE–Total length, 78–90 mm. (3–3.5 in.); weight 3.5–5 gms. (.1–.17 oz.).

DESCRIPTION–This is a **small brownish** shrew with a relatively short tail (27–33 mm.; 1–1.3 in.). The tail is indistinctly bicolor, dark brown above, slightly paler below. There are six mammae. The first and second unicuspids are about equal in size and distinctly larger than the third and fourth.

HABITAT–These shrews have been taken in open fields and in woods.

HABITS–About all we know of the habits of this rare shrew is that it frequents different habitats, its nest may be a simple one in a shallow depression in the ground, and four young may be born in a litter some time in early April.

ECONOMIC STATUS–It is probably wholly beneficial.

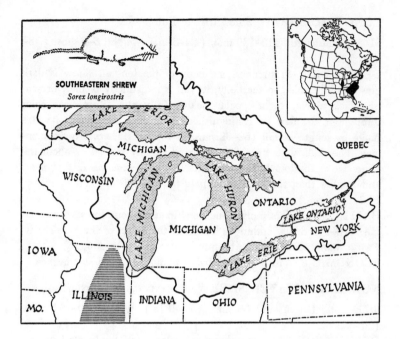

SOUTHEASTERN SHREW
Sorex longirostris

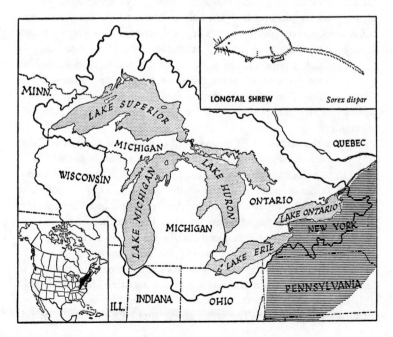

LONGTAIL SHREW   *Sorex dispar*

LONGTAIL SHREW *Sorex dispar* Batchelder

SIZE—Total length, 113–130 mm. (4.4–5 in.); weight, 5–6 gms. (.18–.21 oz.).

DESCRIPTION—In summer, the body of the longtail shrew is dark gray, slightly paler on the belly; its tail is indistinctly bicolor, brownish black above, slightly paler below. In winter, it is **slate color** throughout. It may be distinguished from other shrews in its size range by **length of tail** (52–62 mm.; 2–2.5 in.). There are six mammae. The skull, with the third unicuspid slightly smaller or about the same size as the fourth, is larger than that of S. *cinereus* or S. *fumeus* and smaller than the skull of S. *palustris* (length of skull of *dispar*, 17.3–18.2 mm.).

HABITAT—It prefers moist conditions in coniferous forests.

HABITS—Practically nothing is known of the habits of this rare shrew. Two or more young may be born in a litter as late as August.

ECONOMIC STATUS—It is probably of no economic significance.

NORTHERN WATER SHREW *Sorex palustris* Richardson

SIZE—Total length, 143–58 mm. (5.6–6 in.); weight, 10–15.5 gms. (.35–.55 oz.).

DESCRIPTION—The water shrew is the **largest** of the longtail shrews. Of its total length, two and one-half inches are tail. The dense, soft fur is black above, silver below. The chief external character by which it may be distinguished from all other mammals in its size range in the Great Lakes region is the presence of **stiff hairs** on its large **hind feet** and toes, hairs which serve the same purpose as webbing of the toes—an aid to swimming efficiency. The middle toes are partly webbed. The mammae are in three pairs, one abdominal and two inguinal.

It has the largest skull of any of the shrews of the Great Lakes region except *Blarina* (greatest width of skull in *Blarina* more than 11 mm., in S. *palustris* less than 11 mm.). The skull of the water shrew, like the skulls of other members of the genus *Sorex*, is smooth and delicate, that of *Blarina* is ridged and heavy, with a prominent sagittal crest. The third unicuspid is smaller than the fourth.

HABITAT—This shrew lives along small streams and in low bogs.

HABITS—The habits of water shrews are little known. It is certain, not only from observation, but also from the structure of their hind feet, that they live near the water and are aquatic. Their food probably consists to a large extent of small aquatic animals.

ECONOMIC STATUS—The water shrew probably is of no economic

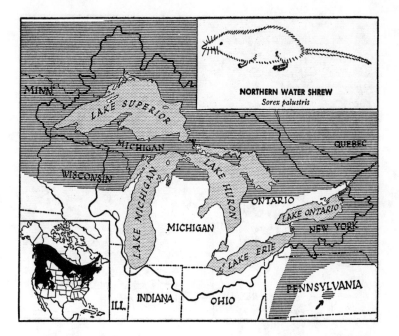

NORTHERN WATER SHREW
Sorex palustris

importance in this area. It is so rare and, in addition, occupies such remote parts of the region that man's interests are in no way affected by its presence.

PIGMY SHREW *Microsorex hoyi* Baird

SIZE–Total length, 78–103 mm. (3–4 in.); weight, 2.3–4.0 gms. (.08–.15 oz.).

DESCRIPTION–In body size this is the **smallest** mammal considered here. It is uniformly light brown above with slightly paler underparts of body and tail. By external characters alone it cannot be distinguished with certainty from the masked shrew. When the skull is viewed from the side, however, there are apparent only three instead of five unicuspids on each side of the upper jaw (Fig. 29d). Although present, the other unicuspids are minute.

HABITAT–Wooded areas and grass clearings bordering them in both dry and wet situations comprise the habitat of the pigmy shrew.

HABITS–Practically nothing is known of the life of this rare shrew. It may be assumed that its habits are similar to those of *Sorex cinereus*. A captive of this species in New York emitted a strong musk odor when excited (Saunders, 1929). A female taken in heavy blue grass

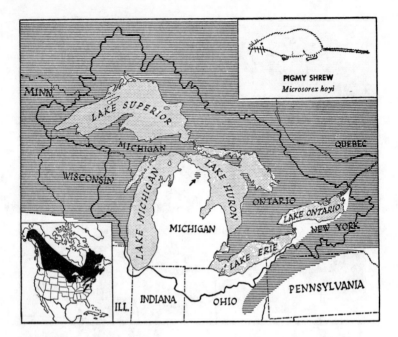

PIGMY SHREW
Microsorex hoyi

in Clay County, Iowa, contained seven embryos (Scott, 1939).

ECONOMIC STATUS–This species, as presently known, is of little or no importance economically.

REMARKS–Three races of this species occur in the Great Lakes region: *M. h. intervectus* Jackson in northern Minnesota, Michigan, and Ontario; *M. h. hoyi* Baird in southern Wisconsin and Ontario; and *M. h. thompsoni* in New York, Pennsylvania, and Ohio.

LEAST SHREW *Cryptotis parva* Say

SIZE–Total length, 69–84 mm. (2.7–3.3 in.); weight, 4.0–6.5 gms. (.15–.23 oz.).

DESCRIPTION–Shrews of the genus *Cryptotis* may be distinguished from all other mammals in the Great Lakes region by their small size, **short tail,** nearly uniform **dark brown** coloration above with ashy gray underparts, small black beady eyes, long nose, and five toes on each foot (Fig. 4). They may be set apart from the other shrews, except *Blarina,* by their short tails; from *Blarina* by their small size and brown instead of dark slate color. The skull may be distinguished from the skulls of all other shrews by the number of teeth, thirty instead of thirty-two.

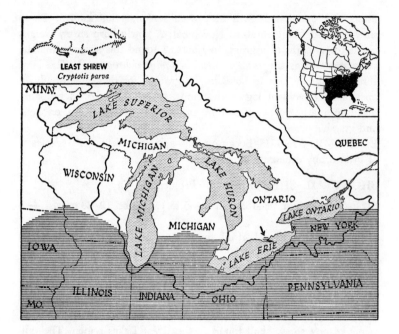

HABITAT–The least shrew lives in open grass and brush.

HABITS–Biologists profess but a sketchy knowledge of the habits of a mammal that has been known to science for more than a hundred years. Three to six young are born in a litter, but the number of

Fig. 4. Least shrew.

litters that one female will bear each season is not known. These shrews breed from March to November. A newly born shrew weighs about three-tenths of a gram. In Kansas I found this shrew using the same runways as the prairie vole (*Pedomys ochrogaster*). The least shrews probably nest in holes in the ground, for they are usually in open areas devoid of logs and stumps. Insects and worms probably make up a large part of their diet. In captivity one ate frogs, crickets, and grasshoppers.

ECONOMIC STATUS–Because of its apparent rarity, this species is of little if any economic importance.

SHORTTAIL SHREW *Blarina brevicauda* Say

SIZE–Total length, 98–132 mm. (4–5 in.); weight, 12–23 gms. (.4–.8 oz.).

DESCRIPTION–The shorttail shrew may be distinguished from all other mammals of the Great Lakes region by its combination of stocky build, five-toed feet, **short tail,** small eyes and ears, long proboscis-like nose, and **dark slate** coloration. The skull of *Blarina,* instead of being smooth and delicate as in the other shrews, is somewhat angular with prominent ridges and crests. It has the greatest width (more than 11 mm.) of any shrew skull found in the Great Lakes region. The unicuspid teeth, viewed from the side, are in two pairs—a large pair in front with a much smaller pair behind. The fifth unicuspid is so small that it is not apparent from a side view. The teeth also are usually dark chestnut, but this feature is not peculiar to *Blarina.*

HABITAT–This shrew is most common in heavy forests and low, damp, swampy areas, but may be expected in practically every land habitat in the area even to the sand dunes of the Lake Michigan shore.

HABITS–These animated bundles of energy make their own burrow systems, but, on occasion, burrows made by moles or microtines probably are appropriated after abandonment by their original owners. In winter shorttail shrews probably make their own runways beneath the leaves and snow, where they are active at all times, although seldom seen by the average person. Their nests, measuring six to eight inches in diameter and made up of dry leaves, grasses, and, infrequently, mouse fur, often are placed under logs at depths of one to twelve inches or more. Five to eight young in a litter have been recorded; although the female has but six mammae, all inguinal. Young are born in spring and later summer, or early autumn, but it is not known how many litters an adult female will produce in one season. The young

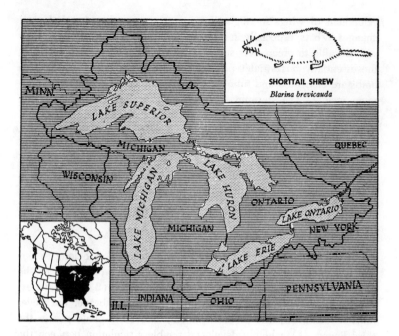

SHORTTAIL SHREW
Blarina brevicauda

are naked and dark pink when born. The period of gestation is twenty-one days or more.

The home range of this animal is probably about one-half acre in area, and populations of twenty-five or more to an acre may occur. The food consists of insects, worms, crustacea, small vertebrates, mollusks, centipedes, arachnids, millepedes, and plant materials. For more extensive accounts of this interesting animal the reader is referred to Shull (1907) and Hamilton (1929 and 1930).

ECONOMIC STATUS—As an insect destroyer, this shrew, because of its abundance, undoubtedly is of considerable economic importance.

BATS (ORDER CHIROPTERA)

The word "chiroptera" means "winged hand" and expresses the one peculiarity that sets this large order of mammals apart from all others. The hand is modified with greatly elongated fingers that serve as a framework to support the thin, leathery skin stretched between them, forming the wing. The bat's wing serves the same purpose, and quite as efficiently, as that of a bird, although it differs structurally. It supports the body in air and makes flight possible. Along with the development of wings for flight there were many other morphological changes in bats, especially in skeleton and musculature. Although they still are able to creep over surfaces with some agility, bats have lost the essentially terrestrial type of locomotion. The bones of the fore limbs are elongated and tubular, giving maximum strength with minimum weight. The sternum is keeled to give better support to the powerful wing (pectoral) muscles. The hind limbs have been diverted backward and upward so that the acetabula of the pelvis face upward rather than downward. An anomalous situation is present in the extremely rudimentary eyes of bats, which are nocturnal. To compensate for their apparently poor vision bats possess extremely acute tactile and auditory senses. They are guided in flight by echoes from supersonic cries emitted at the rate of about thirty a second.

PLAINNOSE BATS (FAMILY VESPERTILIONIDAE)

All of the bats inhabiting the area of the Great Lakes belong to this one family, members of which are distinguished from those of the other families of bats by (1) their simple muzzles, (2) long tails extending to the edge of the wide interfemoral membrane, but never much beyond, (3) the presence of only two bony phalanges in the third finger, (4) a highly developed double articulation between the scapula and humerus, and (5) the rudimentary ulna.

LITTLE BROWN MYOTIS *Myotis lucifugus* Le Conte

SIZE–Total length, 80–95 mm. (3–3.7 in.); weight, 6–9.5 gms. (.2–.34 oz.).

DESCRIPTION–This medium-sized bat is usually olive brown, sometimes yellowish brown, with a distinctly dark spot on the shoulder. The underparts are gray, washed with buffy. The wing and interfemoral membranes, like the ears, are dark brown or black and nearly devoid of hair. There is **no keel** on a calcar. The tragus is long and pointed. The **ear,** when laid forward, **does not extend** noticeably **beyond** the end of the **nose.** The skull is difficult to distinguish without comparing it directly with other skulls of known identity. It is slightly broader in interorbital width (4 mm. or more) than that of *keeni* or *sodalis*, with which it is most likely to be confused.

HABITAT–This bat may live in hollow trees, beneath loose bark, in caves, about buildings, in which it may be found hanging behind blinds or loose siding by day; flying over fields, lakes, and in forests by night.

HABITS–Like most bats, these are night fliers. They appear at dusk

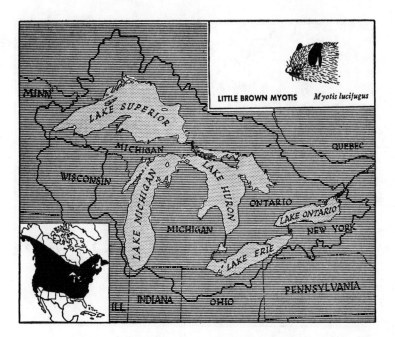

LITTLE BROWN MYOTIS   *Myotis lucifugus*

and fly over water or among trees in search of flying insects, their chief food. During the daytime they hang, head down, in some dark recess. Usually, one bat is born at a time in late June or early July. The young are carried by their mothers for three or four days after birth and are then left in the roost. When about a month old the young take to their wings and become self-supporting. These bats apparently possess a homing sense. They have been known to return to their home cave when released 180 miles away. They leave the roost as dusk approaches and do not return until between four and five o'clock in the morning. In late fall they either hibernate or migrate south.

ECONOMIC STATUS–Little brown bats, destroyers of many insects, are almost wholly beneficial. On occasions they may take up their abode in the attic of a house. This local nuisance is easily remedied by closing the entrances in the evening after the bats have departed to feed.

INDIANA MYOTIS *Myotis sodalis* Miller and Allen

SIZE–Total length, 70–91 mm. (2.8–3.5 in.); weight, 6–9 gms. (.2–.32 oz.).

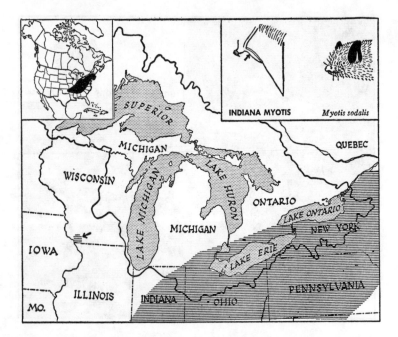

INDIANA MYOTIS   *Myotis sodalis*

DESCRIPTION–This is a small brown bat of about the same size and general appearance as *lucifugus,* with which it might be confused. It differs from *lucifugus,* however, in having **tricolor fur** (three color bands from tip to base) with a pinkish gray tinge instead of olive brown or light brown. The **calcar** (at the side of the foot) also has a **definite keel.** In the skull there is a slight median crest, and the interorbital constriction is always less than 4 mm., whereas in *lucifugus* it is 4 mm. or more.

HABITAT–The known specimens were taken mostly from caves.

HABITS–This bat was not known until 1928. Before that time it was confused in collections with *lucifugus.* About all that is known of it is that it lives in caves. Most of the specimens in collections were taken during hibernation.

KEEN MYOTIS *Myotis keeni* Merriam

SIZE–Total length, 79–90 mm. (3–3.5 in.); weight, 6–9 gms. (.2–.32 oz.).

DESCRIPTION–In coloration and size this bat is similar to the little brown myotis previously described. It differs in having **larger ears** which, when laid forward, extend 3 or 4 mm. beyond the tip of the nose instead of just reaching the tip, as in *lucifugus.* The tragus is

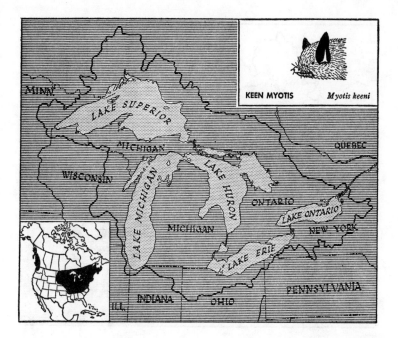

KEEN MYOTIS   *Myotis keeni*

long and pointed. The skull is slightly longer and is narrower at the interorbital constriction (less than 4 mm.) than that of *lucifugus*, but direct comparison is necessary to be certain of the identity.

HABITAT–The keen myotis may be found in forested areas.

HABITS–The habits of this bat probably are similar to those of the little brown myotis. The keen myotis is apparently the less common of the two—at least it is represented in collections by fewer specimens—and is considered rare in the area.

ECONOMIC STATUS–As far as is known it is entirely beneficial.

SMALL-FOOTED MYOTIS *Myotis subulatus* Say

SIZE–Total length, 73–82 mm. (2.9–3.2 in.); weight, 5–8 gms. (.17–.28 oz.).

DESCRIPTION–This is a small, brown bat with black ears and membranes and a **blackish mask** across the face. The calcar has a definite keel. It is the smallest myotis in the Great Lakes region (length of forearm, 31–34 mm.; 1.2 in.). The delicate skull may be difficult to identify, but the number of teeth (thirty-eight) and the small size (greatest length, 14.2 mm. or less) should place it. There are two mammae.

HABITAT–It lives in natural caves, chiefly in mountainous areas.

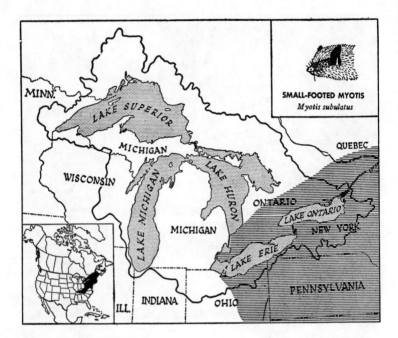

SMALL-FOOTED MYOTIS
Myotis subulatus

HABITS—These bats hang with the wings partly outstretched, not close to the body. One is born, probably in May, to each adult female. Apparently these bats migrate, or move, from one cave to another, in late winter.

ECONOMIC STATUS—It is probably beneficial.

SILVER-HAIRED BAT *Lasionycteris noctivagans* Le Conte

SIZE—Total length, 90–115 mm. (3.5–4.5 in.); weight, 6–11 gms. (.2–.39 oz.).

DESCRIPTION—The silver-haired bat is of medium size with short, rounded ears and a blunt tragus. Its outstanding character, which at once distinguishes it from other bats, is its **color; blackish brown** with many of the hairs of the belly, interfemoral membrane, and especially of the back tipped with **silvery white.** The interfemoral membrane is furred above for at least the basal half. The skull differs from that of any other bat of the area by the number of teeth, thirty-six in all. Its combination of teeth is present in no other mammal of the Great Lakes region.

HABITAT—The silver-haired bat lives in forest areas, preferably along streams and lakes.

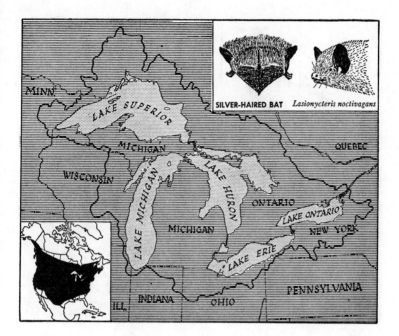

SILVER-HAIRED BAT *Lasionycteris noctivagans*

HABITS–This is one of the solitary bats. It is not found in colonies, but hangs alone in trees or other shelter during the daytime. The young, usually two, are born in late June or early July. They start flying at about three or four weeks of age. Their food, like that of other bats, consists of insects, which are taken over water or in and about trees. These bats are rather late fliers and seldom are seen before deep dusk, at which time they are difficult to collect. They probably migrate south for the winter, but the dates of their arrival in the spring and of their departure in the fall are unknown.

ECONOMIC STATUS–These bats never, as far as is known, interfere with man's interest and must be classed as wholly beneficial because of the many insects they consume.

EASTERN PIPISTREL *Pipistrellus subflavus* F. Cuvier

SIZE–Total length, 81–89 mm. (3.2–3.5 in.); weight, 3.5–6 gms. (.12–.2 oz.).

DESCRIPTION–The eastern pipistrel is one of our **smallest** bats. It is yellowish brown to drab brown above, and slightly paler below. The **tragus** is short and **blunt,** not sharply pointed as in *Myotis*. The delicate skull may be distinguished from all other bat skulls of this

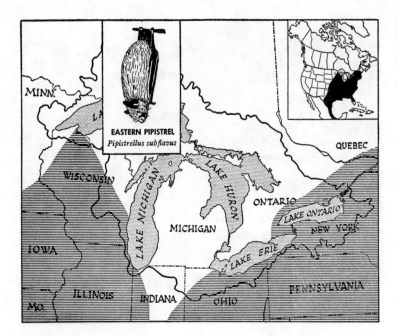

EASTERN PIPISTREL
Pipistrellus subflavus

area by the number of teeth, thirty-four in all. There are two mammae.

HABITAT–It is found in caves, buildings, and crevices in rocks or trees.

HABITS–The eastern pipistrel is an early evening, erratic flyer. It hibernates during the winter in caves or other sheltered places. In this area it spends about four months, November through February, in hibernation. In June or July two young are borne by each female. She may carry the young with her until they become too great a burden. When about three weeks of age, the young take to the air on their own. They may live seven years or more in the wild. Their food consists of small insects taken on the wing.

ECONOMIC STATUS–They are probably entirely beneficial.

BIG BROWN BAT *Eptesicus fuscus* Peale and Beauvois

SIZE–Total length, 96–117 mm. (3.7–4.6 in.); weight, 11–17 gms. (.39–.6 oz.).

DESCRIPTION–This bat is easily distinguished from all others of the area by its **large** size and uniformly **dark brown** body, with black ears and membranes (Fig. 5). The ears are broad and rounded, and the **tragus** is rather **blunt,** not sharply pointed as in *Myotis*. The skull

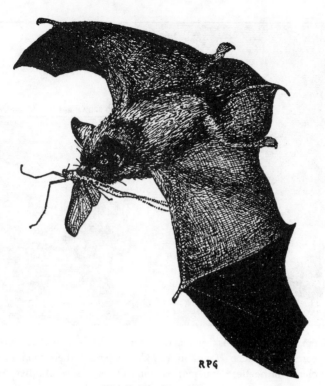

RPG

Fig. 5. Big brown bat.

is large and has a peculiar dental formula. Although it has the same total number of teeth as has that of *Lasiurus*, the arrangement is different. In *Eptesicus* there are two upper incisors and one upper premolar on each side instead of one incisor and two premolars, as in *Lasiurus*. The big brown bat is distinguished from specimens of *Nycticeius*, with which it might be confused, by its larger size and by its dental formula.

HABITAT–This bat has taken up residence about buildings, where it is common, especially in winter. Before the advent of man it occupied hollow trees, caves, or crevices in rock cliffs.

HABITS–Some individuals of this species remain throughout the year. During the winter they hang in sheltered spots and are fairly inactive, although on occasion they have been seen flying in Ann Arbor in the middle of winter. One or two young are born to each breeding female, probably in June. These bats, as a rule, fly late and are seen

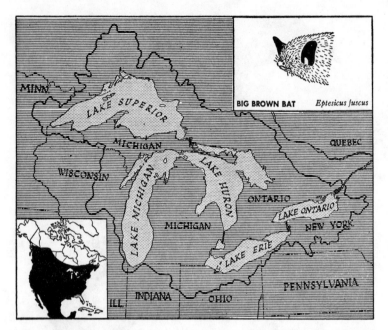

BIG BROWN BAT   *Eptesicus fuscus*

seldom before late dusk, when they come relatively near the ground in search of insects. Hamilton (1933a) reported their food to consist chiefly of beetles, Hymenoptera, and Diptera; several other groups of insects are eaten in smaller numbers. Little is known of their social habits; groups of four to six may semihibernate together during the colder months, but they are somewhat solitary during the summer. ECONOMIC STATUS–Except as an occasional annoyance to some household, these bats are wholly beneficial. Their diet consists partly of flies.

EVENING BAT *Nycticeius humeralis* Rafinesque

SIZE–Total length, 95 mm. (3.7 in.); weight, 10 gms. (.35 oz.).
DESCRIPTION–Externally, the evening bat is like a miniature big brown bat, with the same uniform **dark brown** above and black ears and membranes. The underparts are washed with buffy. The ears are rounded, and the **tragus** is short and **blunt**. This bat is distinguished from specimens of *Eptesicus* by its size (forearm less than 40 mm., 1.6 in., long). The skull differs from that of any other bat of the area in the dental formula. From *Myotis*, which is about the same size and color, it is set apart by its shorter (less than 4.5 mm.) tragus, which is blunt rather than pointed.

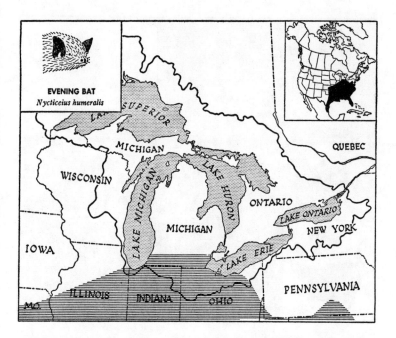

EVENING BAT
Nycticeius humeralis

LAKE SUPERIOR

MICHIGAN

WISCONSIN

LAKE MICHIGAN

LAKE HURON

IOWA

ILLINOIS

MO.

INDIANA

MICHIGAN

OHIO

ONTARIO

QUEBEC

LAKE ONTARIO

NEW YORK

LAKE ERIE

PENNSYLVANIA

HABITAT–Wooded areas and buildings are included in its places of refuge during the daytime.

HABITS–In some areas this bat is colonial, at least during part of the year. A female, taken on May 23, 1938, by H. R. Becker in the window of his home at Climax, Michigan, contained two well-developed embryos.

RED BAT *Lasiurus borealis* Müller

SIZE–Total length, 93–115 mm. (3.7–4.5 in.); weight, 6.5–13.5 gms. (.23–.48 oz.).

DESCRIPTION–This is a medium-sized, brick-red or yellowish **red** bat. The hairs have dark brown or black bases followed by a broad band of golden yellow, then a narrow band of red, usually faintly tipped with white. The males are much more reddish than are the females. The membranes are black; the **interfemoral** is **completely furred** above. The females have four mammae, an unusual number for bats (most bats have two). The combination of teeth and the small size (less than 15 mm., .6 in., long) serves to distinguish the skull. The first upper premolar is small and may be overlooked without the aid of a lens.

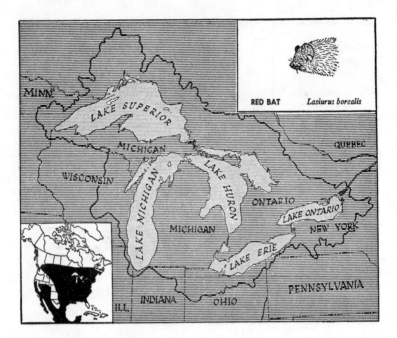

RED BAT   *Lasiurus borealis*

HABITAT–The red bat lives in wooded areas.

HABITS–This solitary bat, as a rule, spends the daytime hanging alone in a tree. In the evening, several red bats may be seen flying over the same general area. If an individual red bat is watched closely, it will be noticed that it flies over a definite part of the general area under observation. There may be two bats, but rarely more, flying the same course at the same time. They may shift their hunting area as the evening progresses, depending somewhat on weather conditions, but I am of the opinion that each bat has its particular area, which it hunts night after night. The young, one to four for each female, are born in June. They cling to their mother until their total weight becomes too much for her to support on her travels. It is not unusual to find a mother stranded on the ground, unable to take flight, because of the heavy burden of young clinging to the fur of her breast. These bats apparently migrate south in autumn. If any remain through the winter, I am not aware of their ever having been noticed at that season. In other parts of the country they have been observed in large numbers, flying as do migrating birds.

ECONOMIC STATUS–They are wholly beneficial.

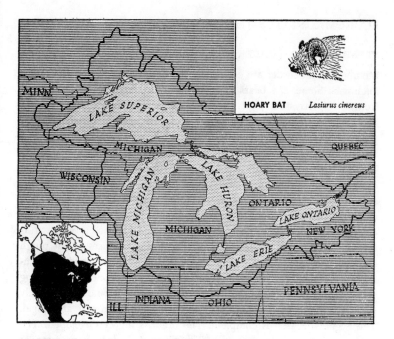

HOARY BAT   *Lasiurus cinereus*

HOARY BAT *Lasiurus cinereus* Beauvois

SIZE–Total length, 130–49 mm. (5–5.9 in.); weight, 26–31 gms. (.9–1 oz.).

DESCRIPTION–The hoary bat is the largest and most strikingly colored of the bats that are found in the Great Lakes region. It is easily distinguished by the combination of large size, furred inter-femoral membrane, and coloration. As in *borealis,* the basal parts of the hairs are dark brown or black followed by a broad band of golden yellow, but the subterminal band is dark brown or black, and the hairs are broadly tipped with white, giving the animal a dis-tinctly **hoary appearance.** The **throat** is **yellow.** The skull is like that of *borealis* but larger. Although the skull is slightly shorter than that of *Eptesicus,* the brain case is much larger. There are four mammae.

HABITAT–It inhabits forested areas.

HABITS–The hoary bat, like the red bat, is solitary and migrates south for the winter. It is not as common as the red bat. Owing to its relative scarcity and its habit of not appearing until late in the evenings it is one of the bats least often seen. Usually, two young are born in June; they cling to the mother on her excursions for food until they are too heavy for her to support.

ECONOMIC STATUS–This bat is wholly beneficial.

FLESH EATERS (ORDER CARNIVORA)

Members of this order are essentially the flesh eaters among Eutherian mammals. Some, the bears and raccoons for instance, have deviated from the strictly flesh diet and now are omnivorous. Their teeth are correspondingly modified, but the primary flesh-eating adaptation still persists. The incisors are small, more or less pointed, and set in a transverse row between the large, sharp, conical, recurved canines. The premolars usually, except the fourth upper premolar, are simple, compressed, pointed teeth with one or two roots. In all modern carnivores the fourth upper premolar and the first lower molar are enlarged and specialized as shearing teeth (except where this specialization has been lost, in bears and raccoons); these are known as the carnassials, and are the teeth that a dog or cat uses to cut tough tendons. The last molars are sometimes reduced. The mandible articulates with the cranium by close-fitting transverse condyles, allowing only for a vertical movement. The orbits open behind, but usually there are prominent postorbital processes on the frontal and jugal. The zygomatic arch is complete. The brain is highly developed. The leg bones are of moderate length. The radius and ulna are separate, as are also the tibia and fibula. The feet normally have five digits (pollex and hallux often reduced) tipped with claws, and are plantigrade (bears) or digitigrade (dogs). Carnivora vary in size from the least weasel, hardly larger than a mouse, to bears and lions.

BEARS (FAMILY URSIDAE)

The bears are large, plantigrade, bob-tailed mammals that have lost the primary flesh-eating adaptations of the teeth. They still retain the large canines, but the molars are low, flat, crushing teeth similar to the teeth of man in some respects. The molars are progressively enlarged, and the last molar is much larger than the one directly in front of it. Accordingly, the premolars are much reduced, the front ones being mere pegs, which are usually lost in old age. An adult bear rarely has the full complement of teeth. The bears are the largest carnivores in the Great Lakes region. They have five toes on each foot.

BLACK BEAR *Ursus americanus* Pallas

SIZE–Total length, 5–7 ft.; weight, 225–475 lbs.

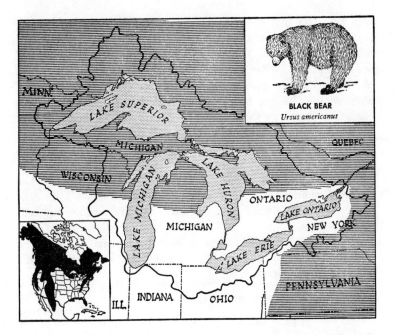

BLACK BEAR
Ursus americanus

DESCRIPTION—The bear is one of the larger mammals of the area. So common is it in zoos that nearly everyone is familiar with this **bulky, black** or dark brown, bob-tailed animal. Its feet are five-toed, and, like man, it walks on its entire foot (plantigrade). Adult bears are two to three feet in height when standing on all fours. The mammae are in three pairs, one in the inguinal and two in the pectoral region. The skull may be distinguished easily from the skulls of all other mammals of the Great Lakes region by its combination of large size, the presence of long, pointed canine teeth, and by its last molar tooth, which is larger than the one in front of it. The only skull with which it might be confused is that of a wolf, and the character of the last molar teeth is sufficient to separate these two.

HABITAT—It resides in heavily wooded areas and swamps.

HABITS—The bear is not a sociable animal. The father bear probably never sees his offspring except by accident. The mother bear dens up alone and in late January or early February gives birth, in alternate years, to one or two, rarely three, cubs, weighing nine to twelve ounces each. When she comes out in the spring she brings her cubs with her. This part of the family remains together until the young are weaned in August, after which time the individuals become, as a rule, solitary animals. The gestation period is seven to seven and one-half months. When bears emerge from the long winter period of hibernation they appear to be in good condition. Shortly after this, however, they become thin and unkempt while shedding the winter coat. Omnivorous in their habits, bears will eat anything—carrion, fresh berries, or tender roots. Individual bears, especially old males, are said to range as much as fifteen miles from their homes. On this point there is very little definite information. The mother bear with her cubs would not be expected to range so far. Whether or not they display territorial behavior is unknown, but it is possible that the mother maintains a small protected area while her cubs are still with her.

ECONOMIC STATUS—As a game animal, the bear holds an important place among the fauna. An occasional raid on livestock should not be taken too seriously.

RACCOONS (FAMILY PROCYONIDAE)

In this family, as in the Ursidae, the carnassial specialization of the teeth has been lost in varying degrees. There are only two lower molars, whereas bears have three. The canines are well developed, but the molar teeth are low-crowned with rounded cusps. In the raccoon, the only representative of the family in the area, the five-toed feet are plantigrade, and the short tail is ringed or annulated. Raccoons are semiarboreal in habits.

RACCOON *Procyon lotor* Linnaeus

SIZE—Total length, 655–960 mm. (26–38 in.); weight, 12–36 lbs.
DESCRIPTION—The raccoon is a medium-sized animal, about the size of a Boston bulldog. Its fur is long and grizzled gray. The **black mask** over its eyes and the **ringed tail** are distinctive characters found in no other mammal of the area. The raccoon is plantigrade, has a lumbering gait when on the ground, and is quite at home in the water or in trees. There are six mammae. In the skull, the large canines are present, but the molar teeth are not typical of the carnivora. Instead of sharp teeth for cutting flesh, the teeth of the raccoon have low rounded cusps for crushing, fitting the animal for an omnivorous diet. The bony palate extends back noticeably beyond the last molars. This is also true in some mustelids, but they have only one upper molar on each side, whereas the raccoon has two.

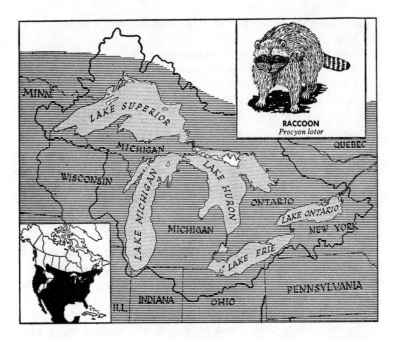

HABITAT–The raccoon prefers wooded areas, especially along streams and near lakes where large hollow trees are present.

HABITS–This primarily nocturnal animal on occasion is seen abroad during the daytime. Raccoons prefer hollow trees for their dens. They are omnivorous in their diet, eating a great variety of foods, including nuts, fruits, grains, insects, crayfish, frogs, and bird eggs.

During the cold winter months, raccoons go into a partial hibernation either alone or in groups, coming out on warm days. They mate in late January or early February and the three to seven young are born in late April or early May. The gestation period is about sixty-three days. When about two months old, the young accompany the mother on her excursions for food and may either remain with her through the year or disperse for a distance of several miles from the home den during the first fall. Wood (1922) described the call of the raccoon as "a shrill tremulo cry, almost like a whistle, and on a still night [it] may be heard for a long distance. When caught by a dog it sometimes utters a snarling cry, from rage or pain." The raccoon is a sociable animal, at least within the family group, which usually forages and dens together. The raccoon does not look for trouble, but when it is hard-pressed by dogs and cannot reach a tree, it fights valiantly. It is a good dog that can dispatch a raccoon without help.

ECONOMIC STATUS–On occasions rogue raccoons will raid poultry houses and during "roasting-ear" time they may damage cornfields. For some people, the fur value of the pelts and the pleasure derived from hunting the animals with dogs far outweigh the harm they do.

WEASEL-LIKE MAMMALS (FAMILY MUSTELIDAE)

A rather large and varied group of carnivores makes up the family Mustelidae. All members have the molars reduced to one on each side of the upper jaws and two on each side of the lower jaws. The carnassial teeth are specialized and well developed. The single molars back of the carnassials are usually broad with the transverse diameter as great as, or greater than, the longitudinal diameter. The auditory bullae are flattened or elongated, a characteristic that carries through the entire skull. Members of this family usually are digitigrade or semi-digitigrade, sometimes plantigrade. The legs are short, and the body usually is elongate. There are five well-clawed toes on each foot. A pair of musk glands in the anal region is characteristic of the family. In size, they range from the least weasel (the smallest living carnivore) to the wolverine, which is as large as a medium-sized dog. It is in this group that the greatest disparity in size is found between sexes, especially in the genera *Martes* and *Mustela*. In some, the male is twice as large as the female.

MARTEN *Martes americana* Turton

SIZE–Total length, male, 610–30 mm. (24–25 in.), female, 550–60 mm. (21.5–22 in.); weight, 2–4 lbs.

DESCRIPTION–The marten, one of our finest fur-bearers, and now either extremely rare or absent from the southern part of the area (recently introduced [1955] in Wisconsin and Michigan), has soft, thick, rich yellowish brown fur shading into blackish on the tail and legs, **pale buff** on the **throat** and breast, and dull white on the inner sides of the ears. Its body is long and slender, and its tail, about half as long as the body, is distinctly bushy. The legs, as becomes the mustelids, are relatively short, and the feet are large. The female is about three-fourths the size of the male and has eight mammae.

The skull of *Martes*, being dog-like in general appearance, deviates somewhat from the typical mustelid type; the brain case is less flattened, and the auditory bullae are more rounded than is usual in

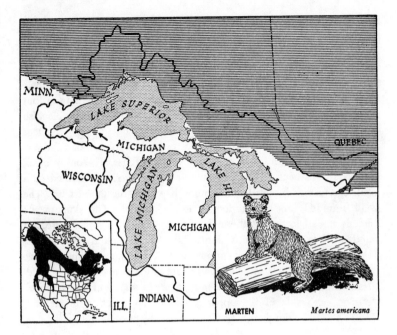

MARTEN   *Martes americana*

the family. The broad molar teeth, however, are typically mustelid in character.

HABITAT–The marten lives in large, dense coniferous forests.

HABITS–It is an arboreal representative of the carnivores and is more at home in the trees than on the ground. Its staple food is, according to most authorities, mice and other small rodents. Included in its menu, however, are squirrels, rabbits, shrews, birds and their eggs, amphibians, reptiles, fish, insects, nuts, and fruit. It is truly omnivorous. The marten prefers a hollow tree for its den; three or four young are born in April. There is one litter a year. The gestation period is about nine months. From all accounts the marten is one of the least sociable of mammals. Little is known of this aspect of its activity except what has been learned from observations of captive animals. The mother apparently assumes the entire responsibility for bringing up the young. The interest of the old male goes no further than the short period of mating. The marten is primarily nocturnal, but spends some time abroad during the day. Its special habitat requirements (coniferous forests), its retreat before the advance of civilization, and its extreme curiosity (making it easy to trap) have combined to reduce its numbers.

ECONOMIC STATUS–Where the marten is numerous enough to permit trapping it is an important fur animal.

FISHER *Martes pennanti* Erxleben

SIZE–Male: total length, 1,000 mm. (39 in.); weight, 4.5 to 10 lbs.

DESCRIPTION–The fisher is really a large edition of the marten, but is of a different color. The body is **dark brown,** approaching blackish down the middle of the rump, on the tapering tail, and on the legs and feet. The nose is blackish also, and the underparts are dark brown, slightly grizzled, with occasional small white patches. The entire **head, shoulders,** and **back** (nearly to the rump) are heavily **grizzled** as a result of the broad whitish subterminal bands on the guard hairs. The small, rounded ears are bordered with light buffy. The skull of the fisher is similar to that of the marten except that it is larger (greatest length always more than 100 mm., 3.9 in.). The skull may be distinguished from that of any other mustelid in the area by its size (about 118 mm., 4.6 in., long), the greatest diameter of the small infraorbital foramen (less than 6 mm., from *Lutra*), and its five cheek teeth on each side of the upper jaw only (from other mustelids). HABITAT–It is found in large forests, usually near water.

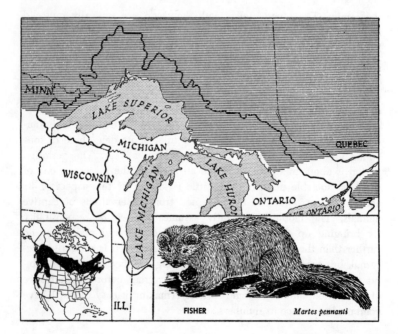

FISHER   *Martes pennanti*

HABITS–The fisher is reported to be a solitary animal, chiefly nocturnal, but often abroad during the day. It is at home in trees or on the ground. The den usually is in a hollow tree or log. Forests are essential to its well-being. Two to four young are born about the first of April. The gestation period is 351 to 358 days. The food of the fisher, like that of the marten, includes practically everything edible. Although omnivorous, it probably subsists chiefly on small rodents, but other animals are eaten when available. Like all of the weasel tribe, the fisher is a courageous fighter both in defense of its life and in subduing its prey.

ECONOMIC STATUS–The fisher, like the marten, is an important fur animal in some areas. Several were introduced in northern Wisconsin in 1956.

SHORTTAIL WEASEL *Mustela erminea* Linnaeus

SIZE–Total length, male, 277–315 mm. (11–12 in.), female, 242–45 mm. (9.5 in.); weight, male, 68–105 gms. (2.4–3.7 oz.), female, 45–74 gms. (1.6–2.6 oz.).

DESCRIPTION–The shorttail weasel has a relatively long, slender body, long neck, and small head. Its legs are short, and the front ones

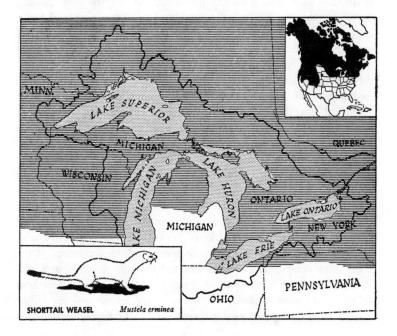

SHORTTAIL WEASEL   *Mustela erminea*

are set well back. The slightly bushy, black-tipped tail is usually less than one-third of the total length. In summer this weasel is uniformly dark brown above, on the outsides of the legs, and on the feet, except as noted below. The underparts are white, usually washed with pale yellowish. The white continues down the inside of the hind legs and feet. The toes are often tipped with white. In the winter the animal is white except for the black tip on the tail. The males are appreciably larger than the females. By its relatively short tail and the white on the inside of its hind feet, this weasel usually can be distinguished from *Mustela frenata*. There are eight mammae.

The skull is relatively long, narrow, and flattened. The auditory bullae are inflated and noticeably longer than wide. The short rostrum tapers abruptly from the zygomatic arches. It is chiefly in size and in the blunt instead of sharply pointed postorbital processes that it is separated from *frenata*. The skull may usually be distinguished from that of *frenata* by size alone, if the sex is known; however, an adult male *erminea* and a female *frenata* may be of about the same size.

HABITAT—The shorttail weasel lives primarily in woodlands, but also, on occasion, in open country.

HABITS—This weasel is chiefly nocturnal, but may be seen hunting during the day. Its food consists mainly of small mammals and birds. It is a born killer and is reported, by numerous authors, to destroy more than it can consume. A captive female ate nearly half its weight in mice every twenty-four hours. An occasional raid on the poultry yard may be disastrous, but most of its killing is done some distance from habitation. It is a mouser of the first order; its long slender body enables it to enter the burrows of these small rodents. Four to eight young of this weasel are born about the first of May. The gestation period is not definitely known, but is probably about seventy-seven days. Young shorttail weasels have a distinct mane on the neck, which disappears in the adults. The den may be in the ground or beneath a rock pile, wood pile, or abandoned building. Although chiefly terrestrial, the weasel can and does climb trees.

ECONOMIC STATUS—All weasels are condemned for their occasional raids on poultry. The few fowl killed are small payment for the hordes of mice kept under control by these energetic little carnivores. If the mice were uncontrolled they undoubtedly would destroy, in actual value, much more in the way of grains than the value of a few hens killed by renegade weasels. The farmer may be excused for killing a weasel around the barnyard if there are no rats or mice making raids on his granary. Otherwise, the weasel is a definite asset to him. The trapper also derives some income from the "ermine."

LONGTAIL WEASEL *Mustela frenata* Lichtenstein

SIZE–Total length, male, 345–405 mm. (13.6–16 in.), female, 284–335 mm. (11–13 in.); weight, male, 170–267 gms. (6–9.4 oz.), female, 85–99 gms. (3–4.4 oz.).

DESCRIPTION–In general coloration, the longtail weasel is similar to the shorttail weasel just described. The upper parts are uniformly dark brown; the underparts are white, washed with dull yellowish. The white usually does not continue on the foot or toes. The tail has a black tip both in summer and winter pelage. This weasel normally turns white in winter in the northern part of its range; in the south, it retains the brown coat. In southern Michigan and Wisconsin some turn white, some remain brown, and others become roan during the winter. In specimens of comparable age and sex, these weasels are distinctly larger and have longer tails (more than one-third of the total length) than do the shorttail weasels. The lack of white on the feet and toes further distinguishes most individuals. The skull is

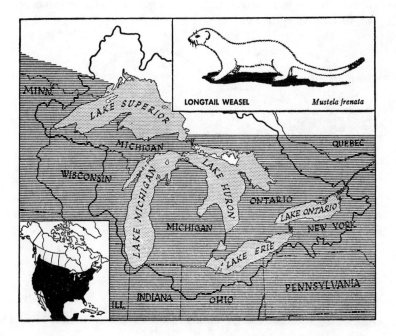

LONGTAIL WEASEL   *Mustela frenata*

larger and more angular, with more sharply pointed postorbital processes, than that of *erminea*. There are eight mammae.

HABITAT–The longtail weasel inhabits forests, brushland, and prairies, especially near water.

HABITS–The habits of this weasel, as far as is known, are essentially the same as those of the shorttail weasel. It is both diurnal and nocturnal. It feeds chiefly on small rodents, but also takes any animal it can overpower. Five to eight young are born in a litter, either in late April or early May. The gestation period is 103–337 days; with an average of 279 days. The reason for the great variation is that there is delayed implantation of the embryo. The young of this species do not possess the well-developed mane present on the young of the shorttail weasel. The father apparently brings food to the young and remains with the family at least until the young can shift for themselves.

ECONOMIC STATUS–As stated for the shorttail weasel, this species also is undoubtedly beneficial to agricultural as well as fur interests.

LEAST WEASEL *Mustela rixosa* Bangs

SIZE–Total length, male, 189–205 mm. (7.4–8 in.), female, 172–76 mm. (6.8–7 in.); weight, male, 40–50 gms. (1.4–1.8 oz.), female, 40–49 gms. (1.4–1.7 oz.).

Fig. 6. Least weasel.

DESCRIPTION–The least weasel is the smallest of the carnivores; the short tail is one to two inches long. The body is of about the thickness of a man's thumb. In summer the animal is dark brown

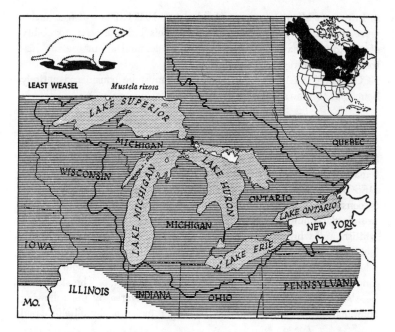

LEAST WEASEL *Mustela rixosa*

above, white or brown spotted with white beneath. It molts in the fall and the new pelage is white throughout, except for occasional scattered black hairs at the tip of the tail (Fig. 6). The tail, unlike that of the other weasels, is not black-tipped, either in winter or summer. There are eight mammae. The skull is similar to that of other weasels except in size. It is smoother, with less ridging than is present in the skulls of the larger weasels.

HABITAT–The least weasel resides in meadows, fields, and possibly woodlands.

HABITS–The food of this little carnivore is, supposedly, mice, insects, and possibly small birds. The weasel enters holes in the ground which customarily are less than one inch in diameter. Old mole runs may be used as den sites. Whether or not the weasels dig their own holes is unknown. Nests of dry grasses and other vegetation have been seen about six inches below the surface of the ground in Iowa. A den of five young was plowed out in a field in Allegan County, Michigan, and I found a dead least weasel in a tree nest-box six feet above ground near Ann Arbor. Four to ten young are born in a litter, and two or more litters may be born in a single season. The gestation period is not known. The winter home range of males, as determined in Iowa, was about two acres (Polderboer, 1942). Dens of four males were spaced forty to sixty rods apart. This indicates the possibility of territorial behavior. Much is yet to be learned about the life history of this interesting animal.

ECONOMIC STATUS–The least weasel must be considered entirely beneficial to man's interests.

MINK *Mustela vison* Schreber

SIZE–Total length, male, 520–620 mm. (20–25 in.), female, 420–520 mm. (17–20 in.); weight, male, 567–964 gms. (20–34 oz.), female, 665–850 gms. (23.5–30 oz.).

DESCRIPTION–The mink is weasel-like in general appearance, but is considerably larger and has a bushier tail. It is uniformly **dark brown**, darkening to nearly black at the tip of the tail. The **chin is whitish,** and white spots are occasionally present on the belly (Fig. 7). The mink does not turn white in winter; however, an occasional white, albinistic individual may be found. The tail is about half as long as the head and body. There are eight mammae. The skull may be distinguished from the skulls of other carnivores by the following combination of characters: the last upper molar is dumbbell-shaped

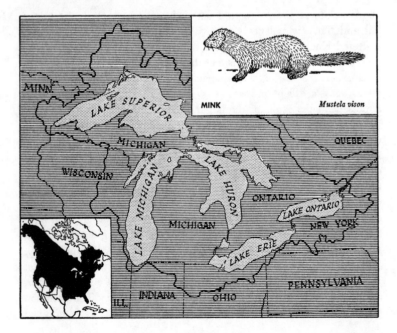

MINK   *Mustela vison*

and is smaller than the tooth in front of it; there are four cheek teeth on each side of the upper jaw; the bony palate extends posteriorly beyond the last molars; and the skull is 58–70 mm. (2.3–2.8 in.) long. The fur is thick, an adaptation for aquatic life.

HABITAT–This mammal is found along streams and lakes, especially where wooded.

Fig. 7. Mink.

HABITS–The mink is chiefly nocturnal. It is at home on land or in water. It is an expert swimmer, although its toes are not webbed. Its home is usually in a burrow along the bank of a stream or lake, or under stumps or logs. The mink may dig its own burrow, or it may appropriate one made by some other animal. Females and males are said to live in separate dens. Three to ten, usually five or six, young are born in late April or early May. The gestation period is about forty-eight to fifty-four days. The young are naked and blind when born. To the regular weasel bill-of-fare—small mammals, birds, eggs, and frogs—the mink adds fish. The major part of its food probably consists of mice and muskrats.

During the time the young are in the nest the female probably does not go far afield in search of food. The extent of the home range is unknown. Old males probably wander several miles along streams or across country.

ECONOMIC STATUS–The only serious damage done by the mink is an occasional raid on the poultry yard. As a fur animal, it is highly prized.

REMARKS–There are two subspecies of mink in the Great Lakes region. *Mustela vison mink* Peale and Beauvois occurs in the southern part and *M. v. vison* Schreber in the north.

RIVER OTTER *Lutra canadensis* Schreber

SIZE–Total length, 1,000–1,130 mm. (39–44 in.); weight, 10–20 lbs.

DESCRIPTION–The legs of the otter are short, and it is built on the lines of a weasel. The tail is thick where it joins the body, then tapers gradually to the tip. The large **feet** are completely **webbed,** the ears are small, and the fur is short and dense—all adaptations for aquatic life. The fur is a rich, glossy, dark brown, slightly paler (silvery gray) on the throat and around the mouth. The female has six mammae. The skull of the otter is flattened dorsoventrally and is broad with a short rostrum. It is the only carnivore of the Great Lakes region that has five cheek teeth on each side of both upper and lower jaws. The teeth, in all but young animals, are usually badly worn, and in some specimens one or more incisors or front premolars have been lost. The bony palate extends posteriorly beyond the last molars, the auditory bullae are flattened, and the infraorbital foramen is large (more than 6 mm., in greatest diameter).

HABITAT–It lives along streams and lakes.

HABITS–Of all the carnivores of the Great Lakes region the otter is the most nearly adapted for an aquatic life. Although present chiefly near the water, it occasionally wanders across country. I have seen its tracks in deep snow several hundred yards from the nearest water. Because of its short legs, the body drags in the snow, and the otter leaves a furrow-like trail. Its home is in a burrow in the bank of some lake or stream, with the entrance usually below water. It is in this burrow that one to three, usually two, blind young are born in late April or early May. The young otter is dark brown. The gestation period is believed to be about eleven to twelve months.

The spring food of the otter in Michigan as determined by examination of stomach contents of 187 animals from trout waters and 105 from nontrout waters was as follows (Lagler and Ostenson, 1942): by volume from trout waters—forage fishes, 35.9 per cent; amphibians, 25.3 per cent; game and pan fishes, 22.7 per cent; crayfishes, 7.4 per cent; the remainder, miscellaneous vertebrates, insects, and snails; by volume from nontrout waters—game and pan fishes, 65.3 per cent;

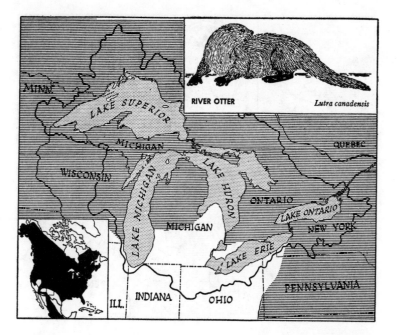

RIVER OTTER   *Lutra canadensis*

amphibians, 14.4 per cent; forage fishes, 11.2 per cent; crayfishes, 3.7 per cent; the remainder, miscellaneous vertebrates and insects. Its diet may vary with the season and with the availability of certain food items. One conclusion is apparent: the otter gets most of its food from the water.

The home range of the otter has been estimated variously to include fifteen to one hundred miles of shore line along the borders of streams or lakes. Here again more definite information is needed.

ECONOMIC STATUS–This mammal was at one time a more valuable fur bearer than it is at present. Its depletion in numbers, however, brought about action for closed seasons in some places. It is questionable whether the otter can withstand heavy cropping. Although it eats game fish, the importance of this may be magnified by the fisherman. The enjoyment of seeing such a splendid animal as the otter should not be overlooked.

BADGER *Taxidea taxus* Schreber

SIZE–Total length, 720–75 mm. (28–31 in.); weight, 13–25 lbs.
DESCRIPTION–In general, the badger is yellowish gray and has a narrow white stripe from its nose over the top of its head, **white cheeks,**

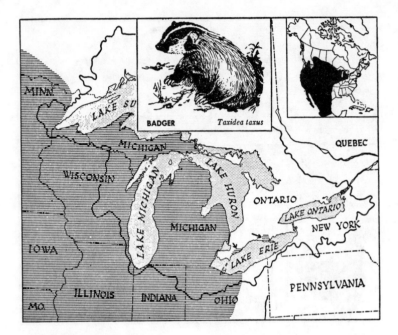

and a black spot in front of each ear. The **feet** are **black.** The long, shaggy hairs of the upper parts are yellowish at the bases, banded with black, and tipped with white. The underparts and the short tail are yellowish. The badger is about the size of a Boston bulldog. Its forefeet are large, with long, powerful claws (longest about 38 mm., 1.5 in.), and its ears are small. The female has eight mammae.

The skull of the badger may be distinguished from the skulls of other carnivores by the dental formula (four cheek teeth above and five below on each side), the triangular last upper cheek tooth, the bony palate extending posteriorly beyond the last upper molars, and its size.

HABITAT–It thrives in open country, preferably grassland.

HABITS–The badger is a fossorial animal, as displayed not only in its structure (small ears, short tail, large, digging front feet), but also in its habits. It lives in deep, long burrows, which it digs. It not only excavates its own living quarters, but also digs for its food, which consists chiefly of small rodents. Although nocturnal for the most part, the badger may be seen abroad during the day, especially in the mornings. Badgers are believed to pair for long periods. It is not known when they mate, but young may be abroad in late May or early June. There are two to five young in a litter. Badgers have been known to live for as long as twelve years in captivity. The span of their natural life is unknown.

Badgers are so rare in this area that they are seldom seen. Their nocturnal habits add to the unlikeliness that they will be encountered. ECONOMIC STATUS–About the only harm done by the badger results from excavations made while digging, possibly for a ground squirrel or a nest of mice. The badger is not sufficiently numerous to be of importance as a fur bearer.

SPOTTED SKUNK *Spilogale putorius* Linnaeus

SIZE–Total length, 400–550 mm. (16–22 in.); weight, 450–1,250 gms. (1–2.75 lbs.).

DESCRIPTION–The spotted skunk, which is somewhat smaller than an ordinary house cat, is black with a **white spot on** its forehead and **broken white stripes** over its back and sides. The bushy tail contains considerable white, particularly at the tip. It is plantigrade, and the claws on the front feet are long. The mammae number eight, two pairs pectoral, one pair abdominal, and one pair inguinal.

The skull may be distinguished from the skulls of all other car-

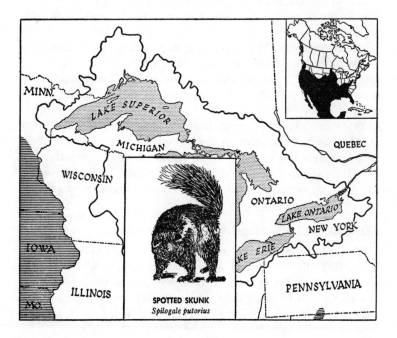

SPOTTED SKUNK
Spilogale putorius

nivores except *Mephitis* by the teeth, one squarish molar above and two molars below on each side, and by the bony palate terminating at or anterior to the plane at the posterior borders of the last molars. From *Mephitis*, it may be distinguished by size (greatest length less than 55 mm., 2.2 in., usually less than 50 mm., 2 in.).

HABITAT–It inhabits open or semiopen areas, and frequents farm buildings where rats and mice are present.

HABITS–The spotted skunk is more like the weasels than the striped skunk in habits. Its food during winter and spring consists mostly of small mammals with a few insects and birds. During summer and fall, insects make up most of the food items with small mammals, birds, and some vegetable matter rounding out the diet. Seldom seen during the daytime, this little skunk is almost wholly nocturnal. For its nesting site, or daytime retreat, it requires a dark place. Four to seven young are born in late May or early June. The young weigh about 9 or 10 grams each at birth, are weaned when about fifty days of age, and attain nearly adult weight in three months.

Population densities, as determined in Iowa farm country, may run as high as thirteen per square mile (Crabb, 1948). The home range of both sexes in winter is usually confined to about 160 acres or less. In summer, males may wander farther and range over three or four square miles. Usually, two or more nests are available to each skunk.

When threatened by an enemy, such as a dog, these skunks do a handstand on their front feet and discharge their protective musk up over their backs in the direction they are facing. Unlike their larger relative, the striped skunk, they take readily to trees to get out of reach of ground enemies.

ECONOMIC STATUS–Except for their occasional raids on poultry or their discharge of scent in the vicinity of farm buildings, these active mousers are beneficial to the farmer on whose property they live. They kill many rats and mice—particularly during the winter months—that certainly would otherwise destroy much stored grain as well as poultry and eggs.

STRIPED SKUNK *Mephitis mephitis* Schreber

SIZE–Total length, 509–665 mm. (20–26 in.); weight, 4–10 lbs.

DESCRIPTION–The striped skunk is familiar to nearly everyone by odor if not by sight. It is about the size of a large house cat. It has a small head, large deep body, relatively short legs, plantigrade feet with long claws on the front feet, and a long bushy tail. It is **black**

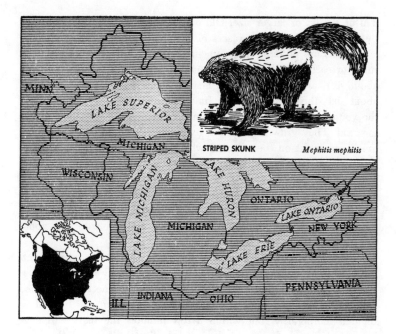

STRIPED SKUNK   *Mephitis mephitis*

with a narrow **white stripe on** its **forehead,** a white patch on the top of its head and **two** broad (or narrow) **white stripes** forking on the crown and extending over the back for varying distances, usually to the tail. The long hairs of the tail are mixed black and white. The mammae usually number twelve, six on a side.

The skull is distinguished from other carnivore skulls (except *Spilogale*) by having the molars reduced to one above and two below on each side, and by having the bony palate terminate at, or anterior to, the plane at the posterior borders of the last upper molars. A further character of the skull is the squarish last upper molar. It may be distinguished from *Spilogale* by larger size (over 55 mm., 2.2 in., in greatest length).

HABITAT–Semiopen country with a mixture of woods, brushland, and open grassland, preferably not more than two miles from water is the habitat of this mammal.

HABITS–The striped skunk comes out from his daytime sleep shortly after sundown and starts his search for insects, grubs, mice, eggs, berries, and a variety of small animal life that he may encounter in his wanderings. He is omnivorous. The den is normally a hole in the ground, either made by the skunk or abandoned by some other animal of similar or larger size. Old outbuildings are readily taken over by skunks and utilized as places of shelter.

Skunks are probably polygamous. Mating takes place in late February or early March, and the young, two to ten in a litter (usually about six), are born about the first of May. The gestation period is about sixty-three days. By late June or early July the mother brings the young out of the den to accompany her on her nightly searches for food. They grow rapidly and usually are in good condition, with much excess fat on their bodies, when the cold of winter sets in. At this time, in late December, the females den up, sometimes eight or ten in a den, and seldom appear above ground until the winter is broken. Males do not remain in the dens, except in extremely cold weather, but sally forth at intervals throughout the winter months. The normal winter population of skunks in good territory is about one skunk to each 10.4 acres.

The skunk is a fearless animal, apparently depending on its scent-spraying mechanism for protection. This is used only in emergencies. If a person is so unfortunate as to be sprayed in the eyes, he need fear no lasting deleterious effects. His eyes will burn, and he will be blinded temporarily, but within a few minutes the tears will have washed the eyes clean, and the painful effects, albeit not the odor, will have disappeared. To this I can attest from personal experience. ECONOMIC STATUS—The skunk is not only one of the most important of our fur-bearing animals, but also one of the most important animals that prey on small rodents. In addition, it destroys many insects. Rarely does the skunk destroy poultry. It is one of our most valuable wild animals.

REMARKS—Two races of skunk occur in this area, *Mephitis mephitis nigra* Peale and Beauvois in the south and *M. m. hudsonica* Richardson in the north. Specimens of *M. m. hudsonica* differ from those of *nigra* in usually having a black-tipped instead of a white-tipped tail. In the skull, specimens of *nigra* commonly have a small median projection on the posterior edge of the bony palate that is absent in specimens of *hudsonica*.

DOGS, FOXES, AND WOLVES (FAMILY CANIDAE)

The dogs, foxes, and wolves which comprise this family hold a central position among the carnivores as regards adaptive specializations. They have a nearly complete Eutherian dentition, missing only one upper molar on each side. The carnassials are well-developed, strong, shearing teeth. The molars back of the carnassials are progressively reduced, low-crowned, crushing teeth. The mandibles are long, with compressed two-rooted premolars, except the small one-rooted first premolar. All but the first premolar in the lower jaw usually have accessory cusps in front and behind the main central cusp. As a cursorial adaptation the limbs are long, and the feet are digitigrade, with four toes well developed (the pollex is reduced and situated high on the foot; the hallux is vestigial and not apparent). Members of this family possess a sebaceous gland on the dorsal part of the tail, near the base. The position of the gland is marked by coarse, black-tipped hairs, which have no underfur at the bases. These stiff hairs are known as a mane and have their greatest development in the gray fox. The gland is the animal's "identification card."

RED FOX *Vulpes fulva* Desmarest

SIZE–Total length, 955–85 mm. (37–38 in.); weight, 10–15 lbs.

DESCRIPTION–The red fox is known to most people from fur pieces if not from having seen the animal in life. It has many color variations; usually it is reddish yellow, somewhat darkened down the middle of the back, with black in the long **tail**, which is **tipped with white,** and with black legs and feet. The outer sides of the ears also

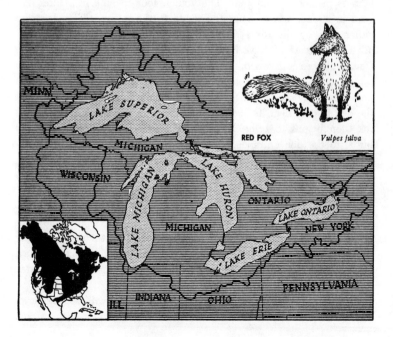

RED FOX   *Vulpes fulva*

are blackish. The belly, throat, and cheeks are whitish. The more common variations are: (1) dark crosses on the withers (cross fox); (2) black, frosted with white hairs (silver fox); and (3) entirely black. The mammae number eight.

The skull may be distinguished from the skulls of other carnivores by the following combination of characters: the total number of teeth is forty-two (ten on each side above and eleven on each side below); the last upper molar is smaller than the tooth in front of it; the bony palate ends slightly anterior to the posterior borders of the last molars; the parietal ridges often form a sagittal crest; if the ridges are present, they are separated at the suture between the frontals and the parietals by a space of less than 10 mm. (more than 10 mm. in *Urocyon*); the dorsal surfaces of the postorbital processes are slightly concave, forming shallow pits (no pits in *Canis*).

HABITAT–It prefers broken, sparsely settled country.

HABITS–Although chiefly nocturnal, the red fox often ventures forth by day, especially in early morning or late evening. During midday it usually rests in solitude in some sheltered spot from which it may detect approaching danger. The male and female probably pair for the year. The gestation period is about fifty-one days, and but one litter is produced each year. The young, four to nine in a litter, are born in a den, which is usually made in the ground. The dens are either dug by the foxes themselves or are the abandoned dens of other animals which have been taken over and enlarged by the foxes. Usually, there are two or more entrances to the den. One or more refuge dens are near-by, enabling the mother to move her pups promptly if the home den is disturbed. The young foxes come out of the den to play near its opening when about a month old. The parent fox then begins to bring food, in the form of small mammals and birds, to the den entrance. By the middle of summer the many un-eaten fragments strewn about give the den entrance an untidy appearance and a not too pleasing odor. The food of foxes is chiefly meat, with berries and fruits in season. Although they eat some birds, the bulk of their food consists of small mammals. I have found remains of shrews, moles, chipmunks, squirrels, rabbits, and pheasants at fox dens. The list of diurnal food species indicates much hunting during the day. Foxes often cache food in the snow or in the ground —sometimes it will be an entire animal, at other times a partly eaten one.

ECONOMIC STATUS–An occasional renegade fox will raid the farmyard and do considerable damage. There is no more reason to condemn the entire fox tribe for this than there would be to condemn the entire human race because of a few outlaws. If the value of fox fur and the value of the fox as a "mouser" is considered, the local damage done is insignificant. Some misinformed administrations have seen fit to pay a bounty on the fox in recent years.

GRAY FOX *Urocyon cinereoargenteus* Schreber

SIZE–Total length, 988 mm. (39 in.); weight, 8–13 lbs.
DESCRIPTION–The gray fox, although somewhat lighter in weight than the red fox, has about the same body measurements. It has longer legs and a smaller body. Its distinguishing characters are: general gray upper parts—resulting from the white bands and black tips on the guard hairs—with the buff of the underfur sometimes showing through; long bushy **tail, with** a median **black stripe** (mane) down nearly the entire dorsal surface, and **tipped with black;** yellowish on sides of neck, back of ears, and on legs and feet; whitish throat and belly; and brownish patches on the sides of the nose in front of and below the eyes. The claws of the front feet are distinctly more curved than they are in the red fox.

The skull, in addition to the regular dental formula of the family

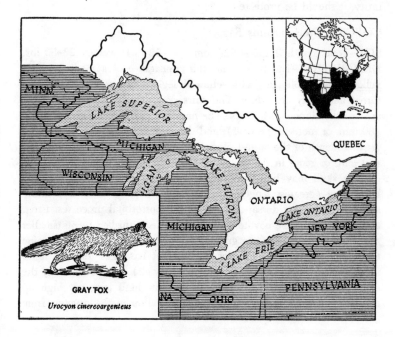

GRAY FOX
Urocyon cinereoargenteus

Canidae, possesses the following characters: deep, concave pits on the dorsal surfaces of the postorbital processes; distinct parietal ridges, 1–3 mm. high and separated at the suture between the frontals and parietals by a space of 15 mm. or more, not forming a sagittal crest; the upper incisors without lobes; the mandible with an angular emargination below.

HABITAT–It lives in forests and fairly open brushland.

HABITS–The gray fox is a sly, cunning creature and a desperate fighter when at bay. Unlike the red fox it is quite at home in a tree and will seek refuge there when hard pressed. When caught in a trap it often gives up, knowing perhaps that the odds are against it. Its den may be in a hollow log or tree, or under a rock pile. Occasionally, this fox dens in burrows in the ground. Three to seven young are born in April. The care of the young is probably similar to that of the young red fox. The young first play about the den, then, when about two-thirds grown, they may accompany the parents on their nightly excursions in search of food. The gray fox, although primarily a carnivore, is nearly as omnivorous as man.

ECONOMIC STATUS–So rare is the gray fox in much of the Great Lakes region that it now has no economic value here. Because of its rarity, it should be protected.

COYOTE *Canis latrans* Say

SIZE–Total length, 1,155–1,320 mm. (45–52 in.); weight, 23–50 lbs.

DESCRIPTION–The coyote has the appearance of a medium-sized, yellowish gray collie dog with **yellowish** legs, feet, ears, and muzzle. Its **throat** and **belly** are **white**. The hairs down the middle of the back are broadly tipped with black. The nose pad is less than 25 mm. wide (30 mm. or more in the wolf), and the nose is long and pointed. The greatest depth of the largest claw on the front foot is less than 8 mm. (10 mm. or more in the wolf). There are eight mammae.

The skull may be distinguished from the skulls of foxes by its larger size (greatest length over 150 mm., usually about 200 mm.) and by the convex dorsal surfaces of the postorbital processes. From that of the wolf, the coyote skull may be distinguished by its smaller size (less than 225 mm., in greatest length) and smaller upper canine tooth (greatest antero-posterior diameter at base less than 12 mm.; in the coyote, more than 12 mm. in the wolf). When running, the coyote carries its tail well down between its hind legs, not high up as does the wolf. There is much color variation in the coyotes, from

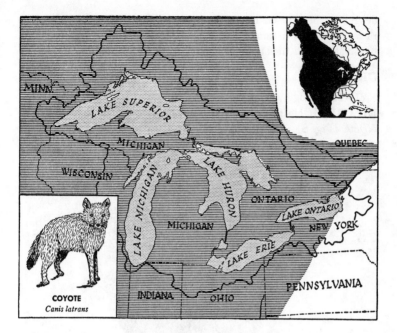

COYOTE
Canis latrans

nearly white to nearly black with varying amounts of yellowish and tawny.

HABITAT–This mammal prefers open or semiopen country.

HABITS–The coyote is a wild dog, chiefly carnivorous in food preferences, and subsisting in large part on small mammals and birds. Carrion and domestic animals round out its bill of fare if other prey is not readily available. Corralled and well-cared-for domestic animals probably suffer little from the coyote. It gets the blame, however, for much damage done by its tame relative—the domestic dog. The coyote mates in late January or early February. Five to ten young are born in early April, after a gestation period of about nine weeks. Dens are made in the ground in some concealed spot. More than one den is the rule—probably a precaution against danger.

ECONOMIC STATUS–The coyote is and has been the subject of controversy throughout the country. Bounties have been paid on the coyote because of a belief that it is a harmful animal and that it should be exterminated. According to recent studies in other parts of the country the coyote, as a scavenger and a "mouser," probably does more good than harm. Although local control measures may be desirable, there is no reason to condemn the coyote throughout its range. It is a wise animal, and I see little danger of its becoming exterminated even though rigid control methods are employed.

GRAY WOLF *Canis lupus* Linnaeus

SIZE–Total length, 1,570–1,650 mm. (61–65 in.); weight, 70–100 lbs. DESCRIPTION–In general coloration, the wolf is similar to the coyote (Fig. 8). It is distinguished from the coyote by its **larger size**

Fig. 8. Gray wolf.

(total length over 1,300 mm., 55 in., and tail more than 375 mm., 15 in.), **wider nose pad** (usually 30 mm. or more), larger feet and claws (depth of claw on front foot more than 8 mm.), and larger skull (total length more than 225 mm.; the antero-posterior diameter

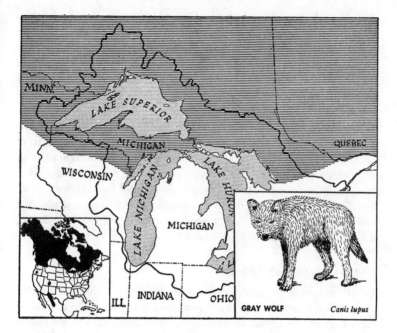

GRAY WOLF *Canis lupus*

of the upper canine at the base is more than 12 mm.). When running, the wolf carries its tail high, not low as does the coyote. Females have five mammae on each side.

HABITAT–Unlike the coyote, the wolf prefers forested regions, but may also be found in semiopen country.

HABITS–This vanishing carnivore, most majestic of the local fauna, has habits similar in general to those of its smaller cousin, the coyote. Its diet consists of fish, fruit, insects, snails, birds, and mammals. To the list of small mammals and birds, the main items in its diet, it adds deer. In late fall and winter, bands of three to a dozen or more wolves may travel together in search of food. These bands, in many instances, are assumed to represent family groups rather than gatherings of unrelated individuals. There is also a possibility that some of them may be "bachelor bands" made up of young nonbreeding animals. Wolves do not breed until they are two to three years old. They mate, for the season and possibly longer, in late January or February. The gestation period is about nine weeks. The den may be any suitable shelter—a natural cave, hollow tree, or a den in the ground. Here the three to fourteen (usually six or seven) sooty-brown young are born and spend the first six weeks of their lives, unless moved to another den. The young are then started on solid foods, and the old male becomes a provider. The pups are at first confined to the immediate vicinity of the den, but soon accompany the mother on her daily rounds for food. Wolves have "runways," circular in outline and twenty to sixty miles in diameter. Scent posts are along these feeding routes. When traveling in the snow, wolves go single file and step into the leader's tracks, making it difficult for anyone to know the number in the band.

ECONOMIC STATUS—In the Great Lakes region the wolf has been nearly extirpated. The few that remain are in the wildest parts of northern Michigan and Wisconsin, and in Ontario, where there is little or no stock raising. To be sure, they take a few deer, but there are usually too many deer for the available winter food. It is my opinion that this magnificent carnivore should be protected. I doubt if it will ever come back in sufficient numbers to be a problem. If it should, a bounty could again be placed on it.

CATS (FAMILY FELIDAE)

Of all mammals the cats are the most highly specialized for eating flesh. The canines are well developed, long, and sharp; the carnassials have the extreme development in the order Carnivora, and the molars back of them are lost or reduced to vestiges. The premolars in front of the carnassials likewise are reduced both in number and in complexity. The skull of a modern cat is short, especially in the facial region, with broad arches and rounded convex forehead. The lower jaw has a comparatively deep abrupt chin. The body is relatively long, and the limbs are of moderate size. The tail is well developed, except in the genus *Lynx* and in some domestic varieties. Cat feet are relatively large and digitigrade, with long, sharp, retractile claws. There are five toes on the front foot and four on the back. The first toe on the front foot is high on the wrist and does not touch the ground when the cat is walking. The young of the native cats are spotted at birth.

LYNX *Lynx canadensis* Kerr

SIZE—Total length, 915 mm. (36 in.); weight, 15–30 lbs.
DESCRIPTION—The lynx is the largest of the bob-tailed cats. It is easily distinguished by the **black tip** that goes around its short tail, and by long black **ear tufts**. The general coloration is yellowish gray with scattered black-tipped guard hairs down the back. The legs are yellowish, indistinctly spotted. The animal is somewhat paler in winter than in summer.

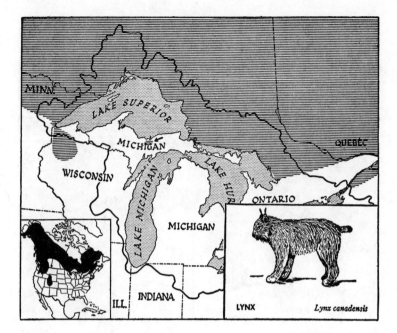

LYNX   *Lynx canadensis*

From that of the bobcat (*Lynx rufus*), the skull of the lynx differs in having the anterior condyloid foramen distinct and separate from the foramen lacerum posteriorus (Fig. 35) and in having a wider presphenoid (more than 5 mm., greatest width) and a longer upper carnassial (more than 16.6 mm.). Many large bobcat skulls are larger than small lynx skulls.

HABITAT–It is confined to primitive forests.

HABITS–The lynx, even where common, is seldom seen. The little that has been surmised of its habits has been based on indirect evidence. Apparently, these animals mate in January or February, and the young are born in March or April. The gestation period is sixty days or more. Since the females have four teats, one may judge that the litter consists of one to four young. These are indistinctly spotted on the legs and belly and have faint streaks over the tops of their heads; their eyes are believed to be open at birth, an unusual situation among the cat family. The food of the lynx is in large part the snowshoe hare. Undoubtedly, many kinds of small mammals and birds are eaten when procurable.

ECONOMIC STATUS–The lynx was once a valuable fur bearer, but now is being reduced in numbers except in the far north.

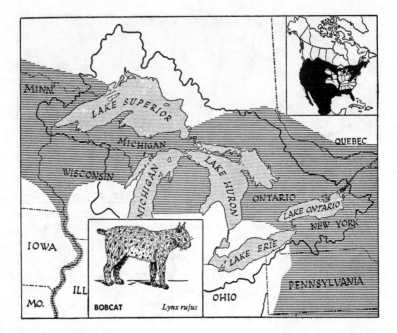

BOBCAT   *Lynx rufus*

BOBCAT *Lynx rufus* Schreber

SIZE–Total length, 755–890 mm. (30–35 in.); weight, 15–30 lbs.

DESCRIPTION–The bobcat is similar to the lynx in general coloration. It differs, however, in appearing somewhat smaller, and in having shorter, less conspicuous ear tufts, more distinct spotting on the
legs, and **black on the tip of the tail only on top.** The summer coat of
the bobcat is rufous, the winter coat is more nearly gray.

The skull is similar to that of the lynx, but differs from it as pointed
out on page 206 (Fig. 36).

HABITAT–The bobcat lives in swamps and broken country with an
adequate cover of brush.

HABITS–Again, knowledge of the life history and habits of a common
mammal is incomplete. Dens are made in hollow trees or logs or in
other sheltered spots. One to four young are born in late April or
early May. The gestation period is not known; mating probably occurs
from January to July. The young are blind at birth. The food of the
bobcat is mostly small birds and mammals, many of which it catches
alive. Although chiefly nocturnal, the bobcat often sallies forth during
the day. It is seldom seen by man, unless treed by dogs or caught in

a trap. When cornered the bobcat is a formidable foe, but it does not go out of its way to fight.

ECONOMIC STATUS–The bobcat is present in the wilder parts of the area, where very little opportunity is afforded for predation on domestic animals. For the sportsman, bobcat hunting with dogs is unsurpassed.

GNAWING MAMMALS (ORDER RODENTIA)

The rodents are readily recognized by the reduction in number and specialization of the incisor teeth into two gliriform or gnawing teeth in each jaw. This diprotodont specialization is present in some other groups of mammals, especially in certain Australian marsupials, but in no other group has the specialization been carried so far. In the rodents, these central gnawing incisors have become rootless, growing throughout the life of the animal from a persistent pulp, and the enamel is developed on and restricted to the anterior face of the tooth. The softer dentine of the back of the tooth wears more rapidly than does the hard enamel; the result is a sharp, chisel-like structure. With the enlargement of the central incisors there has been a loss of the lateral incisors, canines, and some or all of the premolars, resulting in a distinct diastema (gap) between the incisors and the cheek teeth. There has also been a considerable change in the relative positions of the bones of that region. The most important change has been the shifting forward of the anterior root of the zygoma so that, instead of arising behind the last molar or opposite the last two molars as it does normally in mammals, it springs from opposite the front of the cheek-tooth row. This also involves a radical change in the musculature. Correspondingly, in the lower jaw, the angular region is expanded into a broad plate and the glenoid articulation is altered from a transverse one with a postglenoid process to an oval one without the process, allowing for an antero-posterior as well as a rotary, side to side movement of the jaw. The fossa is so constructed that when the lower jaw shifts forward to engage the incisors, the cheek teeth disengage. Similarly, when the jaw falls back to engage the cheek teeth for crushing or grinding food, the incisors are disengaged. The animal chews with a side to side or slightly rotary motion of the lower jaw. It cannot chew with a fore-and-aft motion of the jaw as this disengages the cheek teeth. Further, the lower tooth rows are closer together than the uppers, and only the teeth of one side will fully occlude at one time. The cheek teeth of rodents may be low-crowned, rooted, with low rounded enamel-covered cusps (for crushing) or high-crowned, not rooted, with cross ridges of enamel (for grinding).

In the skeleton, the clavicle is usually present, the radius and ulna are always separate, but the tibia and fibula are often ankylosed at the distal ends. There are usually five toes on the front foot, but the pollex is much reduced and without a claw (sometimes with a nail) in many instances. The only rodents of the Great Lakes region with claws on all five toes are the beaver and muskrat. The hind foot usually has five toes, all with claws; these may be reduced to four or three in some kinds, but all rodents of this area have five. Representatives of this order of mammals in our area vary in size from the small western harvest mouse to the beaver. Although chiefly terrestrial in habits, rodents have also become adapted to the following ways of life: arboreal (the squirrels), fossorial (woodchuck), semiaquatic (beaver and muskrat), and volant (flying squirrel). The rodents have a nearly world-wide distribution and constitute the largest order of mammals, both in individuals and in species. They are of much economic importance in many sections of the country.

SQUIRRELS (FAMILY SCIURIDAE)

Included in this family are the woodchucks, ground squirrels, chipmunks, tree squirrels, and flying squirrels. Members of this family may be distinguished at once from other rodents by their thickly haired tail with the longest hairs 10 mm. or more in length, lack of spines in the fur, the presence of four cheek teeth below, and four or five cheek teeth above on each side of the jaw. The cheek teeth are rooted and have low rounded cusps or crests on their surfaces, adapted for crushing, not grinding. The arboreal members of this family have long bushy tails, which serve as balancing organs while the animals are passing through the treetops. The ground-dwelling woodchucks and ground squirrels have shorter, less bushy tails.

WOODCHUCK *Marmota monax* Linnaeus

SIZE–Total length, 530–645 mm. (21–25 in.); weight, 5–10 lbs.

DESCRIPTION–The woodchuck is the largest member of the squirrel family. It has a compact, heavy body supported by relatively short powerful legs. The **front foot** has **four** well-developed **toes** with long, slightly curved claws, an adaptation for digging. The pollex is small, high on the foot, and tipped with a nail. The hind foot has five clawed toes. As is characteristic of fossorial animals the **ears** are **small**, and the **tail** is **short**. The general coloration of the upper parts is

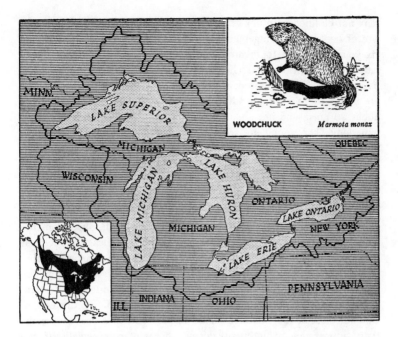

WOODCHUCK   *Marmota monax*

grizzled yellowish gray. This color is produced chiefly by the cover hairs, which are banded successively from the base—black, buff, black, light buff, and black. The yellowish tips of the underfur give the yellowish cast. The underparts and upper legs are suffused with rufous, whereas the **feet are black**. Albino and melanistic (black) woodchucks are not uncommon. The skull, which is of large size, is flattened or depressed between the postorbital processes, and the posterior borders of these project laterally at right angles to the longitudinal axis of the skull. The incisors are pale yellow or whitish on their front surfaces.

HABITAT–This mammal inhabits forests and areas of heavy brush. In the farming districts, it is found along creeks and brushy ravines.

HABITS–The woodchuck is primarily a diurnal animal that spends most of the daylight hours during the summer eating green vegetation and storing up fat so that it may sleep through the long winter in hibernation. Nocturnal wanderings are common in early spring before mating. In its adaptation it is a combination of the fossorial and terrestrial types; it digs complicated burrow systems up to forty feet or more in length and four feet in depth. Usually, there is a front and back entrance, and occasionally side entrances to the burrow; the back one is concealed in brush or other vegetation. The nest chamber may or may not be lined with dry grasses or leaves. Woodchucks breed at the age of one year. Mating takes place in March and April, and two to six young (usually four) are born in April or May. Yearlings breed later than do old females. The gestation period, as determined in captive animals, is thirty-one or thirty-two days. The naked, blind young are about the size of an adult pine vole (*Pitymys*) at birth, weigh about 26 gms., and are about 105 mm. long, the tail being about 16 mm. long. The young are weaned in late June or early July. There is one litter a year. The age which they attain in the wild is not known, but is supposedly about four or five years. The home range of an individual is about one-quarter to one-half mile in diameter, but again this has not been worked out in detail. It is known that a woodchuck will protect his own den if it is entered by a stranger, but it is not known whether he will protect a territory for any distance from the actual den site. Most wild animals are sanitary, at least about their home sites, and the woodchuck is no exception. The feces are buried in small pits and covered with soil. When young are in the den, the nest is cleaned out and materials are replaced or added to it at intervals; the offal of the young is kept well covered. By the end of October most of the woodchucks are in hibernation. A few may make their appearance at intervals during the winter, especially if the weather is mild, but they do not come out as a rule until February.

ECONOMIC STATUS–The woodchuck can do considerable damage if it becomes sufficiently numerous in an agricultural district. At the present time woodchucks are comparatively rare and inflict only slight damage to crops. To the hunter and trapper they are definitely an asset. The woodchuck is not a game animal, but his numerous burrows afford shelter for rabbits and skunks. The revenue derived from hunting and trapping these other animals is considerable. The attractiveness of the woodchuck cannot be translated into dollars and cents.

REMARKS–Two subspecies of woodchuck are present in the area. The race *Marmota monax monax* Linnaeus inhabits the southern part and a more reddish subspecies, *Marmota monax rufescens* Howell, lives in the northern part.

THIRTEEN-LINED GROUND SQUIRREL *Citellus tridecemlineatus* Mitchill

SIZE–Total length, 215–94 mm. (8.5–12 in.); weight, 82–207 gms. (2.9–7.3 oz.).

DESCRIPTION–This small, rat-sized ground squirrel, or gopher as it

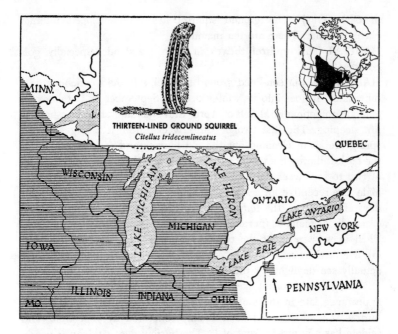

THIRTEEN-LINED GROUND SQUIRREL
Citellus tridecemlineatus

is known in this area, may be distinguished from all other mammals of the region by the number of **stripes,** alternately **dark brown** and **cream-colored,** running lengthwise of the body, but not extending on the face as they do in the chipmunks. From its name one would gather that there are thirteen of these stripes. Actually there are twenty-three, twelve dark ones and eleven light ones. The light stripes are continuous in the shoulder region, but five of them break up into rows of spots over the back and rump. The ears are little more than fleshy rims about the opening. There are four well-developed toes with long claws (for digging) on the front foot and five clawed toes on the hind foot. The tail is about one-half as long as the head and body, is slightly bushy, and is held straight out behind when the animal is running. With its long round body and small head the ground squirrel has a snakelike appearance as it goes through the grass.

Size (p. 224) and dental formula will distinguish the skull from any but that of a flying squirrel of the genus *Glaucomys.* The skull of the ground squirrel may be distinguished from that of specimens of *Glaucomys* by pale yellow instead of dark orange incisor fronts, broad rostrum, small auditory bullae, and larger third upper premolar (nearly half the size of the fourth premolar in *Citellus,* much smaller in *Glaucomys*). The ground squirrel has well-developed internal cheek pouches. There are ten mammae.

HABITAT–This squirrel thrives in open grassland, especially golf courses.

HABITS–The thirteen-lined ground squirrel, like the woodchuck, is a hibernator. It goes into its winter sleep in September or October and emerges sometime in March or April, thus spending about one-half its life sleeping. The first two or three weeks after it emerges in the spring are spent cleaning out the old burrow and regaining some of the fat lost during the winter's sleep. After this there is a rutting period of two to four weeks in which the males are sexually active. The females are receptive for a somewhat longer period. About twenty-eight days after mating, the female gives birth to seven to ten young, occasionally as many as fourteen. These are naked and blind when born. Their eyes open about the twenty-sixth day after birth. When they are five or six weeks old they come from their subterranean nest and actually see daylight for the first time.

The ground squirrel likes warm days with sunshine and makes its appearance late in the morning; it retires early in the evening. The burrow is a small round hole, usually concealed by vegetation, and seldom has any dirt in front of it. The burrow goes straight or nearly straight down for six or more inches, then angles off. The ground squirrel is omnivorous and takes seeds and insects alike. The insects are eaten on the spot, but seeds usually are stuffed into internal cheek pouches and carried to some underground storage place. It is not known when or how much of this stored material is eaten. On one occasion I observed a ground squirrel digging something from a lawn. A closer approach enabled me to watch its activities in detail. Apparently by its sense of smell it located the position of a white grub (larva of the June beetle), dug it out, sat up with the grub between its paws, turned it over and over, then bit off the head and proceeded to consume it. I watched it dig four or five of these larvae in fifteen minutes. Each time it started digging it secured a grub.

ECONOMIC STATUS–On occasion, in a garden area, these squirrels can and do become a nuisance. They are easily trapped either with large rat snap traps or with live traps baited with rolled oats. In general they probably do as much good as harm. I suspect that their presence in such great numbers on golf courses is because of the white grubs there. The many grubs that they eat should compensate somewhat for the few burrows they make. Further, I suspect that some of the golfers enjoy seeing these friendly little striped squirrels on the otherwise monotonous course.

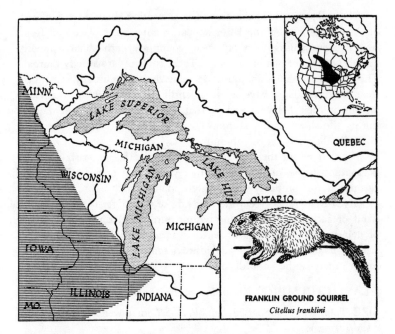

FRANKLIN GROUND SQUIRREL
Citellus franklini

FRANKLIN GROUND SQUIRREL *Citellus franklini* Sabine

SIZE—Total length, 355–430 mm. (14–17 in.); weight, 370–500 gms. (13–18 oz.).

DESCRIPTION—This is a relatively **large** ground squirrel with a **slightly bushy tail** that is about half as long as head and body. The fairly short body hair is a mixture of browns, whites, and blacks so that the over-all color is a salt and pepper mixture with a **brownish** cast. The belly is yellowish white, as are the feet and inner sides of the legs. There are ten or twelve mammae; two pairs pectoral, one or two pairs abdominal, and two pairs inguinal.

The skull may be distinguished from those of other squirrels with twenty-two teeth by size, length 52–55 mm. (about 2 in.).

HABITAT—Though it prefers open prairies or prairie-like areas, in the north, the Franklin ground squirrel lives along edges of wooded areas.

HABITS—Although its food consists primarily of seeds, fruits, and green vegetation, as much as one-third of this squirrel's diet may be made up of animal matter in the form of insects, bird eggs, birds, and mammals.

This is one of the true hibernating mammals. It is active above ground from late March or early April to November, depending on the latitude.

The males appear above ground in the spring about a week ahead of the females. When the latter appear, mating takes place and from four to eleven, usually six or seven, young are born about a month later. There is but one litter a year. These squirrels are strictly diurnal. They prefer sunshine, and on dark, rainy days they usually remain in their burrows. They have a rather shrill, bird-like whistle. Little is known of their behavior except that males fight among themselves during the short mating season. They can, and do, climb trees, but normally they stay on the ground.

Populations, in the northern part of the range at least, seem to fluctuate, with peaks about every four years. Four or five adult squirrels per acre is probably a fairly high population.

ECONOMIC STATUS—On the bad side of the ledger is the squirrel's habit of eating eggs of ground-nesting birds, including poultry, and of doing a certain amount of harm to farm crops. To compensate in part for its destructive habits, it destroys some insects and mice which might otherwise be harmful to crops.

LEAST CHIPMUNK *Eutamias minimus* Bachman

SIZE—Total length, 185–222 mm. (7.3–8.7 in.); weight, 42–53 gms. (1.5–1.9 oz.).

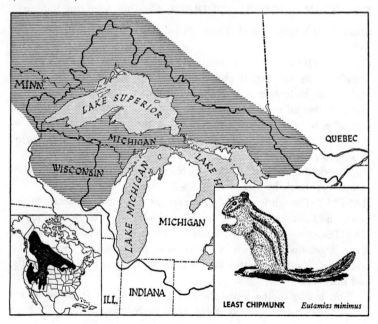

LEAST CHIPMUNK   *Eutamias minimus*

DESCRIPTION–This colorful little forest inhabitant may be recognized by its small size, by the three dark and two light **stripes on** the sides of its **face,** and by five dark and four light stripes, extending **to** the **base of** the **tail,** on its back and sides (Fig. 9). The long, bushy tail is bright fulvous beneath, dark brown mixed with fulvous above.

RPG '42

Fig. 9. Least chipmunk.

Internal cheek pouches enable it to carry quantities of seeds from the place of harvest to its subterranean granary. In addition to the dental formula and small size, the skull is characterized by being highly arched on the dorsal surface; the incisors are dark orange on their front surfaces, and the third premolar is little more than a peg. There are eight mammae—two inguinal, four abdominal, and two pectoral.

HABITAT–The least chipmunk is found in cedar, spruce, and hemlock forests, and semiopen broken country. It also lives around old buildings and sawmills.

HABITS–This little chipmunk, where it occurs, is one of the most active of the diurnal animals. During the summer months, from April to October, much of its time is spent in search of food. When a supply is found it carries the surplus away in its cheek pouches to its underground granaries. It probably breeds soon after it comes out of hibernation. There is little definite information on the life history of this species, but from inference one may assume that the gestation period is about a month. Two to six young are born in a litter. Whether more than one litter is produced in a season is not known. The nest is usually under an old stump or log, where the animal makes its own burrow. Although much of its time is spent on the ground, this little animal readily climbs trees. Its food consists of seeds, nuts, berries in season, and probably a great variety of insects. The home range has not been determined, nor is much known about its social behavior. It readily adapts itself to camp conditions, and with a little encouragement, by means of food, it will become fairly tame and make regular visits to pick up crumbs.

ECONOMIC STATUS–The value of the least chipmunk cannot be measured in dollars and cents, but there is no doubt that the pleasure derived by tourists and campers from watching this colorful little animal constitutes a real asset. There is little that it can do that could be interpreted as harmful to man.

EASTERN CHIPMUNK *Tamias striatus* Linnaeus

SIZE–Total length, 225–66 mm. (9–10.5 in.); weight, 66–113 gms. (2.3–4 oz.).

DESCRIPTION–The eastern chipmunk is another small mammal that adds color to the out-of-doors. Somewhat bulkier than the least chipmunk, it is similarly striped, except that the two light and three dark stripes on the face are less distinct and the **body stripes** are less extensive. On the back is a median, narrow, dark brown stripe bordered on each side by a broad grayish stripe of the same color as the neck and shoulders. Along each side, from the shoulders to the hips, are two dark brown stripes separated by a cream stripe. All of the **stripes end at the rump,** which is bright fulvous. The tail is fulvous beneath, grayish above. The belly is whitish. Like individuals of *Eutamias,* these chipmunks possess internal cheek pouches. The skull is distinguished from the skulls of other mammals in its size range by the

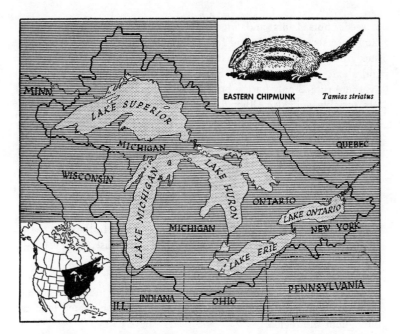

EASTERN CHIPMUNK   *Tamias striatus*

dental formula—one premolar on each side above instead of two as in specimens of the ground squirrel. As in the least chipmunk, there are eight mammae.

HABITAT–It usually lives in large hardwood forests and semiopen brushland and rarely is in swamps. It sometimes frequents old outbuildings and rubbish heaps.

HABITS–The habits of the eastern chipmunk are similar in general to those of the least chipmunk. It is more of a ground dweller and is less likely to be seen in trees. Breeding activity starts about April 1, and young are born in an underground nest about May 1. The gestation period, as determined by one marked individual in the wild, is thirty-one days. Young remain in the nest for at least a month after birth and may be expected to make their first appearance above ground about June 1, when they are nearly two-thirds grown. There is a second breeding period in late July or early August, at which time young females born in the spring breed also. This fall litter appears above ground in late September or early October. Two to eight young are born in a litter. Storage of food is one of the chief daily activities of eastern chipmunks. If a supply of food is located they will work tirelessly carrying it away to their subterranean granaries. Many kinds of seeds, nuts, fruits, and insects are eaten. These animals are definitely not sociable. Male and female become antagonistic a few minutes after mating. Except for the period when young are in the nest and about a week after they come above ground, they lead solitary lives interrupted only for the brief periods of mating. I cannot imagine less sociable animals. Although they are active throughout the day, the greatest liveliness takes place in early morning and late afternoon. Nightfall finds them in their burrows. The home range of an individual is seldom more than one hundred yards in greatest diameter. A large proportion of the home range is protected against invaders. Territorial behavior is displayed in this species. Normal populations range from two per acre at the beginning of the breeding season to four or more per acre at the close of the season. There is no information on populations in the fall after the second litter appears. In the wild these chipmunks, if they escape predation, will live at least three years—how much longer is not known.

ECONOMIC STATUS—The eastern chipmunk may damage unoccupied cabins or open supplies of grain, but this is a minor consideration as compared with the pleasure it affords the many tourists throughout the region.

REMARKS—Four subspecies of *Tamias striatus* occur in the area. *T. s. rufescens* Bole and Moulthrop inhabits the southern part; *T. s. peninsulae* Hooper, the northern part of the Lower Peninsula in Michigan; *T. s. griseus* Mearns, the northwestern part of the Great Lakes region; and *T. s. lysteri* Richardson, the northeastern section.

RED SQUIRREL *Tamiasciurus hudsonicus* Erxleben

SIZE—Total length, 283–345 mm. (11–13.6 in.); weight, 120–250 gms. (4.2–8.8 oz.).

DESCRIPTION—This is the smallest tree squirrel in the Great Lakes region. In addition to its small size it may be distinguished from the fox and gray squirrels in summer by the **black line along the side** between the white belly and reddish-gray upper parts. A white eye ring and the bright reddish upper surface of the tail are other characters. In the woods it is often heard before it is seen. Its explosive drawn-out, ratchet-like call informs one that all is not serene with it. In winter the red squirrel gets a new and different coat. The fur is long and thick, and the color is much brighter. The black stripe along the sides is gone, and the back is a bright reddish fulvous somewhat concentrated down the midregion. Small **tufts** decorate the **ears**, and the feet become grayish instead of fulvous. There are eight mammae, one

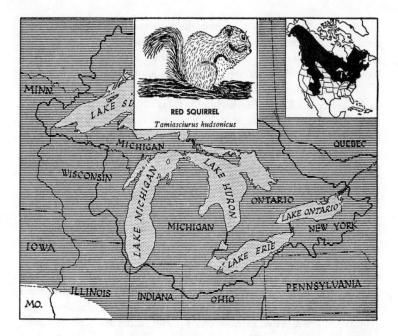

RED SQUIRREL
Tamiasciurus hudsonicus

pair inguinal, two pairs abdominal, and one pair pectoral. The dental formula and the size are sufficient to identify the skull. Some skulls have a very small premolar above, but whether there are twenty or twenty-two teeth no other mammal of the area combines this number of teeth and the red squirrel skull size.

HABITAT–Although it usually inhabits coniferous forests, it is present also in hardwood forests.

HABITS–The red squirrel is active throughout the year. Mating takes place in February or March and again in June or July. The four to seven young from the first mating are born about May 1. Nests may be either in hollow trees or constructed of leaves and shreds of bark among the branches. The young make their first appearance outside the nest when about one-half or two-thirds grown, in the latter part of May. A second litter may be born in August. Whether the fall litter is from old females exclusively or whether females of the spring litter become sexually mature and also breed at this time is not known. I doubt if the male has much to do with the family after actual mating. The old female remains with the young, as a family group, until they are nearly grown. The young may fight among themselves, especially over food, but the mother remains in the background and offers no interference. She will even permit them to cuff her about and take food from her until they are nearly as large as she is. When fighting among themselves, the young squirrels strike with their front feet. I have never seen them attempt to bite one another.

The red squirrel is out at the break of dawn and may continue to be active well into the night. On May 28, 1935, I encountered three young red squirrels at 9:00 P.M. It was extremely dark and a gentle rain was falling. I do not know where they came from, but they remained in the immediate vicinity until July 6, when they disappeared. The food of the red squirrel consists of practically everything available in its habitat, chiefly, however, of nuts and pine cones with mushrooms of various kinds, bird eggs, meat, and sap in season. During seasons of abundance, food is stored for future use. Pine cones and nuts may be stored in caches in the ground, usually while they are green, and mushrooms are stored in crotches in the trees. Cones and nuts are cut from the branches, and fall to the ground. The squirrel then descends from the tree and carries them to his caches. Hickory nuts are buried in the green husks. The home range of the red squirrel probably is less than two hundred yards in greatest diameter. The population is estimated at from one squirrel in twenty acres to ten or more squirrels an acre. The population apparently varies with the type of habitat as well as with the season and possibly other factors not yet understood. A breeding pair to three acres is probably about average. The maximum life span is supposed to be about ten years. Enemies of the red squirrel include hawks, owls, snakes, bobcats, foxes, and even large fish.

ECONOMIC STATUS–Red squirrels may become local pests if they decide to make their homes in the attics of buildings. They compete with the fox squirrel and gray squirrel for food. They are too small to be considered game animals, and the fur is of little or no value. About their only value is the enjoyment they afford to people who watch them. They also plant the nuts and acorns of trees.

REMARKS–Four subspecies are currently recognized for the area. *T. h. hudsonicus* occurs to the north, *T. h. minnesota* to the west, *T. h. loquax* to the south and the east, and *T. h. regalis* on Isle Royale.

EASTERN GRAY SQUIRREL (Black Squirrel)
Sciurus carolinensis Gmelin

SIZE–Total length, 405–510 mm. (16–20 in.); weight, 340–680 gms. (.75–1.5 lbs.).

DESCRIPTION–There are two color phases in the gray squirrel,

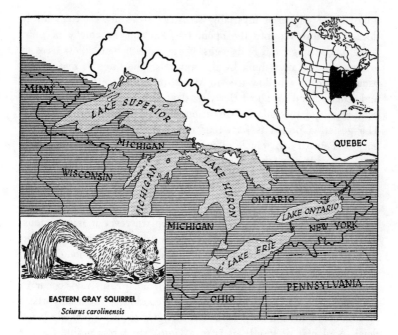

EASTERN GRAY SQUIRREL
Sciurus carolinensis

black and gray. In the black phase the squirrel usually is black, although some individuals are intermediate, with dark grayish underparts. In the gray phase there are distinct summer and winter pelages. The summer pelage is generally grayish with a wash of fulvous especially along the sides and on the feet, the belly is white or light grayish, there is a **white eye-ring**, and the **hairs of** the long **tail** are always broadly **tipped with white**. In the winter pelage there is little if any of the fulvous wash remaining. In addition, there are conspicuous white tufts of fur at the backs of the ears. There are no internal cheek pouches. Eight mammae are present in females. The combination of size and dental formula serves to distinguish the skull. The very small third upper premolar is no more than a spike and is absent in about 1 per cent of the skulls.

HABITAT–Large hardwoods, extensive in area, form the habitat of this mammal.

HABITS–The gray squirrel is typically an arboreal animal. It comes down to the ground to gather and bury nuts, one nut in a place, but much of its time is spent in the trees. Slightly smaller than the fox squirrel, it is distinctly more graceful and more certain of itself as it makes long jumps from branch to branch or from tree to tree. At the approach of danger it invariably scurries to the nearest tree; rarely does it venture far into the open. Its food consists chiefly of nuts, seeds, buds, fungi, and birds' eggs. Nests are either in hollow trees or are outside leaf nests built by the squirrels. The three to five young, usually born in a hollow tree in March or April, are naked at birth and remain blind for about thirty-six days. Shortly after this they may venture out of the hole for excursions up and down the tree trunks. The gestation period is forty-four days. Mating occurs in late January or February. A female may have two litters a year. In captivity these squirrels live for as long as fifteen years; in the wild I suspect that ten years is about maximum; however, there is no definite information on this point.

ECONOMIC STATUS–The gray squirrel was an important game animal fifty years ago. It is still fair game wherever it is numerous, but the concentrations now seem to be restricted chiefly to city and state parks, where hunting is not permitted. Strangely enough, some current game laws permit the shooting of gray squirrels in certain areas, but the blacks are protected. Both color phases may occur in a single litter. If this artificial selection continues, eventually there may be only blacks in some localities. The gray squirrel is wholly beneficial. A planter of forests, it is to a large extent responsible for the hickory trees. In parks it is a source of enjoyment for the tourist, and outside the parks it tests the mettle of the hunter of small game.

REMARKS–Two subspecies of gray squirrel are recognized in the area. *Sciurus carolinensis leucotis* Gapper occupies the southern part and *S. c. hypophaeus* Merriam the northern. I consider the name *S. c. pennsylvanicus* Ord to be invalid (Miller and Kellogg, 1955, p. 239).

EASTERN FOX SQUIRREL *Sciurus niger* Linnaeus

SIZE–Total length, 500–565 mm. (20–22 in.); weight, 544–1360 gms. (1.2–3 lbs.).

DESCRIPTION–This species, largest of the tree squirrels of the area, may be distinguished by its general **fulvous** coloration, which is mixed with grizzled grayish on the back and sides, but is almost pure fulvous on the belly, feet, cheeks, and around the ears. The broad **tips on the tail hairs** and the tufts behind the ears are **fulvous**, not whitish as they are in the gray squirrel. The mammae are in four pairs, two pectoral, one abdominal, and one inguinal. In the skull the small infraorbital foramen (less than 5 mm. in smallest diameter), cheek teeth with rounded cusps (instead of flat grinding surfaces), size range (length

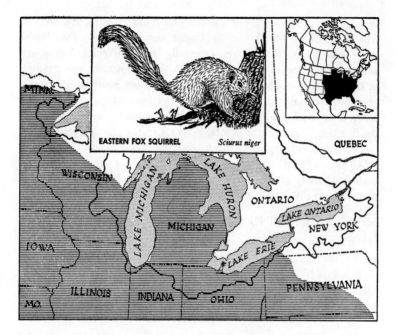

EASTERN FOX SQUIRREL   *Sciurus niger*

QUEBEC

WISCONSIN

LAKE MICHIGAN

LAKE HURON

ONTARIO

LAKE ONTARIO

NEW YORK

IOWA

MICHIGAN

LAKE ERIE

ILLINOIS   INDIANA   OHIO

PENNSYLVANIA

MO.

MINN.

between 60 and 70 mm.), and dental formula serve to set the fox squirrel apart from all other mammals here considered.

HABITAT—This squirrel prefers small areas of hardwoods interspersed with open farm land, and wooded streams.

HABITS—Although primarily arboreal in habits, the fox squirrel spends much of its time on the ground, where it not only searches for food, but also stores nuts in small pits that it digs. The nuts are covered by about an inch of dirt or leaf mold. Whether the squirrel finds the nuts later by smell or by remembering the positions of burial is not known for certain, but it is most likely that those retrieved are located by smell. Many of the nuts sprout and grow. In addition to nuts, the list of food items consists chiefly of buds, mushrooms, birds' eggs and young birds, fruits, and corn. Like other tree squirrels this species has two types of nests—a bulky leaf nest built of green twigs, leaves, and sometimes strips of bark in a crotch or branch of a treetop, and a hollow-tree nest in some cavity. Leaf nests are usually placed about thirty feet above ground and in trees more than ten inches in diameter. Young may be born in either type of nest. Mating takes place from early January to March and again from June to July. Two to five young (average about three), naked and blind at birth, are born in late February or March and in August and September. Two litters may be produced in a season, especially by old females. Young are weaned when ten to twelve weeks old. The maximum age attained in the wild is probably about ten years. The fox squirrel, unlike the gray, will normally cross open fields to get from one wood lot to another, or to reach a cornfield. If pursued it does not necessarily take to the first tree, but may pass several before it reaches its den tree. Foxes, large hawks, and large owls are its chief natural enemies.

ECONOMIC STATUS—As a game animal, the fox squirrel is important. In farming areas it sometimes does considerable damage to corn crops, especially in fields bordering woods.

SOUTHERN FLYING SQUIRREL *Glaucomys volans* Linnaeus

SIZE—Total length, 220–57 mm. (8.7–10 in.); weight, 52–69 gms. (1.8–2.4 oz.).

DESCRIPTION—The southern flying squirrel is about the size of a small rat and may be recognized by the rather **loose fold of skin** which

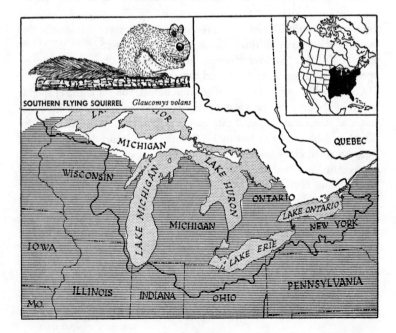

SOUTHERN FLYING SQUIRREL *Glaucomys volans*

extends along the side from the outside of the wrist to the hind foot. A flat, kite-like surface is produced when the animal spreads its legs. Cartilaginous spurlike supports at the wrists make it possible for the animal to extend the skin fold beyond the outstretched legs. The flattened tail is a further aid to a nearly perfect gliding structure. The sharp, curved claws, four on the front foot and five on the hind, help to make this squirrel one of the most agile mammals of the treetops. It has soft thick fur, grayish fulvous on the back and sides, and **large eyes**. The feet are dusky on top, and the belly is pure **white to the bases of the hairs**. The mammae are in four pairs, two inguinal, one abdominal, and one pectoral. In the skull, the combination of the dental formula and of the size (p. 224) is distinct from that of any other mammal of the Great Lakes region.

HABITAT–This squirrel inhabits wooded areas.

HABITS–Flying squirrels are the only truly nocturnal members of the squirrel family in the area. They are never seen abroad in the daytime unless they have been disturbed. Their natural abode is in an old woodpecker hole or some other cavity in a tree. They also build outside leaf nests in the branches of trees. Attics of houses or outbuildings are readily appropriated as homes. Two litters may be born in a season—the first in April or May and the second in August. The gestation period is about forty days. Two to six young, usually three or four, are born in a litter. The young are naked and blind at birth. The food of flying squirrels consists of seeds, buds, nuts, fruits, insects, birds' eggs, and birds, and they are as carnivorous as any of the rodents. Two captive squirrels that I had one summer relished June beetles that came to the lights. Unlike other squirrels, these little gliders are very sociable. Several of them will feed together without any indication of antagonism. In winter they may band together in groups of twenty or more in a single den. The home range of an individual is at least four acres in area. Further studies may reveal it to be considerably larger. The population for the summer of 1936 on an area of slightly less than four acres was 1.6 animals an acre. During winter concentrations the populations, locally, are probably much higher than this. Flying squirrels are tractable and make ideal pets. They have been known to live thirteen years in captivity.

ECONOMIC STATUS–When flying squirrels establish a home in the attic of a house and romp about all night long they may annoy the inhabitants below. Otherwise, because of their nocturnal habits, they are seldom noticed.

NORTHERN FLYING SQUIRREL *Glaucomys sabrinus* Shaw

SIZE–Total length, 245–95 mm. (9.6–11.6 in.); weight, 74–125 gms. (2.6–4.4 oz.).

DESCRIPTION–This squirrel is similar in general appearance to the southern flying squirrel—*Glaucomys volans*. It differs externally in being somewhat larger, in the darker more reddish coloration of the upper parts, and in having the **belly hairs slate at the bases** instead of pure white as in *volans*. There are eight mammae. Characters which, in combination, serve to distinguish the skull from the skulls of other rodents of the area are: dental formula, length of skull (between 35 and 40 mm.), and width of frontals immediately back of postorbital processes (less than 10 mm.).

HABITAT–The northern flying squirrel lives in wooded areas, especially where large trees are present.

HABITS–There is less detailed knowledge of the habits of this squirrel than there is of those of *volans*. By inference it may be assumed that, in general, the habits are similar. There are two litters a season —the first being born in April or May and the second in August. There are probably three to six young in a litter.

ECONOMIC STATUS–This squirrel, like *volans*, is seldom encountered by man unless it takes up its abode in the attic of a house. Trappers report that it may become a nuisance at times by entering traps set with meat bait.

POCKET GOPHERS (FAMILY GEOMYIDAE)

This family of subterranean rodents is strictly North and Central American in distribution. They are powerful diggers and indicate their presence by the mounds of earth that they throw up on the surface above their system of tunnels. Their eyes and ears are small, and their tails are short and naked; all adaptations for an underground mode of life. They all possess external cheek pouches.

PLAINS POCKET GOPHER *Geomys bursarius* Shaw

SIZE–Total length, 230–96 mm. (9–11.6 in.); weight, 200–300 gms. (7–11 oz.).

DESCRIPTION–The plains pocket gopher, about the size of a large rat, is rich brownish or bay, sometimes with white spots. Its **tail** is relatively short, usually less than 100 mm., and **naked**. The eyes and ears are small, as becomes an animal that lives underground, and the

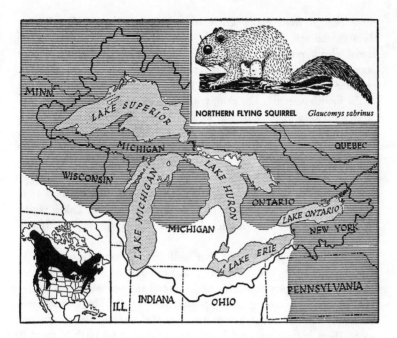

NORTHERN FLYING SQUIRREL *Glaucomys sabrinus*

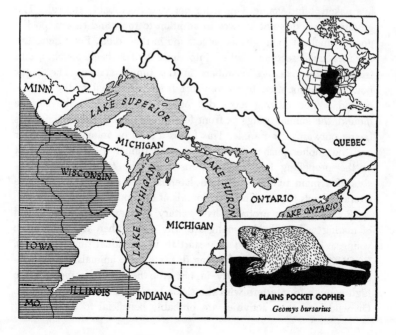

PLAINS POCKET GOPHER
Geomys bursarius

three central front claws are extremely long, adapted for digging through the soil. This is the only mammal of the area that has external cheek pouches opening on either side of the mouth. These pouches are fur-lined and are reversible, like a pants pocket. Another peculiar and interesting feature of the pocket gopher is the structure of the mouth opening. The skin, with hair, extends through behind the large incisor teeth, and the opening is closed by a sphincter muscle. This enables the animal to close its mouth while the gnawing teeth are still free to serve in chipping away hard soil or cutting roots as it tunnels through the ground. The mammae number six, two pairs inguinal and one pair pectoral.

The angular skull with large incisors may be distinguished from all other mammal skulls likely to be found in the Great Lakes region by the presence of two distinct, longitudinal grooves on the front of each upper incisor.

HABITAT–They prefer moist, but well-drained, sandy loam soils. In farming areas they are most likely to be found in hay-crop fields or pastures—also along roadsides and railroad right-of-ways.

HABITS–The pocket gopher spends most of its life underground where it tunnels, about a foot beneath the surface, for tubers and roots. Here, also, is where it builds its nest and gives birth to three to five naked, blind young. One litter per year is probably the rule. The gestation period is not known. In addition to roots and tubers, pocket gophers include some surface vegetation in their diets. Food items are cut into small sections, stuffed into the external cheek pouches, and transported to storage chambers in the tunnel system. The cheek pouches are not used to convey dirt from the tunnel to the surface mound. When moving loose dirt out of the tunnel to the surface mound, the animal brings its front feet under the body with the claws facing outward at an angle. This forms a kind of animated bulldozer and the gopher pushes the dirt along the tunnel with the hind feet as the propelling force. Characteristically, the tunnel system consists of a main tunnel with short laterals. It is at the ends of these lateral tunnels that we find the mounds of dirt, pushed up from below.

Pocket gophers probably live solitary lives except for the period of mating and while the young are with the mother. As soon as the young animals are weaned they start their individual tunnel systems.

ECONOMIC STATUS–In farming districts these animals can do considerable damage particularly in hay-crop fields. Their mounds are high enough to interfere with the sickle-bar, making mowing difficult. On wild land their activities are probably beneficial to the soil.

REMARKS—The presence of these gophers is indicated by large mounds that are somewhat fan-shaped with a round plug of earth usually near one edge. On old mounds the indication of the plug may be obliterated. Gopher traps of different kinds are usually available in stores in areas where these rodents occur. The pocket gopher desires a closed system. Except for the short times that he is pushing dirt from his tunnels, he keeps all outside openings plugged. Trappers take advantage of this habit, open the tunnel, and set the trap in the burrow some distance down from the opening. When the gopher comes to plug the opening he trips the trap. The gopher will sometimes, however, set the trap off with the dirt he is pushing in front of him and avoid being caught. Another method is to locate the main runway by probing with a metal rod, remove a section of soil and set a gopher trap (better, two facing in opposite directions) or a No. 0 jump trap in the bottom of the tunnel. A board is then placed over the opening and loose dirt packed around its edges so that no light is admitted. Poisons have been used to eliminate pocket gophers, but before these are used you should consult with your county agent or write to the Department of Agriculture for instructions.

BEAVERS (FAMILY CASTORIDAE)

This family contains but one genus, which ranges over most of North America and Europe. Its chief characters are its large size (largest of the rodents of this area), broad, flattened (dorsoventrally), scaly tail, webbed hind feet with second claw double, massive skull, and high-crowned, flat-surfaced, grinding cheek teeth.

BEAVER *Castor canadensis* Kuhl

SIZE—Total length, 875–1,020 mm. (34–40 in.); weight, 30–60 lbs.
DESCRIPTION—Its large size, rich brown coloration, and **broad spatulate tail** serve to distinguish the beaver from all other rodents. The skull is large and has massive incisors (chestnut on anterior faces) and high-crowned grinding teeth with cross crests of enamel. The female has four mammae—all pectoral.
HABITAT—The beaver is present about wooded streams and lake shores.
HABITS—The beaver combines aquatic and fossorial adaptations in habits and in structure. A lake or stream, bordered by stands of small timber, preferably aspen, poplar, birch, maple, or willow, seems to be essential to its existence. Where dams are constructed to impound the water, in lakes or along small streams, it is customary for the beaver

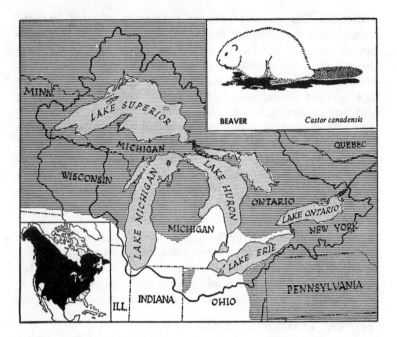

BEAVER   *Castor canadensis*

to build a lodge, which becomes the home of the family group or colony. There may be as many as nine beavers in a colony, consisting typically of parents, kits, and yearlings. Two-year-olds are driven away from the colony by the parents. Along large swift-running streams, where the building of dams or lodges is not feasible, the beaver burrows into the bank for its subterranean home. It is then known as a "bank beaver" and is considered by some trappers to be different from the common dam-and-lodge building beaver, but there is no evidence to substantiate this opinion.

Because of its ability as an engineer, especially in the construction of dams, the beaver has received more attention in the literature than has any other mammal of the area, except man. The dam is made up chiefly of small sticks and mud mixed with a few rocks, if these are available. The upstream surface is smoothly plastered with mud, the downstream side is chiefly the projecting ends of sticks that are otherwise worked into and form the framework of the structure. Dams usually are three to four feet in height and fifty to two hundred feet in length, depending on the condition of the stream and terrain. All members of the colony, except the small kits, help in keeping the dam in repair, so that a uniform water level is maintained in the pond.

Although the food of the beaver is primarily the bark and small twigs of trees, it eats many other kinds of plants, both water and land, if they are available. In captivity a beaver requires on the average one tree (one to three inches in diameter) a day for sustenance. In the wild each beaver cuts an average of one tree in two days (Bradt, 1938). If the supply of trees near the pond or lake becomes depleted, beavers will travel as far as two hundred yards for them. If it becomes necessary to go farther than this the beavers usually move to a new location. The kits number one to eight, usually two to four, in a litter and are born between April and July. There is but one litter a year. The gestation period is not known for certain, but is probably about 128 days (Bradt, 1939). The old male leaves the main lodge when the kits are born.

Defense of territory by a colony of beavers has been observed. More than one colony may occupy a large lake or pond, but there is little overlapping of colonies. Two colonies may share in keeping a dam in repair, but there is no trespass on the feeding areas and lodges. A beaver may live eleven years or more in the wild.

ECONOMIC STATUS–The beaver is an important fur animal. The beaver has been a subject for serious controversy between the fishermen and other groups. It does damage at times by flooding certain areas; it destroys many trees, most of which are of little value except as pulpwood; old beaver ponds may become warm and unsuitable for trout. But all these add up to little as compared to the fur and to the scenic value of the beaver, not to mention the role it plays in maintaining the water table and in forming rich meadows. The fisherman must look to the past. Residents had their best fishing in the early days when beavers were numerous over the entire area.

MICE AND RATS (FAMILY CRICETIDAE)

This family consists mostly of small to medium-sized rodents, diversified in habits and morphology. The infraorbital foramen is wider (rounded) at the top than at the bottom (V-shaped). A strand of muscle, part of the masseter, passes through the upper part of the foramen. A broad, oblique zygomatic plate and the absence of the postorbital processes of the frontal are additional characters. There are two subfamilies in the Great Lakes region.

The subfamily Cricetinae is represented by *Reithrodontomys, Peromyscus,* and *Neotoma;* and the genera *Synaptomys, Clethrionomys, Microtus, Phenacomys, Pitymys, Pedomys,* and *Ondatra* comprise the Microtinae. The Cricetinae are small to medium-sized terrestrial mammals with long tails, large ears and eyes, four toes on the front foot, and five on the hind foot. The cheek teeth are low-crowned, rooted, with low rounded cusps (in two longitudinal rows) for crushing and a more or less omnivorous diet. All in this area have white or whitish bellies (although the hairs are tipped with white they are lead colored at their bases) and feet, and gray, fawn, or brown upper parts. The tail is from one-third to about one-half the total length and usually is sharply bicolored, white below, brownish above. Internal cheek pouches are present. The young of all the species are slate gray and difficult to distinguish.

The subfamily Microtinae contains either small rodents combining the terrestrial and fossorial specializations or medium-sized animals of semi-aquatic adaptation (*Ondatra*). The cheek teeth are high-crowned with prismatic enamel patterns on the flat grinding surfaces. The roots remain open at the tip until late in life (this is commonly known as a rootless tooth, a misnomer inasmuch as they actually are rooted in the jaw). The angular skull usually is ridged. The eyes are small, and the ears are nearly concealed by the long coarse fur. The tail is relatively short (except that of *Ondatra*, which is long and flattened laterally). There are either four or five toes on the front foot, five on the hind foot.

WESTERN HARVEST MOUSE *Reithrodontomys megalotis* Baird

SIZE–Total length, 120–152 mm. (4.7–6 in.); weight, 8–15 gms. (.28–.53 oz.).

DESCRIPTION–This is the **smallest** of the long-tailed mice of the area. It is rather **uniform brown** on the back and sides with pale gray or whitish-tipped hairs on the belly. The tail is indistinctly bicolor. There are three pairs of mammae, one pair pectoral and two pairs inguinal. In the skull, the size (length less than 22 mm.), number of teeth (sixteen), and deep, longitudinal grooves on the front of the upper incisors, will set it apart from all others in the area.

HABITAT–This mouse inhabits grassy or herbaceous areas.

HABITS–The western harvest mouse may build its nest on the ground or in small bushes above ground. The globular nest of dry plant materials is about three inches in outside diameter and the inner chamber about two inches across. We have little knowledge of the breeding season in this area, but it probably is confined to spring and summer. The gestation period is twenty-three or twenty-four days, and the number of young per litter is one to seven (usually four). The young

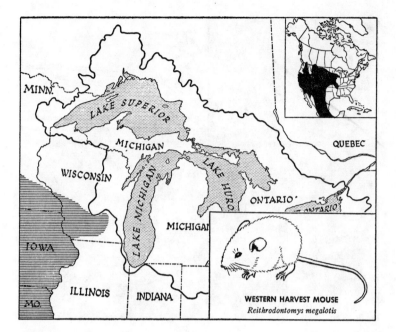

WESTERN HARVEST MOUSE
Reithrodontomys megalotis

open their eyes on about the eleventh day and are weaned when about three weeks old. Seeds and insects are the main items in their diet.

ECONOMIC STATUS–Probably neutral, usually occupy wasteland.

DEER MOUSE *Peromyscus maniculatus* Wagner

In the Great Lakes region there are two populations (subspecies) of the deer mouse that behave as though they were separate and distinct species. This situation is of great interest to the student of evolution and/or geographic distribution of animals. Were it not for the connecting populations of these mice to the south, west, and north, through which we can demonstrate gradual changes in structure and habits from the short-tailed, small-eared, pale prairie type to the long-tailed, large-eared, dark, woodland type, we would undoubtedly look upon them as distinct species in our area. As a matter of fact, the prairie form (*Peromyscus maniculatus bairdi*) is more easily distinguished from the woodland form (*P. m. gracilis*), the geographic range of which it overlaps, than either is from a different species, the white-footed mouse (*P. leucopus*). Although the two (*P. m. bairdi* and *P. m. gracilis*) overlap geographically in the northern part of the

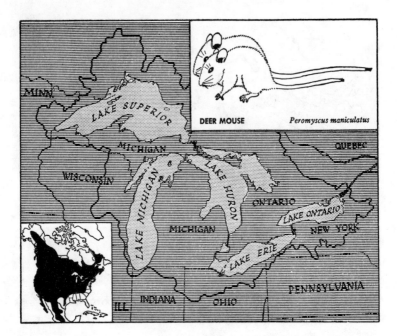

DEER MOUSE   *Peromyscus maniculatus*

Lower Peninsula of Michigan and in northern Wisconsin and Menominee County, Michigan (Upper Peninsula), they occupy separate habitats and are rarely found in precisely the same places. Because of this peculiar and interesting situation, I have thought it advisable to deviate from my method of treating each species under but one heading. Inasmuch as they behave in nature as though they were distinct species (in our area), I feel that it is best to give them separate attention here.

PRAIRIE DEER MOUSE *Peromyscus maniculatus bairdi* Hoy and Kennicott

SIZE—Total length 119–56 mm. (4.7–6 in.); weight, 10–24 gms. (.35–.84 oz.).

DESCRIPTION—This is the smallest *Peromyscus* in the area; it also has the **shortest tail** (usually 65 mm. or less) and smallest ears (16 mm. or less from notch). The upper parts are usually grayish brown, lacking the bright fulvous of the other species. The **tail** is always distinctly **bicolored**, white below, gray above. Other external characters are as given for the subfamily Cricetinae. The skull may be distinguished from the skulls of other rodents in its size class by the following combination of characters: cheek teeth rooted with rounded cusps arranged in two longitudinal rows; incisors without longitudinal grooves on anterior surfaces; interorbital width less than 4 mm.; infraorbital foramen not visible from side view, covered by zygomatic plate.

HABITAT–The prairie deer mouse may be found in open grass-covered areas with or without vines and low brush clumps. It prefers dry uplands to low moist situations.

HABITS–This is truly a grassland species. The nest is in a ground burrow made by the mouse or appropriated from some other animal that has no further use for it. It is likely that several refuge burrows within the home range (usually less than an acre in extent) are in use at various times. The breeding season normally begins in early spring, and the first young are born in early March. Occasionally, litters are produced in the middle of the winter by mice living under corn shocks, where food and shelter conditions are exceptionally favorable. Under ordinary conditions the last litters of the season are born in early November. Females probably do not breed continuously, but have a rest period of about a month in July or August. Old females raise two or more litters in the spring and two or more again in the fall. Young females start breeding when five to ten weeks old. Those born in the spring may give birth to young in the fall of the same year. There are one to seven young in a litter, usually four. The gestation period is about twenty-one days.

During the cold winter months these mice may congregate and live together in groups of as many as fifteen or more. At the end of the winter they disperse, and each breeding female selects an area that is partly exclusive of areas occupied by other breeding females. Although home ranges may overlap in part, most of the range of the breeding female is not traversed by another breeding female.˙ This strongly indicates territorial behavior by the females while breeding.

Populations of these mice during summer months probably do not exceed nine per acre. Their normal life span in the wild rarely exceeds two years, although they may live longer in the laboratory.

There is little detailed information on the food habits of these mice. They store quantities of seeds in their underground retreats in the fall. In addition to seeds they probably eat insects, berries, and nuts in season.

ECONOMIC STATUS–This mouse has little or no economic importance. It eats some weed seeds and insects, but also may destroy some grain if it is left in the field. It is nowhere sufficiently abundant to do appreciable good or harm.

WOODLAND DEER MOUSE *Peromyscus maniculatus gracilis* Le Conte

SIZE–Total length, 155–205 mm. (6–8 in.); weight, 12–31 gms. (.4–1.1 oz.).

DESCRIPTION–Because of its **large ears,** pure **white belly,** and rich fulvous upper parts, this is one of the more striking small mammals of the area. The long tail is distinctly bicolored, white below and brownish above, and is tipped with a small tuft of long hairs. From other kinds of *Peromyscus* occurring with it in the southern part of the area it may be distinguished by its larger ears (more than 18.5 mm. from notch). Other differences do not hold for every specimen. The skull may be set apart from that of *P. m. bairdi* and *P. leucopus* by the position of the anterior border of the zygomatic plate which, when the skull is viewed from the side, does not cover the infraorbital foramen. A space of .5 mm. or more is present in front of the plate.

HABITAT–It is usually confined to forested areas within its general range. Occasionally, young individuals venture out into open areas.

HABITS–This, like the other species of deer mice, is a nocturnal animal. It is rarely seen by man except when it chooses to share a cabin or house with him. It then may become a nuisance or an interesting little neighbor, depending on the attitude of the human occupant of the abode. The food of the mice probably consists chiefly of seeds, nuts, and insects. Seeds may be stored in small caches, especially during autumn. The internal cheek pouches enable the mouse to gather and carry small seeds to its secret granaries. Although mainly terrestrial in habits, these mice readily climb trees. Some of the stores of food as well as nests may be in holes in trees or in or under logs and stumps.

The limits of the breeding season are not known. From what is known, and from analogy, it may be assumed that breeding activities commence about March and that the last litters of the season are born in late September. Adult females may give birth to four or more litters during this time, and young of the spring may raise one or two litters each in the fall. The gestation period is about twenty-one days, somewhat longer in lactating females. Three to eight young, usually four to six, constitute a litter. These mice have been known to live as long as eight years in the laboratory, but I doubt that many live longer than two or three years in the wild.

The home range of this mouse as determined by Blair (1942) may be more than five and one-half acres for adult males and three and three-fourths acres for adult females. The actual area covered by the animal is probably about three-fifths of the above calculated range or a maximum of three and four-tenths acres for males and two acres for females. The possibility of territorial behavior of the females during the breeding season is suggested by the following statement: "The fact that males were taken together 5 times in the traps, while females never were caught together possibly indicates more tolerance among males than among females" (Blair, 1942: 31).

ECONOMIC STATUS–This species is of little economic significance.

REMARKS–In addition to *bairdi* and *gracilis*, a third subspecies, *Peromyscus maniculatus maniculatus* Wagner, occurs on Isle Royale and north of Lake Superior. It is similar to *gracilis* in characters as well as in habits.

WHITE-FOOTED MOUSE *Peromyscus leucopus* Rafinesque

SIZE–Total length, 141–95 mm. (5.6–7.7 in.); weight, 12–31 gms. (.4–1.1 oz.).

DESCRIPTION–The **white feet and belly** (hairs lead-colored at bases on belly) and fulvous (sometimes grayish) upper parts serve to distinguish members of this species from all mice in its size group except those in the same genus. From other members of the genus, the single character that best sets *leucopus* apart is the **size of the ear** (15–18 mm. from notch). The ear is larger than that of *bairdi* and smaller than that of *gracilis* or *maniculatus*. Additional characters usually present in *leucopus* are the dusky upper lip and the indistinctly bicolored tail. For skull distinctions see the key (p. 212).

HABITAT–Although it usually is found in forested and brushy areas, it occasionally is present in open grassy areas that border woods or brush.

HABITS–The white-footed mouse builds its nest wherever there is sufficient shelter and protection. The nest may be in the ground, under old stumps or logs, in holes in trees, in abandoned squirrel and bird nests, or in buildings. Practically any soft materials available are used in nest construction. More than one nest for each animal is probably the rule rather than the exception. A new clean nest is often constructed to hold the two to six naked young. Breeding normally occurs from March to October. Old females give birth to young as early as late March. This litter is followed by a second, after which there is a rest period of four to six weeks in July or August. Breeding

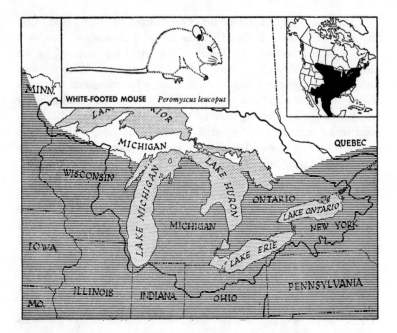

WHITE-FOOTED MOUSE *Peromyscus leucopus*

is again resumed, and two or more litters are born in the fall. These mice occasionally breed in the winter if conditions are favorable. Young females start breeding at ten or eleven weeks of age. The gestation period is about twenty-one days. In the laboratory these mice may live five or more years, but in the wild few reach the age of three years. The home range of adult females is about one-half acre, but old males range over one to one and one-half acres. The food of these mice consists chiefly of seeds, nuts, and insects. Small caches of seeds and nuts are hidden away for future use.

The females seem to display territorial behavior during their breeding season. Populations range from four per acre in the spring to twelve per acre in the fall after the last litters are born. Young leave the nest when about twenty-one days old.

ECONOMIC STATUS–The white-footed mouse serves as a food item for such predators as foxes, weasels, and owls. In this way it may help to relieve the pressure of predation on some game species. Its consumption of insects and weed seeds is beneficial. In late fall these mice commonly enter buildings, where they often constitute a temporary nuisance. A few snap traps set along the walls will eliminate undesirable mice.

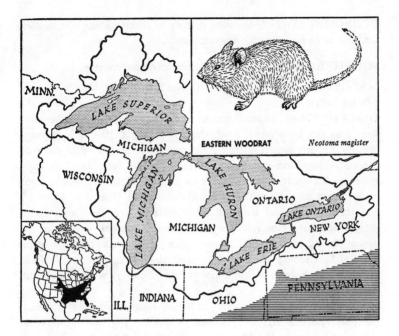

EASTERN WOODRAT *Neotoma magister* Baird

SIZE–Total length, 405–440 mm. (16–17.3 in.); weight, 375–455 gms. (13–16 oz.).

DESCRIPTION–This rather **large rat** barely gets into the area here considered. It is **gray** slightly **washed with buff** above, buffy on the sides, and white on the underparts. The feet are white also, and the tail is distinctly bicolor. The hair is soft and fur-like. The skull has a noticeably long rostrum, three cheek teeth on each side, and the posterior edge of the hard palate does not extend back of the plane of the last molars. Its length is 45–50 mm. There are four mammae, all inguinal.

HABITAT–It is present about rock slides and cliffs in mountainous areas.

HABITS–The eastern woodrat builds nests of sticks and odd bits of vegetation among the rocks. Its presence usually can be detected by these stick houses. They are chiefly nocturnal, although they sometimes venture forth during the day. They breed throughout the spring, summer, and fall. Two, or possibly three, litters are produced each year by an adult female. One to three young constitute a litter, and the gestation period is probably about thirty-three days.

ECONOMIC STATUS–Because it lives in remote areas, the eastern woodrat is of no economic importance.

SOUTHERN BOG LEMMING *Synaptomys cooperi* Baird

SIZE–Total length, 99–132 mm. (3.9–5.2 in.); weight, 14–39 gms. (.5–1.4 oz.).

DESCRIPTION–This small mouse has a **short tail** (about the same length as the hind foot), long, thick fur (about 10 mm.), grizzled gray or grayish brown on the back and sides, tipped with silver on the underparts, and ears nearly concealed in the fur. There are eight mammae, two pairs inguinal and two pairs pectoral. The combination of four toes on the front foot and the short tail (less than 25 mm.) sets this mouse apart from all other mammals of the Great Lakes region except the pine vole (*Pitymys*). The grizzled appearance of the upper parts and the silver-tipped hairs of the underparts of specimens of *Synaptomys* serve to distinguish them from pine voles, which are uniformly auburn on the upper parts and usually washed with buff on the underparts.

The skull of the bog lemming in its size range among the rodents is the only one that has longitudinal grooves on the front surfaces of the upper incisors. Further characters are the flat-surfaced grinding cheek teeth and the length of the entire tooth row, which is greater than the length of the anterior palatine foramina.

HABITAT–It inhabits low damp bogs or meadows in which there is a heavy growth of grass—usually small local areas.

HABITS–The bog lemming is typically a grass eater, although other succulent vegetation and insects are taken on occasion. It is active in the daytime as well as at night. Surface runways and underground burrows are made by these mice or appropriated from *Microtus*. Surface runways may be detected by parting the heavy grass that has grown up and fallen over to form a protective mat. If piles of short green stems and blades of grass and small piles of bright green feces are in the runway, *Synaptomys* is likely to be present. Globular nests, made entirely of dry grass, are built both above and below ground. If above ground, the nests usually are partly concealed in the heavy grass. Two to six young are born in a litter. The gestation period is about 23 days. It is not known how many litters an individual female will bear in a year, but one may expect to find young at any season. I suspect that the height of the breeding season is during spring and fall, but this is not known definitely. An adult female ranges over an area at least forty yards in greatest diameter. Here again information

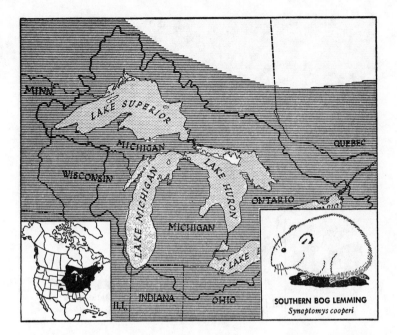

SOUTHERN BOG LEMMING
Synaptomys cooperi

is meager. Practically nothing is known of the home life and social relations of these mice. They are docile when handled and will not bite unless squeezed or otherwise mistreated.

The population of bog lemmings fluctuates from year to year. In one year they may be abundant, inhabiting not only their favorite bog or meadow habitat, but also low woodlands and high grassy areas, and in the next year they may be very scarce in the same area. The reasons for the extreme fluctuations in abundance in this species are not understood. Neither is it known whether the fluctuations are cyclical or whether they are correlated with local phenomena.

ECONOMIC STATUS–I doubt if the bog lemming ever can be considered a harmful mouse. It is local in distribution, rarely occurs on any but wasteland or uncultivated areas, and does not damage crops that might be used by man. During years of abundance it most certainly serves as an important buffer species for predators that might otherwise prey on game animals.

HEATHER VOLE *Phenacomys intermedius* Merriam

SIZE–Total length, 130–150 mm. (5–6 in.); weight, 30–40 gms. (1–1.4 oz.).

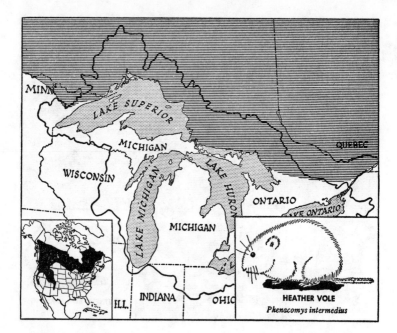

HEATHER VOLE
Phenacomys intermedius

DESCRIPTION–The heather vole is fairly uniform grayish with a wash of **yellow** on the **face and nose.** The underparts are plumbeous washed with whitish. The relatively short tail (less than 42 mm.) and the yellowish nose will serve to distinguish this from other voles in the area. There are eight mammae. The skull, like the skulls of other voles, has flat-surfaced, grinding cheek teeth with enamel ridges and loops. The least interorbital width is less than 4 mm., the dorso-ventral diameter of the audital bulla is less than 6 mm., and the length of the palatine foramina less than 5 mm. On the lower teeth the re-entrant angles go more than halfway across the teeth.

HABITAT–The heather vole lives in relatively dry areas with good ground cover.

HABITS–These voles are present mostly in wild, uncultivated areas and detailed information on their habits is scanty. From three to eight young are born in a litter and probably two or more litters are produced each year.

ECONOMIC STATUS–This vole is probably beneficial. As far as we know, it does not interfere with man's interests.

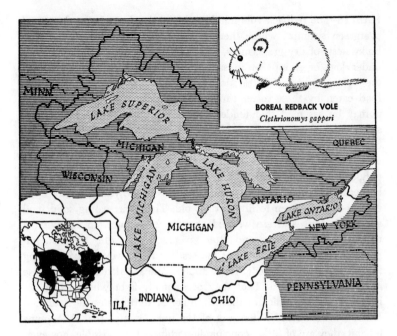

BOREAL REDBACK VOLE
Clethrionomys gapperi

BOREAL REDBACK VOLE *Clethrionomys gapperi* Vigors

SIZE–Total length, 116–58 mm. (4.6–6 in.); weight, 16–37 gms. (.56–1.3 oz.).

DESCRIPTION–The redback vole is the most strikingly colored of the short-tailed microtines of the region. The nose, sides of head, and sides of body are gray, slightly washed with yellowish. Down the middle of the back, from forehead to rump, is a **broad chestnut stripe** which contrasts with the color of the sides. The tail is nearly black above, gray below. The hair of the underparts is black at the base and broadly tipped with white, giving the entire belly a silvery appearance. The ears are partly concealed by the long fur. The skull of the redback vole differs from the skulls of the other microtines in its size range by the character of the palate. In *Clethrionomys* the posterior border of the palate is straight and ends abruptly in a thin bony shelf. It does not have a median projection; it connects with the palatines only at the sides of the posterior narial cavity. Each molar has two distinct roots in adult animals, but in young animals, the molars are rootless as in other microtines.

HABITAT–It may be in hardwood forests and conifer swamps, especially where there are decaying logs and stumps.

HABITS–The redback vole inhabits chiefly the damp forest floors and evergreen swamps, where there is little necessity for runways. The bulky nests of dry grass, moss, and small herbs may be situated in or under logs or stumps or in subterranean chambers connected with the burrow systems. Little definite information is available on the food eaten by these mice. From analogy with other related species it may be assumed that tender vegetation, nuts, seeds, insects, and snails enter their diet. The information on reproduction would indicate that they breed chiefly from April to October, that three to eight, usually four to six, young are born in a litter, and that the gestation period is from seventeen to nineteen days. Two or more litters may be borne each year by the female. The eyes of the young do not open until they are eleven to fifteen days old. They start eating solid food about this time and are weaned about a week later. In captivity, a mother that had her second litter seventeen days after the first, immediately weaned the young of the first litter and would have nothing further to do with them (Svihla, 1930). The social relations of these mice are little known. That they occasionally fight when placed together in a cage indicates the possibility of territoriality in nature.

ECONOMIC STATUS–Because of the wild country that these mice inhabit, they are of little economic importance. It is possible, however, that they help protect the forests through their depredations on insects.

MEADOW VOLE *Microtus pennsylvanicus* Ord

SIZE–Total length, 120–88 mm. (4.7–7.4 in.); weight, 20–68 gms. (.7–2.4 oz.).

DESCRIPTION–The meadow vole is the largest mouse in this area. It is rather uniformly dark brown above, with slightly paler sides and silver-tipped hairs on the belly. The ears are nearly concealed in the thick fur. The eyes are small, black beads a little larger than an ordinary pin head. There are eight mammae, two pairs inguinal and two pairs pectoral. This species may be distinguished from other members of the microtine group by the **long tail** (more than 37 mm.) and the uniform color of back and sides (no distinct reddish band down the back and **no yellowish on nose**). The skull, in addition to size and flat-crowned grinding cheek teeth with folded enamel loops surrounding islands of dentine, possesses the following combination of characters which serves to separate it from the skulls of other rodents of the area: palate with median projection on the posterior border, not ending abruptly in a thin bony shelf; upper incisors not grooved longi-

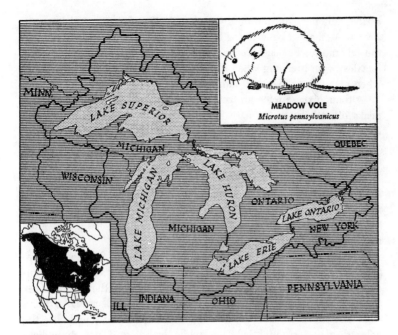

MEADOW VOLE
Microtus pennsylvanicus

tudinally on anterior faces; least interorbital width less than 4 mm.; last upper molar with five or six irregular enamel loops enclosing cement; and length of anterior palatine foramina more than 5 mm.

HABITAT—Meadow voles inhabit moist, low areas with rank growths of grasses. In winter they congregate under corn shocks or other protective covering. They also live on high grassland and near streams, lakes, and swamps. On some of the islands they are found in forests with little ground cover.

HABITS—The presence of these animals may be detected by the numerous runways on the surface of the ground. The runways usually are roofed over by grass or other dense vegetation. Underground burrows also are present with entrances along the surface runways. A large globular nest, six to eight inches in diameter, may be situated above ground and concealed in surface vegetation, or a somewhat smaller nest may be in a pocket connected with an underground burrow. Usually, the nest is made of dry grasses or sedges. One to nine young in a litter have been recorded for these mice. The eyes of the young open at about eight days, and the young are weaned at two to three weeks of age. The gestation period is about twenty-one days. These mice breed throughout the year, but are most active during spring, summer, and autumn. One female may bear several litters in a year. As many as seventeen litters in a year have been recorded in the laboratory, but such fecundity is probably rare in nature. Young females begin breeding when about twenty-five days old, young males when about forty-five days old.

Although these mice are active throughout the day and night, the peaks of activity are in early morning and in the evening with the least activity at midday and midnight. "The home range of an individual seldom encompasses an area in excess of one-fifteenth of an acre" (Hamilton, 1937b).

Their food consists essentially of grasses and sedges. Like most rodents, they undoubtedly consume animal matter when it is available. An individual eats about its own weight in green food every twenty-four hours. Such foods as roots, bulbs, and blades of grass may be stored in and along the runways.

For their size the meadow voles are remarkable fighters. In captivity they sometimes turn cannibalistic. The chewed ears of wild individuals are indicative of unsocial relations. The mother protects her young in the nest against others of her kind. I suspect that if more were known about their social activities it would be found that the voles display territorial behavior while breeding if not throughout the year.

This is one of the most prolific of our mammals. Given proper conditions, the population increases tremendously within a single year. It is one of the so-called "cyclic" species. Populations seem to reach their maxima about every four years. They then fall rapidly only to build up again. Fluctuations may be somewhat local in character. Populations may be high in one area and low in another within the general range of the species. There is much to be learned about these phenomena.

ECONOMIC STATUS–This is probably the most important buffer species in the area. Predatory birds, mammals, and reptiles all take their toll of it. This means a direct benefit to the game species. These mice, especially when the population is high, are capable of doing much damage to farm crops. The consumption of corn in the shock and the girdling of orchard trees are the most obvious of the depredations of these little herbivores. The damage to corn may be prevented by husking in early fall. If left over winter, the crop may be nearly half consumed by these voles. Orchards may be protected in part by eliminating all ground cover within the orchard and around its edge. The damage done to trees may be reduced by placing cinders around

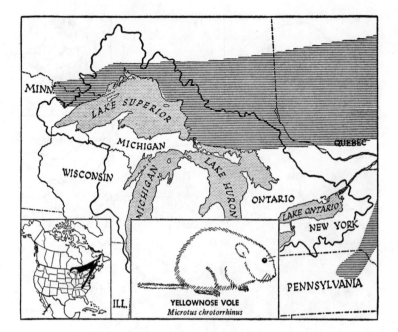

YELLOWNOSE VOLE
Microtus chrotorrhinus

the bases of trees, or the bases may be encircled with hardware cloth. If poison is used for local control it must be used intelligently, preferably under the guidance of an experienced person. Hawks, owls, weasels, skunks, and larger snakes are the natural enemies of these voles and should be encouraged. They are the best controls.

YELLOWNOSE VOLE *Microtus chrotorrhinus* Miller

SIZE–Total length, 140–170 mm. (5.5–6.7 in.); weight, 30–40 gms. (1–1.4 oz.).

DESCRIPTION–This vole of the northern forested area is dark gray above, plumbeous with a whitish wash on the belly. The **face** and **nose** are **reddish orange**. The only other animal with which it might be confused is the heather vole. The length of the tail, more than 45 mm., will distinguish it from the latter. In the skull, the pattern of the enamel in the last upper molar tooth will set it apart from all other voles of the area (Fig. 45). There are eight mammae.

HABITAT–The yellownose vole favors areas with rocky outcrops.

HABITS–Very little is known of the habits of this vole in the Great Lakes region. They probably breed throughout the warmer months and the number of young per litter is usually three or four. They are

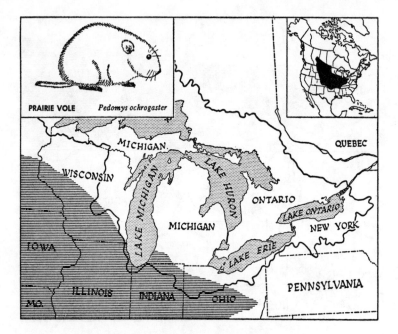

likely to be in small colonies, in which conditions are favorable for their existence.

ECONOMIC STATUS–Inasmuch as these voles occupy untillable lands, they are of little concern economically.

PRAIRIE VOLE *Pedomys ochrogaster* Wagner

SIZE–Total length, 118–55 mm. (4.6–6 in.); weight, 22–35 gms. (.78–1.2 oz.).

DESCRIPTION–The prairie vole is a medium-sized microtine with a tail of medium length. The eyes are small black beads, slightly larger than the head of an ordinary pin, and the ears are nearly concealed in the long fur (Fig. 10). The fur of the upper parts has a distinctly yellowish grizzled aspect not present in other microtines. This **yellowish** color, **mixed with rusty,** is also on the underparts and is especially pronounced **around the base of the tail.** The combination of color and length of tail serves to distinguish the prairie vole from the other closely related species within its range. In addition to the prismatic, flat-crowned grinding teeth and ungrooved incisors, the skull may be distinguished from other skulls in its size class by the following combination of characters: posterior border of palate with median projection which connects with palatines at center as well as at sides of posterior narial cavity; interorbital width less than 4 mm.; last upper molar with four irregular enamel loops enclosing cement; and palatine foramina less than 5 mm. long. There are six mammae.

Fig. 10. Prairie vole.

HABITAT—This vole is restricted to open grassland, fence rows, and cultivated fields. It is seldom in wooded areas.

HABITS—Little is known concerning the habits of the prairie vole. Both underground burrows and surface runways are used, but they probably occupy the underground systems to a greater extent than do the meadow voles. Food consists chiefly of grasses and other herbage, roots, seeds, and possibly some insects. Stores of roots have been found in the underground runways. The nest is usually underground and is made up almost wholly of dry grasses. Three to six young are born in a litter. Females may breed soon after giving birth to young and may raise several litters a year. The breeding season is from March to November. The voles are active both by day and by night, but their peaks of activity are not known. There is no definite information on home ranges, although Kennicott stated that the burrows extend five to ten rods on each side of the nests. The social behavior, from what little is known, is probably similar to that of the meadow vole. They are vigorous fighters and often turn cannibalistic in captivity. Kennicott's (1857: 99) statement that two pairs never occupy the same hole indicates the possibility of territoriality in this species.

ECONOMIC STATUS—Because of its limited distribution in the area, this species is of little economic importance. In the small area where it is found it probably ranks next to the meadow vole in importance.

PINE VOLE *Pitymys pinetorum* Le Conte

SIZE—Total length, 87–128 mm. (3.4–5 in.); weight, 19–35 gms. (.7–1.2 oz.).

DESCRIPTION—The pine vole is a small auburn mouse with a tail scarcely longer than its hind foot. The ears are nearly concealed in long thick fur which is not grizzled, but uniformly auburn-tipped on upper parts and sides. The **underparts** are lightly washed with **buff**. There are four mammae, all inguinal. The combination of the four toes on the front foot, a tail less than 25 mm. long, and the color is sufficient to distinguish this from all other mammals of the area. The bog lemming, the only species with which the pine vole might be confused, is grizzled grayish or grayish brown above. The skull, in addition to having the characteristic microtine cheek teeth with folded enamel loops surrounding islands of dentine on the flat grinding surfaces, may be distinguished from other rodent skulls of similar size and in its range by the following combination of characters: the length of the upper cheek-tooth row is greater than the length of the anterior palatine foramina; the upper incisors are not grooved on the anterior faces; the posterior border of the palate has a median projection, not ending abruptly in a thin bony shelf; and the least interorbital width is more than 4 mm.

HABITAT—This vole prefers deciduous forests and brushy areas where there is a heavy ground cover of either leaves or grass.

HABITS—The pine vole is chiefly fossorial, spending much of its time in its subterranean burrows in search of roots and tubers. These underground burrows usually are no more than three or four inches below the surface, sometimes they are so close to the surface that little ridges, like miniature mole runs, appear above the ground. Sur-

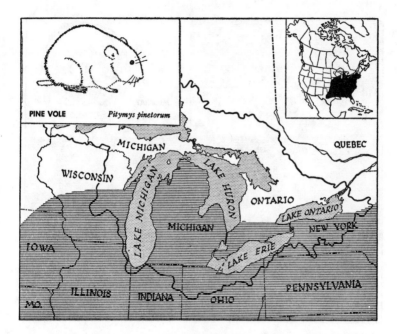

PINE VOLE   *Pitymys pinetorum*

face runways beneath the cover of leaves and grass on the woodland floor are used, but not to the extent that the other voles utilize this type of runway. In addition to making their own runways, these voles often take over the burrow systems of moles and shorttail shrews. Nests are customarily built under the protection of old logs or stumps. Roots and tubers are stored in underground caches.

Two to seven young, usually three or four, are born in a litter. The breeding season is not known definitely, but probably extends from March to October. The gestation period is unknown for this species, but from analogy it may be assumed to be about twenty-one days. The young weigh about 2.2 gms. each at birth, their eyes open when they are nine to twelve days old, and they are weaned on about the seventeenth day after birth. An old female may have several litters during the breeding season.

The home range of an individual is probably about one-fourth acre. The maximum home range recorded for an adult male was ninety-three yards in greatest diameter.

ECONOMIC STATUS–This vole, where abundant, sometimes does considerable damage to orchards by girdling the trees.

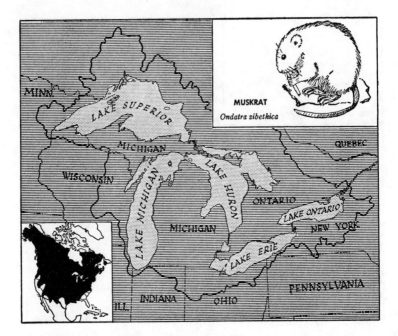

MUSKRAT
Ondatra zibethica

MUSKRAT *Ondatra zibethica* Linnaeus

SIZE–Total length, 477–636 mm. (19–25 in.); weight, 810–1,580 gms. (1.78–3.5 lbs.).

DESCRIPTION–The muskrat is about the size of a small house cat. It is uniformly dark brown on the upper parts, silver-tipped on the belly. It has small beadlike eyes, and the ears are nearly concealed in the dense fur. The hind feet are large, with **webs between the toes.** The black, scaly, nearly naked, laterally **flattened tail** is about as long as the head and body and serves to distinguish the muskrat from all other mammals. There are six mammae, two pectoral and four inguinal. The skull may be distinguished by the following combination of characters: total number of teeth, sixteen; incisors without longitudinal grooves on anterior surfaces; cheek teeth flat-surfaced and high-crowned, with folded enamel loops surrounding dentine; infraorbital foramen less than 5 mm. in smallest diameter; greatest length of skull more than 50 mm.

HABITAT–This mammal inhabits marshes, ponds, lakes, and streams, especially where there are heavy growths of rushes or cattails.

HABITS–The muskrat is chiefly aquatic in adaptation, but still retains some of the terrestrial and fossorial modifications. Open water, at least during part of the year, is essential to its well-being. In our area most muskrats build houses of available aquatic vegetation. These houses vary from three to eight feet in diameter at the base. The entrances, usually below the water level, lead to the dry nest chamber, which is well above the water and near the center of the house. Some muskrats, along streams or where the water is low, burrow into banks and do not build houses. The greatest house-building activity takes place in late summer and early fall. It is at this time of year that muskrats may be seen crossing country far from water, presumably in search of new home sites. The breeding season is normally from April to August. Old females may have as many as three litters in a season. The one to eleven, but usually about six, young are blind at birth, nearly naked, and weigh about 21 gms. each. Their eyes open at fourteen to sixteen days, and they are weaned in the fourth week. They do not breed until the following year. The gestation period is probably somewhat variable. It has been given as twenty-two to thirty days.

The food of these animals consists chiefly of stems and roots of aquatic vegetation. In an emergency they will eat almost any available plant food. Sometimes they turn carnivorous and subsist almost entirely on a flesh diet for certain periods. Mussels, frogs, turtles, and fish, as well as their kind, are eaten on occasion.

The great amount of fighting that takes place, especially in areas where the population is high, indicates that their social relations are not so tranquil as they might be. Much damage is done to the pelts because of this strife. It is believed by those who have studied the muskrat that no more than one family occupies each house. The mink seems to be one of the important enemies of the muskrat. Other predators, bird, mammal, and reptile, probably take their toll, but the muskrat is able to survive and increase in numbers, if suitable habitat is available, in spite of natural enemies and heavy cropping by the trapper.

ECONOMIC STATUS—The muskrat is a valuable fur animal. It usually occupies wasteland and does not enter into competition with man except when it burrows into dikes and causes them to wash out. To the trapper, it is an important source of revenue.

OLD WORLD RATS AND MICE (FAMILY MURIDAE)

There are two representatives of this exotic family in the area, the Norway rat and the house mouse. Both have followed man around the world and now are cosmopolitan in distribution. They are uniform grayish brown above with somewhat paler underparts, never white, and have long, scaly, scantily haired tails. The skull differs from the skulls of other rodents chiefly in that the cheek teeth have small rounded cusps (tubercles) arranged in three longitudinal rows. Also, the hard palate in this family extends posteriorly well beyond the last molar, and the palatine slits extend posteriorly beyond the anterior border of the first molar.

NORWAY RAT *Rattus norvegicus* Berkenhout

SIZE–Total length, 316–426 mm. (12.4–17 in.); weight, 195–287 gms. (6.9–10 oz.).

DESCRIPTION–The Norway rat has been pictured so often that a detailed description seems unnecessary. Size, as given above, and characters given under the family will suffice to distinguish this species from the other mammals. Females have six mammae on each side, total twelve.

HABITAT–This rat resides chiefly around places of human habitation.

HABITS–The Norway rat is omnivorous and draws no lines where food is concerned. It is particularly fond of garbage and refuse.

A prolific species, this rat brings forth litters of six to twenty-two young at a time, and as many as twelve litters may be produced by a single female in a year. The young start breeding when three or four months old. The gestation period as determined in the white rat (an albino of this species) is twenty-one or twenty-two days.

The nests of these rats usually are under buildings, feed stacks, or in old dumps. They prefer a place where they can burrow into the ground beneath protective shelter.

The estimated population in Baltimore was one rat for five to six persons. This, of course, varies with the community. Farming areas and small towns, as a rule, have more rats per capita than do large cities. The rats are colonial in habits. Where one is found there usually are several. Perhaps their social tolerance contributes to their success as a species.

ECONOMIC STATUS–Nothing good can be said of this foreign interloper. It not only consumes and wastes grains, seeds, fruit, and other foods, but is very destructive. It gnaws holes in buildings, chews up equipment and merchandise, kills young poultry for the lust of killing, and is a general nuisance. Further, it is a carrier of many diseases communicable to man and is thereby a menace to health. It costs each person about two dollars a year to support this public enemy. Anyone interested in rat destruction and rat control is referred to the government bulletins listed on page 235.

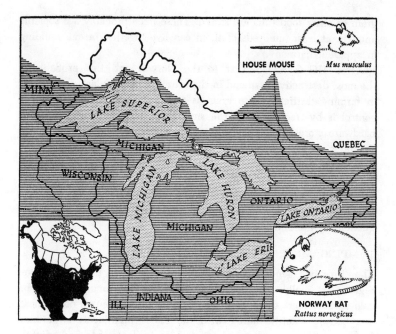

HOUSE MOUSE   *Mus musculus*

NORWAY RAT
Rattus norvegicus

HOUSE MOUSE *Mus musculus* Linnaeus

SIZE–Total length, 150–80 mm. (6–7 in.); weight, 12–23 gms. (.4–.8 oz.).

DESCRIPTION–The family characters and size, given above, separate this mouse from other mammals of the area. The ten mammae distinguish females from other long-tailed mice. The only kinds with which it might be confused are members of the genera *Peromyscus* and *Reithrodontomys*. The **scantily haired tail** and yellowish tinge to the underparts, which are never pure white, set the house mouse apart from *Peromyscus*. The smooth front surface of the incisors sets it apart from *Reithrodontomys*.

HABITAT–It usually lives around places of human habitation, although it often inhabits the fields, especially where there is grain.

HABITS–The house mouse, like the Norway rat, has followed man around the world. It is able to adapt itself to various conditions. Omnivorous in diet and prolific (producing three to eleven young in a litter and breeding the year round), the species has been too successful for the good of mankind. The gestation period is eighteen to twenty-one days, and the young are sexually mature at about six weeks. Nests are constructed of pieces of paper, rags, or anything handy. Buildings are the favorite nesting sites, especially those where grain or other foodstuffs are stored. These mice probably are sociable animals, at least hundreds of them can live together in one building in apparent harmony.

ECONOMIC STATUS–Next to the Norway rat, this probably is the most destructive mammal in the area. It is particularly destructive in farming districts where grain is stored. The simplest method of control is by trapping with the small snap trap procurable at most hardware stores. A farmer wishing to clean out the mice from his buildings should start with no fewer than one hundred traps. A few days of concentrated effort should rid the premises of mice, and the amount of grain saved will pay for the investment in traps many times over. The traps should be baited with a little bacon, cheese, or rolled oats and peanut butter, and set along walls and places frequented by the mice.

JUMPING MICE (FAMILY ZAPODIDAE)

There are two genera in this family of rodents in the Great Lakes region. Externally, they are characterized by the long, distinctly bicolored tail (more than one and one-half times the length of the head and body), scantily haired with the scales prominent; large hind feet, showing the saltatorial or jumping adaptation; and slightly hispid fur on the back. The skull has a large infraorbital foramen (more than 1 mm. in smallest diameter); the zygomatic plate is nearly horizontal and is always narrower than and completely beneath the infraorbital foramen; the upper incisors have longitudinal grooves on the anterior faces.

MEADOW JUMPING MOUSE *Zapus hudsonius* Zimmermann

SIZE–Total length, 182–225 mm. (7–9 in.); weight, 15.0–22.5 gms. (.5–.79 oz.).

DESCRIPTION–This is a small, long-tailed mouse with **large hind feet.** The tail is bicolored, scantily haired so that scales show prominently, and **not tipped with white.** The belly hairs are **white to the bases,** sometimes washed with yellowish. The general coloration of the upper parts is yellowish olive with a distinctly darker dorsal stripe and paler sides. The hair is slightly hispid. This is the only mammal of the area that has a total of eighteen teeth. Other skull characters are given under the family. The mammae are in four pairs, two inguinal, one abdominal, and one pectoral.

HABITAT–The meadow jumping mouse prefers low meadows, but at times is present in nearly every habitat in the area. It is more abun-

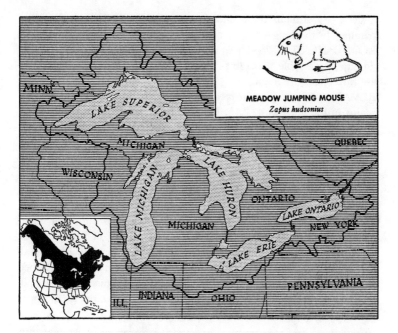

MEADOW JUMPING MOUSE
Zapus hudsonius

dant in the northern than in the southern part of the Great Lakes region.

HABITS—This is a hibernating mammal. In October and November these mice retire to well-drained slopes or prominences, where they curl up in nests two to three feet below the surface of the ground and go into their winter sleep. In this attitude the nose is bent down between the hind legs and the long tail is wrapped round and round the whole body. Here the animals remain in deep sleep until sometime in April or May, when they emerge several grams lighter than they were the previous fall. Plants have already started growing, and an abundant food supply is available to the little jumper. Breeding begins probably in late May, and the first young are born sometime in June. The gestation period is eighteen to twenty-one days. One to eight, usually three to five, young are born in a litter. It is possible that some of the older females, those wintering over, may raise two or three litters a year, but again there is no definite information. Nests usually are in the ground or beneath the shelter of a log or its equivalent, if available. The food consists chiefly of seeds, fruits, and insects. The feeding ground is generally in a low moist place and on occasion may be several yards from the nesting ground higher up on a slope. By autumn these mice have stored fat in their bodies preparatory to the long winter sleep.

ECONOMIC STATUS–These mice are never sufficiently abundant to do any appreciable damage to crops. They may do some good. They are rarely seen by man.

REMARKS–There are four races of this species in the area, *Z. h. hudsonius* in the northwest, *Z. h. brevipes* in the south, *Z. h. americanus* in the extreme east, and *Z. h. ontarioensis* in the northeast.

WOODLAND JUMPING MOUSE *Napaeozapus insignis* Miller

SIZE–Total length, 205–50 mm. (8–10 in.); weight, 19–26.8 gms. (.67–.95 oz.).

DESCRIPTION–This is one of the most colorful of the small mammals of the area. It has **pure white underparts,** bright fulvous sides, a brownish back, and usually a **white tip on** the long **tail.** In general, it is similar to *Zapus,* but its brighter coloration, usually white-tipped tail, and slightly larger average size serve to distinguish it. The skull is similar to that of *Zapus,* except that it does not have the small upper

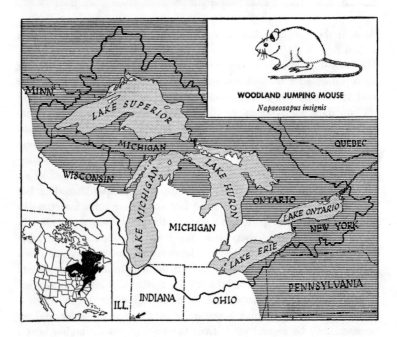

WOODLAND JUMPING MOUSE
Napaeozapus insignis

premolar. Other characters are given under the family. The mammae are in four pairs.

HABITAT–This mouse lives in forests, especially where these border lakes or streams.

HABITS–Like *Zapus*, the woodland jumping mouse hibernates from about November to late April or early May. Young have been reported in June, July, and September. There are one to six, usually four or five, young in a litter. It is possible that two litters are produced in a season. The gestation period is twenty-nine days or more, and young weigh about one gram each at birth. The young are naked, blind, and without the vibrissae which are common in young of rodents generally. These mice may climb small vines and berry bushes in search of food, but their chief adaptation is of a jumping, terrestrial type. Their food consists mainly of seeds, fruits, and a few insects. The home range averages one to two acres in area, and the populations in the fall are about three per acre.

Our knowledge of the life history of this mouse is still relatively incomplete.

ECONOMIC STATUS–This species occurs only in wild areas and is so little known at present that I am not able to evaluate it.

PORCUPINES (FAMILY ERETHIZONTIDAE)

In the United States and Canada the porcupine is the only member of a large group of rodents, chiefly South American in distribution, known as the hystricomorphs. In these rodents, the infraorbital foramen is enlarged, and through it passes not only nerves and blood vessels, but also a considerable muscle (masseter medialis). The zygomatic plate in this family is nearly horizontal in position and lies beneath the infraorbital foramen. There are no postorbital processes of the frontals and very little constriction in the interorbital area. The body is covered with short soft underfur, long coarse overhair, and sharp spines or quills. The spines are most numerous on the rump and short thick tail. There are four toes on each front foot, five on each hind foot. Four mammae are present in the pectoral region.

PORCUPINE *Erethizon dorsatum* Linnaeus

SIZE–Total length, 630–80 mm. (25–27 in.); weight, 9.5–19 lbs.
DESCRIPTION–Same as for the family.
HABITAT–It is confined to forested areas.
HABITS–The porcupine is plantigrade and terrestrial with arboreal

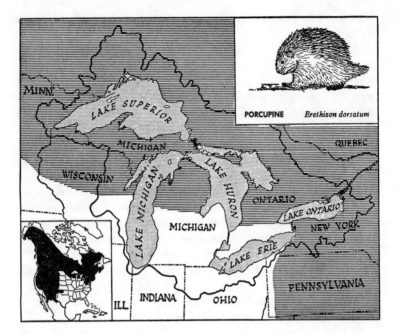

PORCUPINE   *Erethizon dorsatum*

specializations. Because of its well-armored body it is one of the most fearless of mammals. If the porcupine is on the ground and is approached by an enemy, it tucks its head down between its front legs and presents its rear to the foe. With the slightest touch on the rear the tail is swished sideways at lightning speed. If the adversary happens to be within reach of this formidable weapon it receives many **barbed quills.** The inexperienced dog or coyote that walks into this trap often does not live to repeat the experience.

Porcupines den in hollow trees and logs or in caves among rocky outcrops. During a large part of the year they are colonial; as many as twenty or more may live in the same shelter, if it is sufficiently spacious to accommodate them. The rutting season begins in early September and lasts a month or more. Males and females usually pair for the mating season, but one male may mate with two females before the season is over. The gestation period is seven months. Usually, one (rarely two) young is borne by a female. At birth the young porcupine weighs about five hundred grams (over one pound), has its eyes open, is clothed with long silky hair, and is able to climb within a few hours. The short quills are apparent on the second day after birth, and the young porcupine is not only able to shift for himself within a few days, but is able to throw up his "spine screen" against his enemies. The mother pays very little attention to her offspring. The young are sexually mature in their third year. In spite of the extremely slow rate of reproduction, the porcupine is able to hold its own against great odds. Apparently, the infant mortality is extremely low. Man is the porcupine's main enemy. The porcupine is chiefly a vegetarian, eating almost any plant available and relishing the bark of many trees, but it is also fond of meat.

ECONOMIC STATUS—The porcupine does considerable damage to buildings and communication lines in parts of the area. The forester complains, legitimately, of its damage to trees. It is a prodigious gnawer of woods, especially if they are flavored with salt. Outbuildings and cabins that are vacant during the winter are likely to suffer from the depredations of this innocuous-appearing animal.

In the porcupine's favor it may be stated that it is a source of food for the man who happens to be lost in the wilderness. In the past the Indians used the quills as decorative elements in their crafts. Further, the tourist usually derives pleasure from seeing these wild animals in nature. One cannot travel long in the northern woods without glimpsing one of these exotic-appearing creatures.

HARES, RABBITS, AND PIKAS (ORDER LAGOMORPHA)

This order of mammals, nearly world-wide in distribution, includes the rabbits, hares, and pikas. The rabbits and hares (family Leporidae) are represented in the mammalian fauna of the Great Lakes region. One of the chief characters of this order is the presence of two pairs of upper incisors, one directly behind the other (not in a continuous arc as in other mammals).

HARES AND RABBITS (FAMILY LEPORIDAE)

In addition to the ordinal characters given above, this family possesses the following features: the hind feet are large; all feet are covered with dense hair on the entire sole; the hind legs are much longer than the front, a jumping adaptation; the tail is a short cottony tuft; and the ears are long. The skull has an elongate muzzle; the sides of the cranium, in front of the orbits, have a network of bony braces; ossification of the facial bones is incomplete; the cheek teeth are high-crowned with cross crests (lophodont); the palate has only a narrow bridge; the radius and ulna are separate, but with little movement; the tibia is fused distally with the fibula.

SNOWSHOE HARE *Lepus americanus* Erxleben

SIZE–Total length, 380–506 mm. (15–20 in.); weight, 3–4 lbs.

DESCRIPTION–The **yellowish brown** summer pelage of the snowshoe hare is replaced in the fall by a **white coat,** which the animal retains until spring. At all times the majority of the body hairs are slate at the bases. This slate band of the hairs of the upper parts is followed by a buff band tipped with brownish in summer, white in winter. The nape has about the same color as the back. The unusually **large feet** covered with long dense fur, especially in winter, enable the hare to travel on top of deep snows as a man does on snowshoes. Against a background of snow the white pelage of this "ghost" is well-nigh impossible to detect, unless one spots the dark brown eyes of the hare. Its skull may be distinguished by size (length less than 90 mm., 3.6 in.) from that of the European hare and by the flared-out postorbital processes (which are not fused, at their posterior tips, with the frontals) from that of the cottontails. Four pairs of mammae are strung along from the pectoral to the inguinal region.

HABITAT–It inhabits spruce and cedar swamps, and near-by wooded areas.

HABITS–Snowshoe hares prefer dense cover during the day but come out into open areas to feed at night. The food consists chiefly of succulent vegetation during summer months, and of twigs, buds, and bark of small trees during winter. These hares are apparently fond of frozen meat, even of their own kind, but they will rarely bother a carcass on which the skin has not been torn or bloodied. They sometimes become a nuisance to trappers who are using meat baits. Customarily, they sit in forms on the ground, by an old log, or beneath a tree during the daytime. On occasion they seek refuge in hollow logs or burrows in the ground. When startled from a resting spot they usually bound off a short distance and stop. If pursued they almost invariably describe a circle and return to within a few yards of the starting place. Hunters who have good dogs to bring the hares around often take advantage of this habit. Usually, the hare remains within a ten-acre area, and it is difficult to drive one out. This probably is about the size of the home range. Although definite runways are followed, especially in the snow, the hares range in all directions when feeding. They commonly take dust baths, sometimes in the dusting wallows of grouse. On occasion they enter the water and swim to the opposite bank of a stream, but this is a rare incident.

The gestation period is about thirty-six days. The first young appear sometime in May, others may be born as late as August. An old

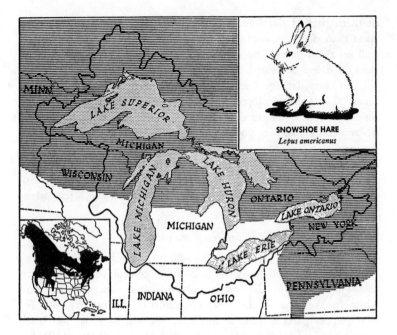

SNOWSHOE HARE
Lepus americanus

female is capable of producing at least two litters a season. One to seven young, usually two to four, are born in a litter. They weigh 70–80 gms. each at birth, are fully furred, and have their eyes open. No nest is prepared to receive the young hares. They start nibbling on green vegetation at about the eighth day and are weaned when between six and eight weeks old, at which time they have reached nearly adult weight.

Although socially inclined during much of the year, the males, during the breeding season, and the females, during pregnancy, are antagonistic toward others of their kind. It is likely that during these times territoriality is displayed. It is well-known that populations of these hares fluctuate tremendously. In a period of ten or eleven years they may increase from about one to a square mile to several hundred in the same area, then within a few months their numbers may be decreased, through disease, predation, or possibly other unknown factors, to their previous low. The snowshoe hare is the classical example in this country, as is the lemming of the Old World, of a fluctuating species. There is yet much to be learned about the causes of, and associated factors in, these great fluctuations.

ECONOMIC STATUS–This is an important game animal in the

northern part of the area. Few small game mammals afford better sport than does the snowshoe. The archer would do well to try his skill on these hares. The swish of arrows passing does not frighten them, and one is assured of several shots.

The chief damage that these hares do is to plantations of small pines. Their habit of nipping the terminal bud is disconcerting to the forester. In wild forests they serve as a thinning agent, but rarely destroy entire stands of young trees. Here there is probably little real damage.

REMARKS–There are two races of *Lepus americanus* in the area. *L. a. americanus* is present on Isle Royale and north of Lake Superior, *L. a. phaeonotus* to the south and on the Lake Michigan islands.

EUROPEAN HARE *Lepus europaeus* Pallas

SIZE–Total length, 714–62 mm. (28–30 in.); weight, 8–9 lbs.

DESCRIPTION–The European hare is in general yellowish brown, somewhat grayish on the cheeks and rump. The **underparts** are **pure white** (unlike those of the other Leporidae of this region). The fur of the upper parts is white at the base, followed by a band of black then a band of fulvous. The short tail is blackish above, white beneath. The large size of the skull (total length more than 90 mm.), and the two sets of upper incisors, one pair directly behind the other, serve, in combination, to distinguish this species from all other mammals of the Great Lakes region.

HABITAT–This hare is found in open fields or low rolling hills affording a good view.

HABITS–The European hare is an animal of the open country. It does not burrow, nor does it customarily seek refuge in an underground passage. Instead, it depends on its keen senses and speed to escape its enemies in the open. During the day it rests in a form, which it hollows out at the base of a shrub or low clump of vegetation. In the evening it comes out to feed on green vegetation or twigs and bark of small trees and shrubs. It is a bold swimmer and will cross creeks and rivers to reach a favored feeding spot on the opposite side. The gestation period probably is thirty days or more. In England it begins breeding in February or March and two to eight, usually four or five, young are produced in a litter. The young are fully furred and have their eyes open at birth. The mother scatters the young, placing one (sometimes two) in a situation, and makes regular rounds to suckle them. After they are weaned the mother usually drives them away and

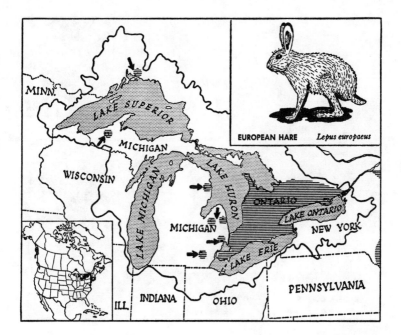

EUROPEAN HARE *Lepus europaeus*

forces them to shift for themselves. They are said to live as long as twelve years in the wild. Old males have a tendency to fight during the breeding season if one encroaches upon the territory of another. These fights commonly terminate with the death of one of the bucks. In England it is estimated that one hare to twelve acres is about the optimum population.

ECONOMIC STATUS—To date the European hare is of little economic importance except in Ontario where it is numerous enough to serve as a game animal. Two or three of these eight-pound hares will consume approximately the amount of food eaten by one sheep.

EASTERN COTTONTAIL *Sylvilagus floridanus* J. A. Allen

SIZE—Total length, 400–485 mm. (16–19 in.); weight, 900–1,800 gms. (2–4 lbs.).

DESCRIPTION—This is the commonest of the leporids of the Great Lakes region. The upper parts are, in general, dark buffy brown washed with grayish and sprinkled with black. A patch on the **nape** is **bright rufous.** The underparts are white, except for the throat, which is buffy. The fur of the body is slate at the base. The extremely short tail is white beneath, brownish above. The skull may be distinguished

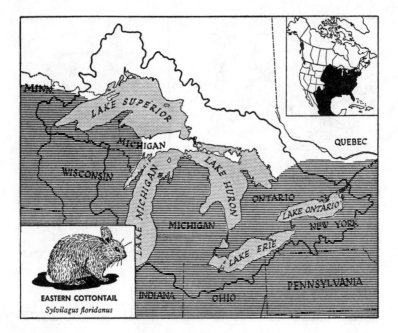

EASTERN COTTONTAIL
Sylvilagus floridanus

from all other mammal skulls having two pairs of upper incisors (with a small pair directly behind a larger pair) by the fusion of the postorbital processes with the frontals (*Lepus europaeus* sometimes has the tips of these processes fused with the frontals, but the skull is more than 90 mm., 3.5 in., in greatest length), and the notch in front of the supraorbital processes (from *S. transitionalis*). There are four pairs of mammae.

HABITAT—Brushy areas, edges of swamps, and open woods are the preferred habitats of the eastern cottontail.

HABITS—The eastern cottontail is chiefly nocturnal in habits. The day is spent in some sheltered spot, either in a form in heavy grass, a hole in the ground, or the shelter of a brush pile. Shortly after sundown these rabbits sally forth to forage on green vegetation in summer, or on twigs and bark of small shrubs in winter. They become sexually active in January or February, and young of the first litter are born in March or April. The gestation period is about thirty days. Before bearing the four to seven young, usually about five, the female excavates a small depression four to six inches deep and four or five inches in diameter. This is lined first with dry grass, then with fur from her own body. The young rabbits, blind, naked, and helpless at birth, are placed in this nest, where they are almost perfectly concealed. The mother returns to the nest to suckle the young, but spends the remainder of her time some distance away. At the end of two weeks the young rabbits, now about the size of chipmunks, emerge from the nest well-furred and with their eyes open. This probably is the most hazardous period in their lives, for they are easy prey to their enemies. Young do not breed until the following spring. An old female will raise three or four litters a season. The home range of an individual averages about three acres for a female and eight to twenty acres for a male, depending on the area. Some animals range much more widely, and others are more restricted in their movements. There is an indication that females display territoriality during the breeding season. They are well spaced at this time of year, whereas in winter they may congregate in large numbers in a place that affords good cover.

There is some indication that they pair off and that a male and female will remain in the same area together for at least part of the breeding season. This is a phase of their life history that needs careful investigation. Populations vary with the seasons, in different parts of the range of the species, and from year to year. In southern Michigan, however, the average is about one rabbit to two or three acres. The life span in the wild is not known, but I doubt if many rabbits live longer than four or five years.

Cottontails are susceptible to many diseases and to parasites. The most serious of these is tularemia, which, fortunately, is rare in the northern states and provinces. Precautions should be taken against this disease, which is transmissible to man. Sickly rabbits should not be handled; the rabbits should not be dressed without rubber gloves if one has cuts on the hands; the meat should be well cooked; and the hunting of rabbits should be delayed until cold weather, at which time there is little danger of getting infected animals.

Chief among the enemies of the cottontail are the red fox and great horned owl. Other mammal and bird predators, as well as snakes, take their toll, but not in significant numbers.

ECONOMIC STATUS–This is the most important game mammal in much of its range. It is the farm boy's "big game."

Cottontails undoubtedly do some damage to farm crops. Gardens and young orchards suffer most from their depredations.

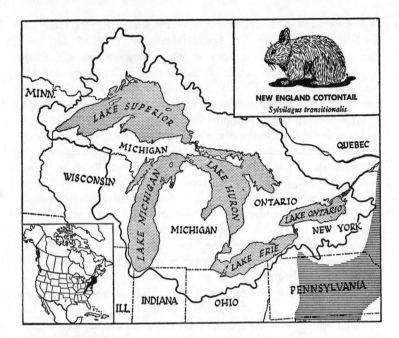

NEW ENGLAND COTTONTAIL *Sylvilagus transitionalis*

NEW ENGLAND COTTONTAIL *Sylvilagus transitionalis* Bangs

SIZE–Total length, 370–450 mm. (14.5–17.7 in.); weight, 900–1590 gms. (2–3.5 lbs.).

DESCRIPTION–This species is similar in general appearance to the eastern cottontail. There are a few characteristics that well serve to separate the two wherever they occur together. The New England cottontail never has a white star on its forehead, there is a **black border** on the anterior **outer edge of the ear,** and a **black area** between the ears. In the skull the anterior supraorbital process present in the eastern cottontail is absent in this species. The entire animal is slightly smaller also.

HABITAT–It lives in woods and brushy areas.

HABITS–This cottontail probably breeds throughout the summer months. It is apparently more nearly nocturnal than the eastern cottontail and prefers thicker cover. Never very abundant, it is considered to be rare over most of its range. As yet, we have very little detailed knowledge of its habits.

ECONOMIC STATUS–As a game animal, this cottontail may be considered beneficial.

COWS, BISON, DEER (ORDER ARTIODACTYLA)

This group, characterized primarily by the arrangement of toes and ankle bones, forms the principal order of hoofed mammals living today. Artiodactyls are known as even-toed hoofed mammals. The third and fourth toes are about equally developed and support the main weight of the body. The other toes are either reduced in size or are entirely lost. The astragalus (an ankle bone) forms a double pulley joint with movement at both ends. This provides extra flexibility of the hind foot and makes it possible for members of this order to get up rear end first instead of front end first, as does the horse (order Perissodactyla), which has a more rigid ankle joint. The skull in the order Artiodactyla is long faced. The premolars are never molariform (like the molars), and the molars are never reduced. In the Great Lakes region this order is, at present, represented by the deer, elk, caribou, and moose. Formerly, the bison also was here. Domestic cattle, sheep, goats, and pigs belong to this order of mammals. In none of these animals, except pigs, are there incisors in the upper jaw.

DEER (FAMILY CERVIDAE)

Members of this family do not have true horns. Instead, they have antlers, bony outgrowths from the frontal bones, confined to the males, except in the caribou, in which females also have them; they are shed each year. Shortly after the old antlers are shed the new ones start growing. At this stage, they are covered with skin richly supplied with blood. When they are fully formed, the skin dries and is rubbed off, leaving the hard bony core. Members of this family have four active mammae. There is no gall bladder.

ELK *Cervus canadensis* Erxleben

SIZE–Males: total length, 7–9 ft.; height at withers, 4–5.75 ft.; weight, 550–800 lbs. Females: total length, 7–7.5 ft.; height at withers, 4.75 ft.; weight, about 500 lbs.

DESCRIPTION–The elk is distinguished by its size and general coloration. The body is grayish brown grading into dark chestnut brown on the head, neck, and legs. The large **buffy white rump patch** extends well above the short white tail. A metatarsal scent gland is situated on the inside of the hock. The hair covering this gland is coarse and ruffled. The nose pad is naked. Old males possess large, many-tined antlers with well-marked brow tines. The neck is maned.

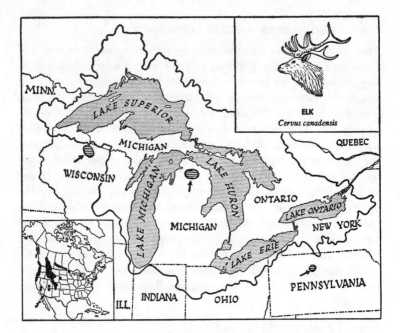

The skull (400–500 mm., 16–20 in., in length) is larger than that of a deer and smaller than that of a moose. There are canines (the teeth which are used as watch charms by the Elk's fraternity) in both sexes. The undivided posterior nares (vomer not attached to palatines) will serve to distinguish it from the skull of a caribou. Fawns are spotted and weigh about 30 lbs. at birth.

HABITAT–It lives in forests with open meadows.

HABITS–The elk is chiefly nocturnal, but may be seen abroad during the daytime, especially in early morning or evening. It is both a grazer and browser, depending somewhat on the season. Grasses, twigs, and leaves make up the bulk of its diet. In the fall, after the antlers are fully formed and polished, the old males round up their harems of cows for the rutting season. Males do battle for these harems, the victor takes possession, and the vanquished goes his way alone or seeks out other unsuccessful males for company. Elk are supposed to be the most polygamous members of the deer family. The gestation period is about eight and one-half months. Young females do not breed until two or three years old, males not until four years. In late spring or early summer the heaviest cows leave the herd one by one and seek secluded spots, each to give birth to a

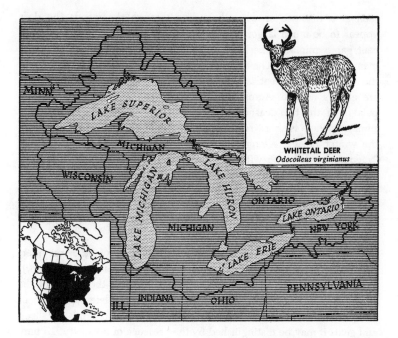

WHITETAIL DEER
Odocoileus virginianus

single fawn, or occasionally twins. For the first few days the fawns (or calves) are hidden by the mother, but within a week they will have gained sufficient strength to follow her. In mountainous areas, elk make regular migrations up the mountains in spring and return to the valleys in fall.

ECONOMIC STATUS–This large game animal at present is chiefly of scientific and aesthetic value. If the herds increase sufficiently there may some day be a restricted hunting season.

REMARKS–Elk have been introduced by private individuals and by conservation departments in several localities since 1909. The only elk now in the area have been introduced. The original elk are all gone.

WHITETAIL DEER *Odocoileus virginianus* Zimmermann

SIZE–Total length, 6–6.5 ft.; height at withers, 3.5 ft.; weight, 150–300 lbs.

DESCRIPTION–This is the smallest and best-known member of the deer family in the Great Lakes region. Some may be surprised to learn that the largest bucks rarely exceed a height of three and one-half feet at the withers. The average buck is nearer three feet in height. When seen at a distance or when bounding through the woods the deer appear to be much larger. The most conspicuous part of this magnificent game animal is the large **white tail** or flag, and this is about all many of us ever see. The summer (red) coat is pure reddish fawn, and the winter (blue) coat is a pepper and salt mixture. The underparts are always whitish. Across the face is a band of dusky brown. The pelages of the two seasons differ in texture as well as in color. The summer pelage is short, relatively thin, and somewhat wiry in texture; the winter pelage is long, thick, and the individual hairs are of the "vacuum bottle" type with air spaces in the core, thereby serving as good insulators. There is a metatarsal gland on the inside of the hock. Its position is disclosed by a patch of coarse ruffled hair. The hoofs are narrow and pointed (the bottom of each front hoof is less than 25 mm. wide). Albinism crops up occasionally in deer, but there are no records of melanism in the whitetail deer.

The skull may be distinguished from the skulls of other members of the deer family by its small size (total length less than 400 mm.), by the width of the audital bulla, which is equal to the length of the bony tube leading to the meatus, and by the complete separation of the posterior nares by the median vomer. From the skulls of sheep and goats it may be distinguished by the presence of a vacuity, 15 mm. or more in width, between the lachrymal and nasal bones.

HABITAT–It is found in border areas between forests and openings.

HABITS–Deer prefer hours of subdued light. On moonlight nights they may feed all night, but in the dark of the moon they are most active during the twilight of evening and dawn of early morning. They are "munchers," rarely remaining in one place to feed their fill. Instead, they nibble a leaf here, a twig there, a tender green shoot or a fungus somewhere else. Their diet changes with the seasons—what is palatable today may not be touched next week. In early spring they graze on tender young grass, they then pass to a variety of herbs, shrubs, trees, and fungi. During the fall they may subsist almost entirely on acorns, while these last. With the coming of winter they turn browsers, consuming small twigs of shrubs, mosses if not covered too deeply with snow, and the green tips of cedar boughs. These are but a few of the many kinds of food taken. On occasion they have been known to eat fish, a rather unusual item in their diet.

The rutting season lasts about two months in the fall. It is at its height in November. Yearling does (and an occasional fawn doe) breed for their first time and give birth to single fawns the following June. Older does usually have two fawns at a time. The gestation period is 205 to 210 days. The spotted fawn is hidden in a thicket or other protective cover, and the mother returns to nurse it. If two fawns are born to a doe she usually hides them in different places, not together. At about the age of a month, the fawns start following the mother on her feeding route. Although they are weaned in the fall, they usually remain with the doe through the winter. Old bucks customarily spend the summers in twos or threes, segregated from the does and fawns. As the rutting season approaches, former companions turn to bitter enemies and much fighting ensues.

ECONOMIC STATUS–There is no question of the economic importance of the deer herd. The money spent by hunters annually on travel, food, lodging, and equipment is an important item, especially to residents of the hunting areas. Deer are known to do considerable damage locally to crops. The state or province can well afford to reimburse the farmer for damage done in order to maintain the huge business of deer hunting. Deer also are of much interest to tourists in the north woods.

MOOSE *Alces alces* Linnaeus

SIZE–Total length, 6.75–8.6 ft.; height at withers, 5.5–5.8 ft.; weight, 725–850 lbs. Spread of antlers, 4–6 ft.

DESCRIPTION–The moose is the most ungainly of the larger mammals of the Great Lakes region. Its long legs, large head with **overhanging snout,** and a small rump give it an unbalanced aspect. Yet it carries itself with a certain grace. Both sexes have a **bell** (200–250 mm., 8–10 in., long) hanging from beneath the throat. In general the moose is blackish brown, slightly paler on the back, shoulders, neck, and head, and whitish on the belly. The tail is very short for the size of the animal. The nose is covered with hair, except for a small spot on the extreme lower part. There is no metatarsal gland. The **antlers** of the male are **broadly palmate.** The young are unicolor, not spotted. The skull is peculiar in that it has a long snout with short nasals (length of nasals less than half length of distance from their anterior tips to anterior tips of premaxillaries). It is the largest of the deer family (length of skull more than 500 mm., 20 in.).

HABITAT–This mammal inhabits forested regions with numerous lakes and swamps.

HABITS–Moose may be seen abroad at any time of day or night; however, their greatest activity centers around twilight and early dawn. Much of their time is spent in shallow water, in which they feed on aquatic vegetation. They are good waders and swimmers. In

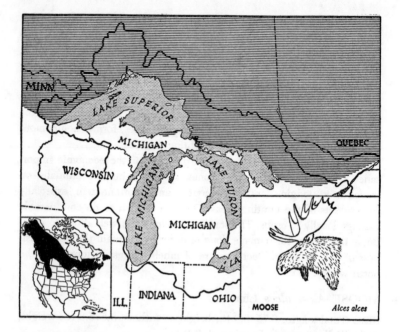

MOOSE   *Alces alces*

addition to aquatic vegetation, they feed on leaves, twigs, and bark of trees, fungi, and a great variety of herbs. They are chiefly browsers, but resort to grazing on occasion.

In early September the males start rubbing and polishing their antlers on small trees in preparation for the rut, which lasts for about a month, with its height in late September. During the rut the bulls seek out the cows, and, although they usually are monogamous, sometimes a bull will be seen with two cows. At this time the bull forgets everything else and becomes extremely curious of every sound in the woods. It may be a cow or it may be a rival bull—in either case worth investigation. The less sportsmanlike hunters take advantage of this habit and call the bulls to them for easy shots. The calves, usually one, sometimes twins, are born in late May and June, following a gestation period of about eight months. The mother hides her calf in the woods for a few days until it is strong enough to follow her. The young moose remains with its mother until the following spring when, just before she is ready to calve again, she drives it away. The old bull is indifferent to the calves until the young bulls are about two years of age. There is then competition for cows, and young bulls are forced to keep their distance during the rut. It is estimated that only about half the cows bear young in any one season. The calves are dull reddish brown and somewhat woolly at birth, but take on another darker coat at two to three months. Adults shed their winter coats in May and June. At this time they have a shaggy appearance. The senses of hearing and smell seem to be well developed in the moose, but most authorities agree that their sight is rather limited.

The home range of a moose is small for the size of the animal. An old bull may spend the entire summer in a hundred acres of swamp. It is during the rutting season that he leaves his haunts to seek out his mate.

ECONOMIC STATUS–At present the moose is of scenic and scientific value only, over most of the area. Hunting is permitted in Canada, where the moose is considered paramount as a game animal.

WOODLAND CARIBOU *Rangifer caribou* Gmelin

SIZE (approximate)–Total length, 6.3 ft.; height at shoulder, 3.5 ft.; weight, 200–300 lbs.

DESCRIPTION–The caribou is intermediate in size between the elk and the whitetail deer. Both sexes possess **palmate antlers** with broad flat **brow plates** extending over the nose between the eyes. The hoofs are broad and rounded, more than half as broad as long, and the side toes are well developed. The nose is covered with short hair. The head and neck are whitish, the back is brown, and the rump patch is whitish. The skull is 400–500 mm. in total length and has the posterior nares completely divided; the width of the audital bulla is about one-half the length of the bony tube leading to the meatus.

HABITAT–The caribou lives in forests and upland bogs or large swamps.

HABITS–This species is a wanderer, apparently keeping on the move in search of food most of the time. When in a hurry the caribou breaks into a trot. It is said to be faster than a good dog and able to continue for great distances. The rut is in October at which time there is much fighting among the males. One male will often serve twelve to fifteen females. The gestation period is probably about seven months and one week. The young, one or two, are born in May or June and follow the mother soon after birth. Although their food consists of almost any green thing, they subsist largely on mosses and lichens during the winter months.

ECONOMIC STATUS–The caribou is of little economic importance in the Great Lakes region. Farther north in Canada it is extremely important as a source of food for the Indians and Eskimos.

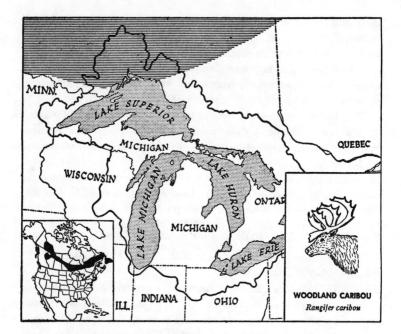

WOODLAND CARIBOU
Rangifer caribou

REMARKS—The caribou has long since gone from the southern areas, but still persists north of Lake Superior.

VANISHED SPECIES

There are three kinds of mammals that have disappeared from the Great Lakes region within historic times, but still exist elsewhere. They are listed below.

WOLVERINE *Gulo luscus* Linnaeus

SIZE—Total length, 36–40 in.; weight, 22–35 lbs.

DESCRIPTION—The wolverine is the largest of the mustelids. The weight of females is about 22 lbs.; that of males, about 30 lbs. The limbs and feet of the wolverine are massive and powerful. The general color is dark brown, paler on the cheeks and head, and two broad yellowish stripes extend from the shoulder region back along the sides and meet above the base of the bushy tail. The skull may be distinguished from other carnivore skulls by the following combination of characters: The total number of teeth is thirty-eight; there are five cheek teeth on each side of the upper jaw, six on each side of the lower jaw; the bony palate extends posteriorly beyond the last molars; the total length is more than 140 mm. In an unbroken skull the lower jaw is so firmly hinged to the cranium that it cannot be removed.

HABITAT–It is confined to boreal forests.

HABITS–The wolverine, although chiefly nocturnal, may be seen abroad in the daytime. Two to four young are born in late spring. Almost any shelter serves for the den. The young are yellowish white. The gestation period is not known. The food of the wolverine consists of practically anything edible. As is true also of the weasels, its regular diet probably is made up of small rodents, birds' eggs, and carrion. The wolverine has a reputation for its cunning, a reputation shared by few mammals. According to the reports of trappers, a wolverine will follow a trap line and will not only kill and devour other trapped animals, but will remove the bait from traps without itself being caught.

MOUNTAIN LION (Cougar) *Felis concolor* Linnaeus

SIZE–Total length, 6–7.5 ft.; weight, 80–200 lbs.

DESCRIPTION–The mountain lion is the largest of the North American cats. The general coloration is pale tawny or light brown, somewhat darker on the back and paler on the belly. The tip of the tail, the backs of the ears, and the patches on the sides of the nose surrounding the whiskers are dark brown.

The skull may be distinguished from skulls of other carnivores of the area by the four cheek teeth on each side above, the first and last of which are very small and single-rooted; by the short broad rostrum; high, arched forehead; and large size (175–200 mm. in length). The mandible is deep, short, and set with three cheek teeth on each side.

HABITAT–The mountain lion stays in forests and rugged country in which deer are plentiful.

HABITS–Little is known of the habits of this graceful cat. It is gone from the local fauna, although there still is a remote chance that it may persist in small numbers in the northern part of the area. Where it exists today, the mountain lion feeds largely on deer, although other mammals as well as birds are eaten. It usually hunts by stalking and, when calculations are complete, by a spring or short dash at the intended victim. Food in excess of what can be consumed on the spot is cached for the future. The gestation period, as determined in zoos, is ninety-one to ninety-seven days. The time of birth seems to vary, but it is thought that in the wild most births occur in early spring.

The young, one to four in a litter, are spotted and have their eyes closed at birth. A shallow cave in a cliff serves as the den site. The male and female are believed to pair for at least the breeding season.

BISON *Bison bison* Linnaeus

SIZE (approximate)–Total length, 11 ft. (male), 7 ft. (female); height at withers, 6 ft. (male), 5 ft. (female); weight 1,800 lbs. (male), 1,000 lbs. (female).

Fig. 11. Bison.

DESCRIPTION–Largest of the native Recent mammals, the bison once roamed the southern parts of the area. Its brown shaggy coat, large head with short curved horns, and high hump on the shoulders set it apart from other mammals (Fig 11). The skull has the lachrymal connecting with the nasal; the length of the cheek tooth row is more than 110 mm.; and the branch of the premaxillary does not extend up to connect with the nasal.

HABITAT–It inhabits open prairies.

HABITS–The bison is a grazer, subsisting almost entirely on grasses and other small herbs. It is gregarious and polygamous. The only conflicts are between old males for leadership. Usually, a cow has one calf (rarely two) sometime during the summer. The calves are able to follow their mothers almost immediately after birth. The gestation period is nine and one-half months.

REMARKS–The bison was probably never as abundant in this area as it was on the western prairies. It must have been a conspicuous part of the landscape when the first white settlers arrived. Being an important game animal and easy prey, the bison was soon eliminated by the white man. It was gone from this region shortly after the beginning of the nineteenth century.

Collecting and
Preparing Specimens

The items in the following list are desirable, but not all are absolutely necessary for the beginner who wishes to collect a few specimens of each species of mammal either for his own private collection or for some museum. The specialist who is to make an extended collecting trip away from home will need much more equipment, especially a greater number of traps and a larger supply of materials used in the preparation of specimens.

EQUIPMENT

 1 spear-type mole trap (obtainable at a hardware store)

25 small mouse traps (snap traps obtainable at a hardware store, or homemade live traps)

 6 large rat traps (snap traps obtainable at a hardware store, or homemade live traps)

 6 No. 1 steel traps (if fur-bearers are to be taken in season)

 1 bag or knapsack for transportation of traps

 1 package rolled oats (bait for small mammals)

 1 pint jar peanut butter (bait, optional)

 1 shotgun (20 ga. or .410 ga., optional) for bats and large mammals, shells of appropriate size (No. 12 or dust shot for bats)

1 rule or steel tape marked in millimeters (see Table I)

1 scalpel (6 in., obtainable at surgical supply house)

1 pair small pointed scissors (obtainable at surgical supply house)

1 pair forceps (6 in., obtainable at surgical supply house)

1 pair pliers with wire cutter

1 package assorted needles

1 package pins (glass-headed pins preferable)

1 spool white cotton thread No. 8 (for chipmunks and larger animals, and for labels)

1 spool white cotton thread No. 24 (for mouse-size animals)

1 spool annealed tin wire No. 24 (for mouse-size animals)

1 spool annealed tin wire No. 20 (for chipmunk-size animals)

4 feet per specimen of galvanized wire for larger kinds (No. 14 for squirrels, No. 9 for rabbits)

1 paint brush, 1 in. (cheapest kind), not essential

1 carborundum stone

1 small roll absorbent cotton (for tail and leg wires)

1 bat long staple quilting cotton for bodies

1 small package powdered arsenic (this is *poison*)

1 pint commercial formalin (40 per cent)

1 can ether (1 lb.), if animals are taken alive

1 collecting chest with trays of soft wood bottoms (may be made from an old suitcase or a tight wooden box)

1 bottle waterproof ink

1 pen and holder

1 loose-leaf notebook and paper (5½ in. × 8½ in.)

1 fishing-tackle box for small tools (optional)

Good grade of water-resistant paper for labels

A copy of the game laws of the state

Proper permits and licenses

COLLECTING MAMMALS

Mammal collecting, if properly done, requires long hours and hard labor. It is necessary in many states and provinces to have a permit, which is issued to reliable persons by the Conservation Department or Department of Lands and Forests, in order to collect mammals. The collector must also have hunting and trapping licenses. The collection of game and fur animals will not be discussed here. The ordinary methods of the game hunter and fur trapper may be employed. It should be stressed, however, that only under unusual circumstances should the holder of a collecting permit take game

TABLE I CONVERSION OF INCHES TO MILLIMETERS

| | Millimeters | |
Inches	Nearest Tenth	Actual Value
1/32	0.8	0.794
1/16	1.6	1.587
3/32	2.4	2.381
1/8	3.2	3.175
5/32	4.0	3.969
3/16	4.8	4.762
7/32	5.6	5.556
1/4	6.4	6.350
9/32	7.1	7.144
5/16	7.9	7.937
11/32	8.7	8.731
3/8	9.5	9.525
13/32	10.3	10.319
7/16	11.1	11.112
15/32	11.9	11.906
1/2	12.7	12.700
17/32	13.5	13.493
9/16	14.3	14.287
19/32	15.1	15.081
5/8	15.9	15.875
21/32	16.7	16.669
11/16	17.5	17.462
23/32	18.3	18.256
3/4	19.1	19.050
25/32	19.8	19.844
13/16	20.6	20.637
27/32	21.4	21.431
7/8	22.2	22.225
29/32	23.0	23.019
15/16	23.8	23.812
31/32	24.6	24.606
1	25.4	25.400

animals out of season, and then only after fully informing the local conservation officer. The abuse of a collecting permit may lead to its cancellation. Further, if one is to collect on private lands permission to do so must be obtained from the owner.

The small, nongame mammals, mostly nocturnal and secretive in habits, may be overlooked entirely in an area unless one makes a special effort to find them. The average individual walking through a forest or meadow may not see a single living mammal, although hundreds of them are quietly passing the day in their various retreats. Nightfall awakens them to activity. The collector must learn from experience where and how to capture the various kinds of mammals that are likely to be present in any area. A few general hints will be offered to the beginner in the hope of making his first efforts more productive.

BATS

Some solitary bats (hoary, red, and silver-haired) hang among the foliage in the branches of trees and are most readily collected in the evening, when they are flying at the edges of trees or near water. A shotgun with light dust loads provides the most effective means of securing them. It requires some practice and skill to hit bats on the wing, especially in the vanishing light of late evening, but this is about the only method of procuring certain kinds. Other bats, colonial in habits, may be found in natural caves, dark recesses of hollow trees, or in attics of buildings. A pair of forceps, twelve inches long or longer, often enables the collector to reach into crevices and extract the bats from their hiding places. The bat, if hanging free, is less likely to take flight if approached by the ends of forceps instead of the hand. With this method one gets perfect specimens which may be etherized and prepared at one's convenience, with no danger of spoilage.

MOLES AND POCKET GOPHERS

The presence of moles may be detected by the ridges of earth that are formed by their tunnels near the surface, and by occasional piles of fresh earth six to eight inches in diameter with no visible opening to the surface or round plug of earth as is found in a pocket gopher mound. Commercial mole traps, especially the spear type, are best for collecting these animals. The ridge of earth above the tunnel is depressed with the foot, and the trap is set across the runway with the trigger touching the ground. When the mole comes through its burrow it lifts the soil and in so doing releases the trap. The prongs are forced down by a strong spring, and some part of the animal is pierced.

Pocket gopher mounds are usually fan-shaped and show the round plug of loose earth at the burrow entrance.

Most hardware stores in farming areas where pocket gophers occur carry traps especially designed for these rodents. Directions for using usually come with the traps. See page 109 for more details.

SHREWS AND MICE

Most of these animals are nocturnal and are seldom seen. Shrews usually inhabit damp situations in woods, swamps, and meadows. Some mice inhabit drier uplands as well as the situations given for shrews. Ordinary snap traps (for mice) or live traps may be used in capturing these animals. In wooded areas and swamps it is best to set the traps along fallen logs or around old stumps. If baited with a small amount of peanut butter and rolled oats (mixed in such proportions that the rolled oats are held together and the peanut butter is no longer sticky), pressed on the treadle, the traps are likely to catch either mice or shrews. In meadows it is well to part the heavy grass covering until surface runways are found. A little experience will enable the beginner to distinguish between used and unused runways. If fresh feces or bits of short green grass are found in a runway one can be certain that it is in use. The grass should be cleared away so that the action of the trap will not be hindered, and if a snap trap is used it should be set across the runway with the treadle in the runway proper. Bait is not necessary, but will increase the catch. For live traps, sunflower seeds are good as bait; however, almost any kind of seeds or rolled oats will do. In warm weather traps should be visited early in the morning before the sun reaches them.

If snap traps or live traps are not available, simple and effective traps may be made from old tin cans or buckets about six inches in diameter and eight inches deep. The container should be placed in the ground sufficiently deep so that the rim is just below the surface of the earth. The sides of the can should be packed solid with earth and only the open top should be exposed. The can should be filled with water to within three or four inches of the top. Small mammals, especially shrews, will fall in the trap and drown. No bait is necessary.

FLYING SQUIRRELS, CHIPMUNKS, AND GROUND SQUIRRELS

The baits used for flying squirrels, chipmunks, and ground squirrels are the same as those for the mice. Larger traps, however, are necessary. The ordinary snap rat traps, procurable at most hardware stores, or live traps with inside dimensions of at least two by two by eight inches are ideal. The traps for flying squirrels should be set on branches or trunks of large trees; for chipmunks the traps may be set on or near old stumps, logs, or rubbish heaps in or near forested areas.

For ground squirrels the open burrow should be located, usually in grassland, and the trap set near the entrance. Chipmunks and ground squirrels also may be taken by shooting, but trapping will yield better specimens. Traps for flying squirrels should be visited early in the morning; those for the others, several times during the day.

TREE SQUIRRELS, RABBITS, AND WOODCHUCKS

The best method of collecting tree squirrels, rabbits, and woodchucks is by shooting them with a shotgun. Number six shot is recommended. Large live traps may be used, but they are too bulky to carry far afield.

HABITATS OF REPRESENTATIVE SPECIES

Some of the more extensive general habitats common to the Great Lakes region, and the mammals characteristic of each of these are as follows:

Prairie (also farmland, chiefly in southern areas).—Eastern mole, least and shorttail shrews, weasels, skunk, badger, pocket gopher, striped ground squirrel, Franklin ground squirrel, prairie deer mouse, western harvest mouse, meadow vole.

Low wet meadows or bogs.—Moles, shrews, weasels, voles, bog lemming, jumping mice.

Southern hardwoods.—Opossum, moles, shrews, raccoon, weasels, skunk, foxes, woodchuck, eastern chipmunk, tree squirrels, southern flying squirrel, white-footed mouse, pine vole, jumping mice.

Northern hardwoods and coniferous forests.—Moles, shrews, black bears, weasels, skunk, wolf, red fox, chipmunks, tree squirrels, northern flying squirrel, deer mice, voles, jumping mice, porcupine, snowshoe hare, deer.

Stream and lake borders.—Opossum, moles, shrews, raccoon, black bears, skunk, weasels, mink, river otter, wolf, coyote, foxes, bobcat, woodchuck, chipmunks, tree squirrels, flying squirrels, white-footed and woodland deer mice, voles, bog lemming, muskrat, beaver, jumping mice, porcupine, cottontail, snowshoe hare, deer.

PREPARATION OF SPECIMENS

The preparation of a specimen begins with securing the animal. If the animal is shot, care should be exercised to avoid blood stains on the fur. Shot holes should be plugged with cotton, and any blood that has issued from the wounds should be wiped off immediately. Animals caught in snap traps usually need little if any attention unless the weather is warm and they are likely to slip (the outer layer of skin, with hair, loosens from the under layer of the skin and peels off if spoilage has started). If there is danger of slipping before the animal is returned to camp and prepared, it is well to open the body cavity along the mid-line of the abdomen (a one-inch slit is sufficient for mice and chipmunks, a two-inch slit for squirrels), remove the intestines with a pair of forceps, and place a plug of cotton in the abdominal cavity. Preparation of specimens should begin immediately on return to camp. Specimens may be preserved in formalin (later to be transferred to alcohol); or they may be prepared as skins and skulls, skins with skeletons (usually partial), or skeletons (complete).

FORMALIN

If it is desired to preserve the soft parts for later dissection of muscles and viscera, the specimen should be preserved in formalin and later transferred to 70 per cent alcohol or to a mixture of alcohol and glycerine. A sufficient amount of formalin should be prepared to cover the animal completely. This mixture consists of one part of commercial (40 per cent) formalin and nine parts of water. Specimens no larger than chipmunks may be preserved by opening the body cavity and immersing them in the fluid. The belly should be punched gently to ensure the entrance of fluid into the body cavity. Additional openings should be made in the skin of the feet and legs of a tree squirrel and a rabbit and in the tail of a squirrel. If a syringe is available injections of fluid may be made into the larger muscles. Injections should be directly into the blood vessels of the larger animals. This requires special apparatus and should not be attempted by the novice.

SKINS AND SKULLS

The beginner should not be discouraged if his first few specimens are not up to standard. It takes practice to perfect any technical skill, and the preparation of study skins of mammals is no exception. Each kind of mammal presents its own special problem. Minor techniques are left to the student, and only a general brief outline, step by step, is presented here. Most of the specimens in museums are prepared as skins and skulls.

RECORDING THE DATA

1. The label (Fig. 12)—(for skin or skeleton).

A specimen without data is worthless. The essential data, to be written on the label before the specimen is prepared, are as follows:

Fig. 12. *Specimen label.*

a. Precise locality: place of capture (state or province, county, specific locality).

b. Date of capture (month written out—April 1, 1942, not 4/1/42).

c. Sex: ♂ = male, ♀ = female.

d. Collector's name and field number; field numbers should never be duplicated.

e. Total length of animal (Fig. 13): All measurements, particularly for small mammals, should be in millimeters. This measurement is taken with the animal lying on its back, straightened out but not stretched, and is the distance from the tip of the nose to the

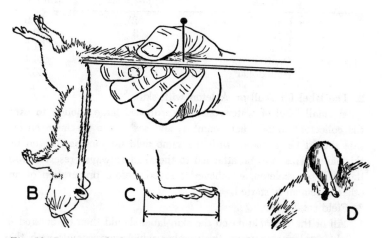

Fig. 13. *Proper method of measuring mammals:* (a) *total length,* (b) *tail vertebrae,* (c) *hind foot,* (d) *ear from notch.*

end of the tail vertebrae; the hairs on the tip of the tail are not included.

f. Length of tail vertebrae (Fig. 13): The animal is hung over a sharp edge of a table or the end of a ruler with the tail bent at right angles to the back of the body and measured to the tip of the tail vertebrae. The tail must be bent at the base. If the body of the animal does not hang vertically, the tail should be released until it does.

g. Length of hind foot (Fig. 13): From heel to tip of claw on longest toe.

h. Length of ear (Fig. 13): Two methods are in use: (1) "height from crown" is the distance from the base of the ear on the crown of the head to the tip of the ear, excluding hair; (2) "height from notch" is the distance from the notch below the ear opening (lowest notch) to the tip of the ear, excluding hair. This is the more usual measurement. The measurement used should be indicated on the label.

i. Weight: If scales are available it is well to record the weight of the animal. Coins may be used to obtain approximate weights (Table II).

TABLE II CONVERSION OF WEIGHTS AND DIAMETERS OF COINS TO GRAMS AND MILLIMETERS

(1 ounce = 28.35 grams)

Coin	Weights in Grams (approximate)	Diameter in Millimeters
Dime	2½	17.9
Penny	3	19
Nickel	5	21.2
Quarter	6	24.1
Half dollar	12½	30.5

2. The label for skull or skeleton with skin.

A small label of water-resistant cardboard large enough to carry the collector's initials, field number, and sex of the specimen on one side should be prepared with the same field number as that on the skin label. This is to be attached to the skull (always preserved with the skin) or skeleton, whichever is saved, before preparation of another specimen is started.

3. Field catalogue.

All of the information on the skin label should then be entered in a field catalogue opposite the number which corresponds with that on the label. In addition, it should be indicated whether the specimen was preserved as a skin and skull, skin and skeleton, skeleton only, or was preserved in alcohol. All entries on labels and in the field catalogue should be made in waterproof ink. A separate section of the notebook should contain all observational information not on the label, such as that concerning habits, habitat, and food.

SKINNING A SMALL MAMMAL

After an animal has been measured and all data have been recorded, it should be skinned. It is best to practice skinning an animal the size of a chipmunk or ground squirrel. One should have cornmeal or fine sawdust from hardwood at hand, not only to absorb excess blood and moisture, thereby keeping the fur clean, but also to make an otherwise slippery skin easy to handle. This absorbent should be used freely and may be reused several times.

1. The animal is placed on its back on the table and, with the scissors, a two-inch slit is made through the skin, but not through the abdominal wall, down the middle of the abdomen to a point about one-half inch in front of the anus.

2. The skin is loosened from the flesh along one side of the cut, and around to the side of the hind legs, by using either the fingers or the blunt end of a scalpel. Cornmeal or sawdust should be applied to the exposed fleshy parts.

3. The knee joint is thrust upward and, if the skeleton is not to be saved, the bone is broken just below the knee (Fig. 14a). With the forceps the leg bone is pulled up and the skin worked from the leg muscle down to the ankle. The entire leg, bone and flesh, is cut off just above the ankle, and the skin is worked away from the leg and hind body nearly to the backbone. The leg skin should be turned right side out to prevent drying, and the opposite leg worked out in similar fashion. In skinning bats, the leg is cut next to the body, the muscles on the upper leg are removed, and the entire leg bone is left in the skin.

4. The stubs of the skinned legs should be grasped with one hand and the skin rolled back over the rump with the other. The tissues and the gut in the anal region are cut with scissors or scalpel to the base of the tail.

5. The skin is worked loose around the base of the tail. The skin of the tail is grasped firmly between the thumbnail and fingernail, and the tail vertebrae are pulled from the skin (Fig 14b) with the forceps. In most mammals the tail will slip out without difficulty. The tail skin should be pulled slightly to take out any folds.

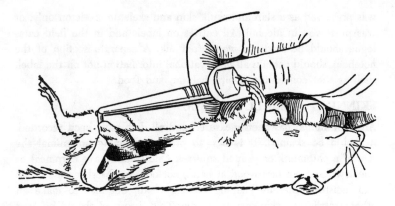

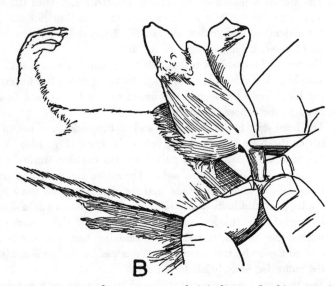

Fig. 14. First stages in skinning a mammal: (a) *skinning hind leg,* (b) *slipping tail from skin.*

6. The skin is then turned back over the body, close to the flesh. Pulling and stretching should be avoided, and plenty of cornmeal or sawdust should be used. The front legs are worked out to the wrists, and the entire leg is cut just above the wrist (Fig. 15a). The entire wing bones are left in bat skins. The wing is cut close to the body and the large muscles are removed.

7. The skin is worked down over the head until the bases of the ears are reached. The ears are cut close to the head with scissors or a sharp scalpel held parallel to the side of the head (Fig. 15*b*).

8. The dark line of the eyelid should then be apparent through the skin. The cut is made between the dark line and the skull (Fig. 15*c*). Care must be taken to avoid cutting the lid.

9. The skin is worked to the nose, and the lips are cut loose from the skull with the scalpel. A cut is made across the nose cartilage, care being taken not to cut the ends of the delicate nasal bones (Fig. 15*d*).

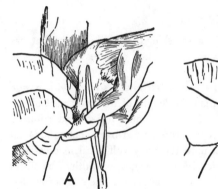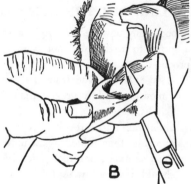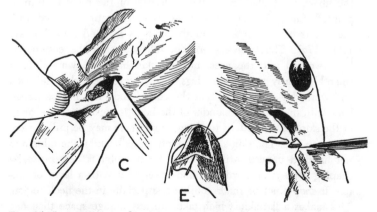

Fig. 15. *Last stages in skinning a mammal:* (a) *cutting front legs above wrists,* (b) *cutting ear from skull,* (c) *cutting around eye,* (d) *cutting nasal cartilage,* (e) *sewing opening of mouth.*

10. The carcass is put aside for the moment, and the excess fat and tissue are removed from the skin; the mouth is sewed by passing a needle transversely through the edges of the upper lip, then through the tip of the lower lip, and tying the thread (Fig. 15e).

11. The skin is now flesh side out except for the hind legs and the tail. The hind legs should be turned flesh side out, but the tail left hair side out. The exposed flesh surface of the skin is dusted with powdered arsenic on a tuft of cotton, and immediately the skin is turned fur side out. If the skin dries out before it is turned back it may be relaxed by applying water to the flesh side with a wad of cotton. The legs must be turned right side out all the way to the feet.

FILLING OUT THE SKIN

A body may now be prepared for the skin. If possible cotton that has a spring to it, that will not pack down when compressed, should be procured.

1. A layer is removed from the cotton bat and a square with a side dimension slightly greater than the length of the body part of the skin is torn out (not cut). For a chipmunk or ground squirrel, about one and three-fourths inches is folded over (not rolled) on one side, then folded again until the body (elliptical in cross section) is about one inch thick by two inches in width. The fibers should run lengthwise. By pulling the fibers out, one end is rounded off for the rump. On the other end, which is to go into the nose, the fibers are folded in on the underside of the body to form a pointed, fairly compact mass (Fig. 16a). This tip is seized with the points of the forceps and the body is inserted into the skin (Fig. 17a). The tweezers are not released until the cotton has been worked into the nose and the skin has been worked back smoothly nearly to the hind legs. The tweezers are then released and worked out gently so that the cotton body will not be pulled back with them. The remainder of the body is tucked into the rump of the skin. If the body is too long, more fibers may be pulled from the rump end. The skin should be left on its back on the table and not handled unnecessarily. A body for a rabbit is best made by shaping a piece of cardboard and covering it with a layer of cotton. It should not be made too large, especially in the neck region. This makes a flat skin which takes up less storage space than one that is high and rounded.

2. Four straight wires for the legs, each wire cut about two-thirds

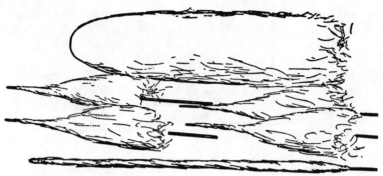

a

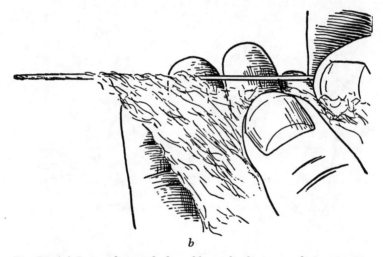

b

Fig. 16. (a) *Prepared cotton body and leg and tail wires, ready for insertion,* (b) *wrapping wire for tail.*

the length of the body, and one cut so that it will reach from the tip of the tail to the front of the incision in the skin should be prepared. Spool wire may be straightened by pulling on it until it gives a little. Bats need only a tail wire. A single wire running from front leg to hind leg is best for rabbits.

3. A small tuft of absorbent cotton is wrapped securely at a point about one-half inch from the end of each of the leg wires (Fig. 16a). By roughening or wetting the wire the cotton may be made to adhere better. The remainder of the cotton should be fluffed back over the wire, but not twisted. This fills out the skin of the leg.

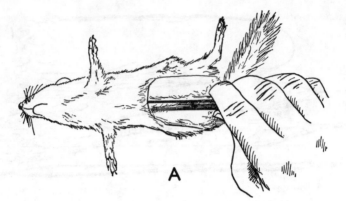

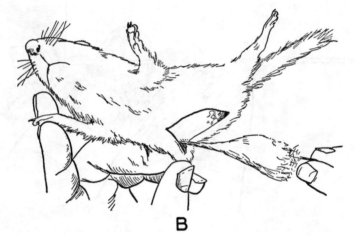

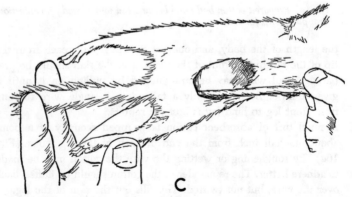

Fig. 17. Inserting: (a) *cotton body into skin*, (b) *leg wire*, (c) *tail wire*.

4. A prepared leg wire is then inserted into each leg, and the uncovered point is forced into the foot just under the skin of the sole (Fig. 17*b*). The wire should then lie along the side of, and parallel to, the body cotton. A slight pressure on the free end of the wire will straighten the leg. To insert the single wire into the front and back feet of a rabbit the wire is bent in the middle and straightened after the ends have been forced into the feet. The single wire adds strength to the delicate skin of the rabbit.

5. For the tail a few strands of a very thin wisp of cotton from the absorbent roll are caught on the end of the wire. By twisting the wire with one hand and feeding the thin strands of cotton on rather loosely with the other, the amount of cotton may gradually be increased for the length of the tail (Fig. 16*b*). The excess cotton not on the wire should be removed, the wire is then twirled in the same direction, and a slight pressure is exerted with the fingers of the other hand on the cotton from the tip to the base of the tail wire. This is repeated several times until the cotton is firmly wrapped on the wire. A little practice will be required to become efficient at wrapping the tail wire. There should not be much cotton on the wire.

6. Arsenic is dusted on the covered tail wire before it is inserted into the tail (Fig. 17*c*). If there is the proper amount of cotton on the wire it will go in easily to the tip of the tail. If the wire binds part way in, it should be removed and rewrapped with less cotton. The free end of the tail wire should lie along the belly surface of the body cotton.

7. The incision is sewed up simply by anchoring the thread with a large knot or by tying a loop at the starting point near the front of the opening and crisscrossing back to the hinder end (Fig. 18*a*). Stitches should be from one-fourth to one-half inch apart. In each stitch the needle should pass from the flesh side through the skin near the cut edge. The thread should be drawn just tight enough to bring the cut edges together. It is well to take the last stitch in the center of the skin in front of the tail before knotting and cutting the thread.

TYING LABEL AND PINNING

1. The skin should not be shaped until it is pinned in the bottom of the tray (Fig. 18*b*). The label should be tied securely with a double knot on the right hind leg just above the ankle.

2. The belly hairs are brushed out straight by stroking from head to

tail, and the belly skin is placed on the soft board of the bottom of the tray. All feet should have the soles down. Bats should have membranes slightly spread. Wings should be pinned in close to the body.

3. A pin should be forced through each front foot and into the board. The front feet should be pushed in under the sides of the head.

4. The specimen should be straightened so that the longitudinal axis runs from the tip of the nose through the body to the tip of the tail; the tail is pinned down by crossing two pins over it at the base.

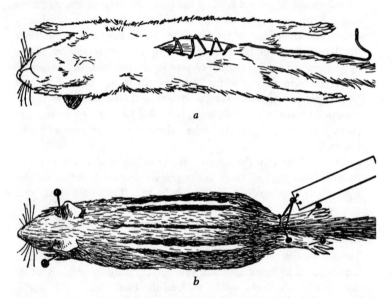

a

b

Fig. 18. (a) *Sewing opening in belly of skin,* (b) *finished skin pinned to board.*

5. The hind feet are pinned in close to the tail, with the soles down.

6. With the thumb and forefinger placed on the outsides of the hind legs in front of the pins, the hind-leg wires should be brought in to parallel the body.

7. The fur should be brushed out with a soft brush and forceps and the body shaped by applying a slight pressure on the spots that bulge. Since the animal will dry the way it is left it must be shaped while green. The pins should not be removed until the skin is dry and firm. A week is ordinarily sufficient to dry small mammals.

SKULL AND SKELETON

1. If the skull (Fig. 19) is the only part of the skeleton to be saved, it should be disarticulated from the vertebral column—the condyles should not be cut at the back of the skull. The tongue should be removed, and the skull label tied through the lower jaw. Skulls the size of a fox skull or larger should have some of the larger muscles removed and the brain taken out either with a wire hook or by forcing a stream of water from a syringe into the brain cavity. Small skulls should be dried as they are. In the field skulls may be carried conveniently in a small container made by folding a rectangular piece of old window screen and catching the open sides with the fine wire. This will keep flies from the skulls, which is important, for maggots will cause the bones to separate. If the basket is suspended from the hood of an automobile, above the engine, and the car is in use, the skulls will dry in a short time. Skulls and skins should always be kept where air can circulate about them until they are thoroughly dry. They should not be placed directly in the sun.

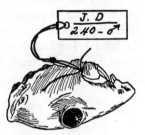

Fig. 19. *Skull with attached label.*

2. If the skeleton is to be saved, the viscera and enough of the flesh should be removed to ensure drying. The label should be securely attached, and the skeleton should be treated in the manner described for the skull.

SKINNING A LARGE MAMMAL

Mammals the size of a woodchuck or larger usually are tanned instead of stuffed. There are two methods of skinning the larger mammals. Those up to the size of a coyote may be cased. One should start with the inside of a hind foot and cut the skin down the inside of the hind leg across in front of the anus to the other hind leg and out to the second hind foot. Then the skin is cut around the anus and the underside of the tail is slit to the tip. The feet are disjointed near the toes (leaving the toe bones and claws on the skin), and the skin is worked off the body according to the method described for a small mammal. For mammals larger than a coyote, in addition to the cuts just described, a cut is made through the skin all the way from the anus to the throat (following the mid-line), angling the cut to tl corner of the mouth. The front legs are cut across from one foot to the other and the body is skinned out. With large mammals it is advisable to skin out the ears (leaving the cartilage attached) and the folds of the lips. The skin should be dried flesh side out, in the shade. There should be no folds in the skin, flies should be kept away from it, and, if the weather is such that rapid drying is not possible, salt should be rubbed in around the head and feet. If convenient, the skin should be shipped to a tanner immediately after being removed from the animal. The labels and measurements are made in the same manner as those for the smaller mammals.

Classification of the Mammals of the World

The mammals living throughout the world today are classified, on the basis of structure, into nineteen orders and 118 families. It should be borne in mind that no classification is rigid. The relationships of many mammals are not yet fully understood. Whenever authorities disagree as to the proper place of some group of animals in the scheme of classification, the group is in need of further study.

The following classification is modified from that given by Simpson (1945) and Ellerman (1949) for the rodents. It enables one to place the mammals of the Great Lakes region in the fauna of the world. Nine orders containing fifteen families starred below are represented in this area. After each family name, the common name and the native region of general distribution are given.

CLASS MAMMALIA

Subclass Prototheria (egg-laying mammals)

Order Monotremata

    Family Tachyglossidae (spiny anteaters or echidnas; Australia, Tasmania, and New Guinea)

    Family Ornithorhynchidae (duck-billed platypus; Australia and Tasmania)

Subclass *Theria*

Infraclass *Metatheria*

Order Marsupialia (Australia and Americas)
* Family Didelphiidae (opossums; North, Central, and South America)
  Family Dasyuridae (carnivore-like marsupials, banded anteaters; Australia)
  Family Notoryctidae (marsupial mole; Australia)
  Family Peramelidae (bandicoots; Australia)
  Family Caenolestidae (shrewlike marsupials; South America)
  Family Phalangeridae (phalangers; koalas; Australia, Tasmania, New Guinea, and New Zealand)
  Family Phascolomiidae (wombats; Australia and Tasmania)
  Family Macropodidae (kangaroos; Australia and Tasmania)

Infraclass *Eutheria*

Order Insectivora (moles and shrews)
  Family Tenrecidae (tenrec; Madagascar)
  Family Potamogalidae (African water shrew; Africa)
  Family Solenodontidae (solenodon; Cuba and Haiti)
  Family Chrysochloridae (golden mole; Africa)
  Family Erinaceidae (hedgehog; North Africa, Europe, Asia)
* Family Soricidae (shrews; northern South, Central, and North America, Europe, Asia, Africa)
* Family Talpidae (moles; North America, Europe, Asia)
  Family Tupaiidae (tree shrews; East Indies)
  Family Macroscelididae (jumping shrews; Africa)
Order Primates (man, apes, monkeys, lemurs)
  Family Lemuridae (lemurs; Madagascar)
  Family Indriidae (woolly lemurs; Madagascar)
  Family Daubentoniidae (aye-aye; Madagascar)
  Family Lorisidae (galagos and slow lemurs; Africa, southern Asia)
  Family Tarsiidae (tarsiers; East Indies)
  Family Cebidae (cebus and howler monkeys; South, Central, and southern North America)
  Family Callithricidae (marmosets; South and Central America)
  Family Cercopithecidae (Old World monkeys; Africa, Asia, Gibraltar)

Family Pongidae (gorillas, chimpanzees; Africa, Asia)
* Family Hominidae (man; world-wide)
Order Dermoptera
Family Cynocephalidae (flying lemurs; Malay Peninsula, Thailand, Sumatra, Java, Borneo, Philippines)
Order Chiroptera (bats)
Family Pteropidae (fruit-eating bats or flying foxes; tropical and subtropical regions of the Old World, east to Australia, Samoa, and the Caroline Islands)
Family Rhinopomatidae (valvenose bats; northern Africa and southern Asia)
Family Emballonuridae (sac-winged bats; tropical parts of both hemispheres)
Family Noctilionidae (fish-eating bats; tropical America)
Family Nycteridae (longtail bats; Africa, Malay Peninsula, Java, Timor)
Family Megadermatidae (large-winged bats; Africa, southern Asia, Australia)
Family Rhinolophidae (crestnose bats; Europe, Africa, Asia, Australia)
Family Hipposideridae (horseshoenose bats; Africa, southern Asia, Australia)
Family Phyllostomidae (leafnose bats, large-lipped bats; tropical America, northward to southern United States)
Family Desmodontidae (vampire bats; tropical America)
Family Natalidae (straw-colored bats; tropical America)
Family Furipteridae (funnel-eared bats; tropical South America)
Family Thyropteridae (disk-thumbed bats; tropical America)
Family Myzopodidae (bats with suctorial disks on thumbs and feet; Madagascar)
* Family Vespertilionidae (plainnose bats; nearly world-wide)
Family Mystacinidae (mustache-lipped bats; New Zealand)
Family Molossidae (freetail bats; world-wide in tropical and subtropical regions)
Order Carnivora (flesh-eating mammals)
* Family Ursidae (bears; Europe, Asia, North and South America)
* Family Procyonidae (raccoons, coatis, kinkajous, ringtails; Asia, North and South America)
* Family Mustelidae (weasels, minks, skunks, badgers; Asia, Africa, Europe, North and South America)

Family Viverridae (civets, mongooses; Europe, Asia, Africa)
* Family Canidae (dogs, foxes; Africa, Europe, Asia, Australia, North and South America)
Family Hyaenidae (hyenas; Africa, southwest Asia)
* Family Felidae (cats, lynx; Europe, Asia, Africa, North and South America)
Order Pinnipedia (seals; sea lions)
Family Otariidae (eared seals, sea lions; North and South America, Australia, Antarctica)
Family Phocidae (hair seals, sea elephants; all seas)
Family Odobaenidae (walruses; Arctic America, Asia, Europe)
Order Cetacea (marine mammals)
Family Iniidae (fresh-water dolphins; Asia, South America)
Family Ziphiidae (beaked whales; all seas)
Family Delphinidae (porpoises; all seas)
Family Platanistidae (river dolphins; Asia)
Family Monodontidae (white whales, narwhals; Arctic)
Family Physeteridae (sperm whales; chiefly tropical seas)
Family Kogiidae (pigmy sperm whales; all seas)
Family Eschrichtidae (gray whales; North Pacific)
Family Balaenopteridae (finback and humpback whales; all seas)
Family Balaenidae (baleen whales; all seas)
Order Rodentia (gnawing mammals)
Family Aplodontiidae (mountain beavers; northwestern North America)
Family Bathyergidae (mole rats; Africa)
* Family Sciuridae (squirrels; Africa, Europe, Asia, North and South America)
* Family Castoridae (beavers; Europe, Asia, North America)
* Family Geomyidae (pocket gophers; North and Central America)
Family Heteromyidae (kangaroo rats, pocket mice; North and Central America)
* Family Muridae (Old World rats and mice; now world-wide)
* Family Cricetidae (hamster-like rats and mice; Europe, Africa, Asia, North and South America)
Family Lophiomyidae (maned rats; Africa)
* Family Zapodidae (jumping mice; Europe, Asia, North America)
Family Rhizomyidae (bamboo rats; Africa, Asia)
Family Gliridae (dormice; Africa, Europe, Asia)
Family Anomaluridae (spinytail squirrels; Africa)
Family Thryonomyidae (cane rats; Africa)

Family Ctenodactylidae (dassie rats; Africa)

Family Pedetidae (springhaas; Africa)

Family Spalacidae (blind mole rats; Europe, Asia, North Africa)

Family Seleviniidae (spiny dormice; Asia)

Family Dipodidae (jerboas; Africa, Europe, Asia)

Family Hystricidae (Old World porcupines; tropical parts of Africa, Europe, and Asia)

* Family Erethizontidae (New World porcupines; North and South America)

Family Caviidae (guinea pigs and cavies; South America)

Family Dasyproctidae (agouti; South America and southern North America)

Family Chinchillidae (chinchillas and viscachas; South America)

Family Octodontidae (hutia, small rats, tuco tuco, coypu; West Indies and South America)

Family Dinomyidae (pacarana; South America)

Family Cuniculidae (pacas; South and Central America)

Family Hydrochoeridae (capybaras; South and Central America)

Order Lagomorpha (rabbits, hares, pikas)

Family Ochotonidae (pikas; Europe, Asia, North America)

* Family Leporidae (hares and rabbits; Africa, Europe, Asia, North and South America)

Order Pholidota (pangolins)

Family Manidae (Africa, Asia)

Order Xenarthra (New World edentates)

Family Myrmecophagidae (anteaters; South, Central, and southern North America)

Family Bradypodidae (tree sloths; South and Central America)

Family Dasypodidae (armadillos; South, Central, and southern North America)

Order Tubulidentata (aardvarks)

Family Orycteropodidae (Africa)

Order Proboscidea (elephants)

Family Elephantidae (Africa, Asia)

Order Hyracoidea (dassies or hyraxes)

Family Procaviidae (Africa, Asia)

Order Sirenia (sea cows)

Family Dugongidae (dugongs; Red Sea, Indian Ocean, western Pacific Ocean)

Family Trichechidae (manatees; Atlantic Ocean of North and South America, Africa)

Order Artiodactyla (even-toed hoofed mammals)
  Family Tayassuidae (peccaries; North, Central, and South America)
  Family Suidae (pigs; Africa, Europe, Asia)
  Family Hippopotamidae (hippopotami; Africa)
  Family Camelidae (camels and llamas; Africa, Asia, South America)
  Family Tragulidae (chevrotains; Africa, Asia)
  * Family Cervidae (deer; Africa, Asia, Europe, North, Central, and South America)
  Family Giraffidae (giraffes; Africa)
  Family Antilocapridae (pronghorns; North America)
  Family Bovidae (cattle, antelope, goats, sheep; Africa, Europe, Asia, North America)
Order Perissodactyla (odd-toed hoofed mammals)
  Family Equidae (horses; Africa, Asia)
  Family Tapiridae (tapirs; Asia, South and Central America, southern Mexico)
  Family Rhinocerotidae (rhinoceroses; Africa, Asia)

Artificial Key to Mammals
of the Great Lakes Region

The following artificial key, based on adult animals, is designed primarily for identification purposes. Phylogenetic order has been sacrificed for simplicity and workability.

To use the key it is necessary first to have a knowledge of the bones of the skull and of the external features of a mammal. As an aid, illustrations and a glossary of terms are provided. The only instruments needed are a millimeter rule and, for the small skulls, a hand lens. If a millimeter rule is not available, inches may be converted (one inch = 25.4 millimeters). The key is in two parts: based on skins only or the animal in the flesh and on skulls only. Each of the parts is further divided into a key to the orders and a key to the genera and species. In many comparisons, instead of listing a single character to separate two categories, a combination of several characters is given. The user should read all the possibilities, not just the first item given in such a combination, and he should also read the alternatives. If characters given under the first alternative (a) do not fit, those given under the second part of the couplet (b) should be tried. If both skull and skin are at hand, each should be keyed out separately. If they both lead to the same species the identification is fairly certain. The numbers in parentheses refer back to the previous couplet. Thus, the key may be worked backward as well as forward. The genus, if the skull is available, often may be determined by reference to the section on Dental Formulae (p. 219) without recourse to the key. Reference to the distribution maps may be of further aid in the identification of many kinds. *Reithrodontomys* is found, for instance, in a limited area.

The key is based on typical adult animals. Atypical, or abnormal animals are common, and the key should not be expected to work in every case. Occasionally, specimens baffle the experts who have large series of comparative material available. The staff of the Museum of Zoology is glad to be of service in verifying questionable identifications.

KEY TO SKINS ONLY OR ANIMALS IN THE FLESH

KEY TO THE ORDERS (EXCEPT PRIMATES, MAN)

1*a*. Fore limbs modified to serve as wings; a leathery membrane stretched between elongated fingers of fore limb, also between hind legs, including tail. Bats—order CHIROPTERA, III.

1*b*. Fore limbs not modified to serve as wings; no leathery membrane between hind legs . . . 2*a*.

2*a*(1*b*). Toes terminating in hoofs, not claws . . . 7*a*.

2*b*. Toes terminating in claws, not hoofs . . . 3*a*.

3*a*(2*b*). Innermost toe of hind foot thumblike and without claw, other four toes with claws; ears thin, leaflike, and naked; tail round, naked, black at base, whitish on terminal half or more; female with abdominal pouch. Opossum—order MARSUPIALIA, I.

3*b*. Innermost toe of hind foot not thumblike; clawed; tail, if naked, not black at base and whitish on terminal half or more . . . 4*a*.

4*a*(3*b*). Always five, clawed toes on front foot (first toe sometimes reduced and high on inside of foot, not touching ground when walking); tail never flattened (dorsoventrally or laterally) nor a cottony tuft shorter than ear; thumb never a mere knob with a nail, always a claw; no external cheek pouches . . . 5*a*.

4*b*. Usually only four well-clawed toes on front foot (thumb sometimes present as small knob with nail); if five, then tail either naked, scaly, and much flattened (either dorsoventrally or laterally) or a cottony tuft shorter than ear; or external cheek pouches present . . . 6*a*.

5*a*(4*a*). Length of head and body less than 115 mm., or, if more than 115 mm., no ear conch (pinna) present and no white on belly. Moles and shrews—order INSECTIVORA, II.

5b. Length of head and body more than 115 mm., ear conch (pinna) present. Flesh eaters—order CARNIVORA, IV.

6a(4b). Ear shorter than tail; hind foot with five well-clawed toes; bottoms of feet not completely covered with dense fur, tail not a cottony tuft. Rodents—order RODENTIA, V.

6b. Ear longer than tail; hind foot with four well-clawed toes; bottoms of feet completely covered with dense fur, tail a cottony tuft. Hares and rabbits—order LAGOMORPHA, VI.

7a(2a). Two or more toes on each foot; horns or antlers sometimes present. Pigs, deer, cows, sheep, goats—order ARTIODACTYLA, VII.

7b. A single hoof on each foot. Horse—order PERISSODACTYLA, VIII.

KEY TO THE GENERA AND SPECIES BY ORDERS

I. Order MARSUPIALIA—family Didelphiidae. Opossum—*Didelphis marsupialis,* page 24.

II. Order INSECTIVORA—Moles and shrews.

1a. No ear conch (pinna); total length usually more than 155 mm., width of front foot (Fig. 20) across palm more than 6 mm.—family Talpidae—Moles . . . 2a.

Fig. 20. *Front foot of a mole* (Scalopus).

Fig. 21. *Hind foot of a water shrew* (Sorex palustris), *with fringe of stiff hairs.*

1b. Ear conch (pinna) present (sometimes no more than a rim around ear opening); total length usually less than 155 mm.; width of front foot across palm less than 6 mm.—family Soricidae—Shrews . . . 4a.

2a(1a). End of snout with twenty-two small, slender, fleshy, finger-like tentacles around its edge, nostrils open toward front; black; length of tail more than 45 mm.; eyelids do not cover eyes permanently. Starnose mole—*Condylura cristata,* page 30.

2b. End of snout naked, without tentacles; grayish with a silver or copper sheen; length of tail less than 45 mm.; eyes covered by thin lids . . . 3a.

3a(2b). Nostrils open upward; tail naked. Eastern mole—*Scalopus aquaticus,* page 26.

3b. Nostrils open forward; tail conspicuously hairy. Hairytail Mole— *Parascalops breweri,* page 28.

4a(1b). Ear conch (pinna) well developed; tail length 30 mm. or more, exceeding half length of head and body . . . 5a.

4b. Ear conch (pinna) poorly developed, little more than a rim around ear opening; tail length less than 30 mm. (always much less than half length of head and body) . . . 13a.

5a(4a). Hind foot (Fig. 21) with a fringe of short, stiff hairs on outer and inner surfaces; total length more than 135 mm. Northern water shrew—*Sorex palustris,* page 38.

5b. Hind foot without a fringe of short, stiff hairs on outer and inner surfaces; total length less than 135 mm. . . . 6a.

6a(5b). Color of sides sharply different from that of back, especially in winter. Arctic shrew—*Sorex arcticus,* page 35.

6b. Color of sides not sharply different from that of back . . . 7a.

7a(6b). Length of tail more than 52 mm. Longtail shrew—*Sorex dispar,* page 38.

7b. Length of tail less than 52 mm. . . . 8a.

8a(7b). Found only in Illinois . . . 9a.

8b. Found outside Illinois . . . 10a.

9a(8a). Grayish brown with silvery underparts. Masked shrew—*Sorex cinereus,* page 32.

9b. Reddish brown, underparts not silvery. Southeastern shrew—*Sorex longirostris,* page 36.

10a(8b). Length of tail less than 33 mm. Pigmy shrew—*Microsorex hoyi,* page 39.

10b. Length of tail more than 33 mm. . . . 11a.

11a(10b). Length of tail more than 40 mm., dull brown in summer . . . 12a.

11b. Length of tail less than 40 mm., not dull brown. Masked shrew— *Sorex cinereus,* page 32.

12a(11a). Length of tail more than 44 mm. . . . Smoky shrew—*Sorex fumeus,* page 34.

12b. Length of tail less than 44 mm. . . . Arctic shrew—*Sorex arcticus,* page 35.

13a(4b). Total length more than 90 mm.; tail length more than

17 mm.; slate-black. Shorttail shrew—*Blarina brevicauda,* page 42.

13*b.* Total length less than 90 mm.; tail length less than 17 mm.; brown. Least shrew—*Cryptotis parva,* page 40.

III. Order CHIROPTERA—family Vespertilionidae—Bats.

1*a.* Dorsal surface of interfemoral membrane nearly naked, except sometimes basal one-fourth; color of fur on back uniform brown, hairs of back never tipped with white . . . 2*a.*

1*b.* Dorsal surface of interfemoral membrane thickly furred entirely or for basal half or more; color of fur on back not uniform brown; hairs of back sometimes tipped with white . . . 8*a.*

2*a*(1*a*). Length of forearm more than 40 mm. Big brown bat— *Eptesicus fuscus,* page 50.

2*b.* Length of forearm less than 40 mm. . . . 3*a.*

3*a*(2*b*). Tragus pointed (Fig. 22); more than 4 mm. high from notch in front of base to tip . . . 4*a.*

3*b.* Tragus rounded (Fig. 24); blunt, end curved inward; less than 4 mm. high from notch in front of base to tip . . . 7*a.*

4*a*(3*a*). Ear from crown more than 13 mm.; when laid forward extends well beyond end of nose. Keen myotis—*Myotis keeni,* page 46.

 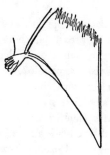 

Fig. 22. Ear of a bat (Myotis), with long pointed tragus.   Fig. 23. Interfemoral membrane and calcar of a bat.   Fig. 24. Ear of an evening bat, with short rounded tragus.

4*b.* Ear from crown less than 13 mm.; when laid forward, may extend to, but not noticeably beyond, end of nose . . . 5*a.*

5*a*(4*b*). Calcar (Fig. 23) with definite keel. Indiana myotis—*Myotis sodalis,* page 45.

5*b.* Calcar usually without definite keel . . . 6*a.*

6*a*(5*b*). Length of forearm more than 35 mm.; no distinct black mask across face. Little brown myotis—*Myotis lucifugus,* page 44.

6b. Length of forearm 35 mm. or less; distinct black mask across face. Small-footed myotis—*Myotis subulatus*, page 47.

7a(3b). Rich brown in color; length of forearm more than 34 mm. Evening bat—*Nycticeius humeralis*, page 52.

7b. Pale brown in color; length of forearm less than 34 mm. Eastern pipistrel—*Pipistrellus subflavus*, page 49.

8a(1b). Dorsal surface of interfemoral membrane not heavily furred to tip of tail; hairs on back not banded with buff; general coloration blackish chocolate. Silver-haired bat—*Lasionycteris noctivagans*, page 48.

8b. Dorsal surface of interfemoral membrane heavily furred to tip of tail; hairs on back banded with buff; general coloration not blackish chocolate . . . 9a.

9a(8b). Length of forearm less than 44 mm.; general coloration reddish or yellowish red; color of throat about same as rest of underparts. Red bat—*Lasiurus borealis*, page 53.

9b. Length of forearm more than 44 mm.; general coloration yellowish gray; throat yellow. Hoary bat—*Lasiurus cinereus*, page 55.

IV. Order CARNIVORA—Flesh eaters.

1a. Five clawed toes on both front and hind feet . . . 2a.

1b. Four clawed toes on hind feet; five on front (first toe reduced and high on foot) . . . 16a.

2a(1a). Color uniform black except for brown muzzle and sometimes a small white spot on breast; tail short and concealed in long fur of rump; size larger than a collie dog—family Ursidae. Black bear—*Ursus americanus*, page 57.

2b. Color not uniform black with above exceptions; tail conspicuous; size smaller than a collie dog . . . 3a.

3a(2b). Tail with a series (five or six each) of buff and black rings with tip black; a black mask across forehead and eyes—family Procyonidae. Raccoon—*Procyon lotor*, page 58.

3b. Tail without series of rings; no black mask across forehead and eyes —family Mustelidae—Weasels and skunks . . . 4a.

4a(3b). Claws of front feet partly concealed by fur; no median white stripe or white spot on forehead . . . 5a.

4b. Claws on front feet not partly concealed by fur; a median white stripe or spot on forehead . . . 14a.

5a(4a). Entire underparts not white or white washed with yellowish . . . 6a.

5b. Entire underparts white or white washed with yellowish, or entirely white with or without black tip on tail. Genus *Mustela* (except *M. vison*) . . . 10*a*.

6*a*(5*a*). Ears brown with a narrow border of light buff on edges . . . 7*a*.

6*b*. Ears uniform brown, not bordered with buff . . . 8*a*.

7*a*(6*a*). Color uniform light brown with a patch of buff on throat and breast; length of longest claw on front toes less than 13 mm. Marten—*Martes americana,* page 60.

7*b*. Color not uniform light brown; no patch of buff on throat and breast; length of longest claw on front toes more than 13 mm. Fisher—*Martes pennanti,* page 62.

8*a*(6*b*). Total length more than 800 mm.; tail length more than 250 mm. and noticeably thickened at base; toes completely webbed. River otter—*Lutra canadensis,* page 70.

8*b*. Total length less than 800 mm.; tail length less than 250 mm., not noticeably thickened at base; toes not webbed . . . 9*a*.

9*a*(8*b*). Tail more than 50 mm. Mink—*Mustela vison,* page 68.

9*b*. Tail less than 50 mm. Least weasel—*Mustela rixosa,* page 66.

10*a*(5*b*). Tail not tipped with black (sometimes a few black hairs on tip of tail); tail length less than 40 mm. Least weasel—*Mustela rixosa,* page 66.

10*b*. Tail tipped with black (not just a few black hairs); tail length more than 40 mm. . . . 11*a*.

11*a*(10*b*). Male adult . . . 12*a*.

11*b*. Female adult . . . 13*a*.

12*a*(11*a*). Total length more than 320 mm.; tail length more than 100 mm. Longtail weasel—*Mustela frenata,* page 65.

12*b*. Total length less than 320 mm.; tail length less than 100 mm. Shorttail weasel—*Mustela erminea,* page 63.

13*a*(11*b*). Total length more than 275 mm.; tail length more than 75 mm. Longtail weasel—*Mustela frenata,* page 65.

13*b*. Total length less than 275 mm.; tail length less than 75 mm. Shorttail weasel—*Mustela erminea,* page 63.

14*a*(4*b*). General color yellowish gray; longest claw on front toes more than 25 mm. Badger—*Taxidea taxus,* page 71.

14*b*. General color black with white stripes or spots on back or sides; longest claw on front toes less than 25 mm. . . . 15*a*.

15*a*(14*b*). Median white stripe on forehead; white on top of head, and usually two white stripes diverging over back; no broken white stripes on sides. Striped skunk—*Mephitis mephitis,* page 74.

15*b*. Median spot on forehead; more than two broken white stripes on back and sides. Spotted skunk—*Spilogale putorius*, page 73.

16*a*(1*b*). Claws not retractile and not entirely concealed in fur; tail bushy with a mane of stiff, black-tipped hairs on dorsal surface —family Canidae—Dogs . . . 17*a*.

16*b*. Claws retractile and concealed in fur; tail short, less than 200 mm., not bushy, and without mane—family Felidae—Cats . . . 20*a*.

17*a*(16*a*). Tail (without hair) more than half as long as head and body; hind foot less than 157 mm.; width of nose pad less than 19 mm. . . . . 18*a*.

17*b*. Tail (without hair) less than half as long as head and body; hind foot more than 175 mm.; width of nose pad more than 19 mm. . . . 19*a*.

18*a*(17*a*). Legs and feet reddish brown; tail tipped with black. Gray fox—*Urocyon cinereoargenteus*, page 79.

18*b*. Legs and feet blackish; tail tipped with white. Red fox—*Vulpes fulva*, page 77.

19*a*(17*b*). Total length less than 1,400 mm.; tail less than 400 mm.; width of nose pad less than 25 mm.; greatest depth of claws on front toes less than 8 mm. Coyote—*Canis latrans*, page 80.

19*b*. Total length more than 1,400 mm.; tail more than 400 mm.; width of nose pad more than 25 mm.; greatest depth of claws on front toes more than 8 mm. Gray wolf—*Canis lupus*, page 82.

20*a*(16*b*). Tip of tail black all around; hind foot over 200 mm.; ear tufts more than 35 mm. long. Lynx—*Lynx canadensis*, page 84.

20*b*. Tip of tail black only on top; hind foot less than 200 mm.; ear tufts, if present, less than 35 mm. long. Bobcat—*Lynx rufus*, page 86.

V. Order RODENTIA—Rodents.

1*a*. Hair on body mixed with sharp quills on back, sides, and tail— family Erethizontidae. Porcupine—*Erethizon dorsatum*, page 139.

1*b*. Hair on body not mixed with sharp quills on back, sides, and tail . . . 2*a*.

2*a*(1*b*). Tail thickly haired, longest hairs on tail 10 mm. or more in length—family Sciuridae—Squirrels . . . 3*a*.

2*b*. Tail naked or closely haired, longest hairs on tail less than 10 mm. in length . . . 12*a*.

3*a*(2*a*). Feet black; length of head and body over 350 mm.; tail less than one-fourth total length. Woodchuck—*Marmota monax*, page 88.

3b. Feet usually not black; length of head and body less than 350 mm.; tail more than one-fourth total length . . . 4a.

4a(3b). Back and sides with five or more longitudinal stripes . . . 5a.

4b. No longitudinal stripes on back; sides sometimes with one black stripe . . . 7a.

5a(4a). Stripes do not continue on side of face; thirteen narrow stripes (some broken into series of whitish dots) down back and sides; color of tail about same below as above; longest claw on front toes more than 5 mm. Thirteen-lined ground squirrel—*Citellus tridecemlineatus,* page 90.

5b. Stripes on side of face, as well as on body, not broken into series of whitish dots; color of underside of tail not like top; longest claw on front toes less than 5 mm. . . . 6a.

6a(5b). Rump reddish; white and black stripes do not continue to base of tail. Eastern chipmunk—*Tamias striatus,* page 96.

6b. Rump similar to back; stripes continue to base of tail. Least chipmunk—*Eutamias minimus,* page 94.

7a(4b). No loose fold of skin extending between front and hind legs on each side of body . . . 8a.

7b. A loose fold of skin extending between front and hind legs on each side of body . . . 11a.

8a(7a). Total length less than 350 mm.; a black stripe on each side in summer. Red squirrel—*Tamiasciurus hudsonicus,* page 98.

8b. Total length more than 350 mm.; no black stripes on sides at any time . . . 9a.

9a(8b). Length of tail hairs less than 45 mm.; belly nearly same color as remainder of body; never black. Franklin ground squirrel—*Citellus franklini,* page 93.

9b. Length of tail hairs more than 45 mm.; belly of different color from back and sides; sometimes black or blackish . . . 10a.

10a(9b). General coloration gray (sometimes faintly mixed with rust) with whitish underparts and white-tipped hairs on tail, or, entirely black or blackish. Eastern gray squirrel—*Sciurus carolinensis,* page 100.

10b. Underparts and feet fulvous, and hairs of tail always tipped with fulvous, sometimes with feet and underparts black. Eastern fox squirrel—*Sciurus niger,* page 102.

11a(7b). Hairs on belly and breast white to roots. Southern flying squirrel—*Glaucomys volans,* page 104.

11b. Hairs on belly and breast lead-colored near roots, white tipped. Northern flying squirrel—*Glaucomys sabrinus,* page 106.

12a(2b). Tail broad, naked, and flattened dorsoventrally; second claw on hind foot double; total length more than 700 mm.—family Castoridae. Beaver—*Castor canadensis*, page 109.

12b. Tail round or flattened laterally; no double claws; total length less than 700 mm. . . . 13a.

13a(12b). External cheek pouches present (Fig. 40)—family Geomyidae. Plains pocket gopher—*Geomys bursarius*, page 106.

13b. No external cheek pouches . . . 14a.

14a(13b). Hairs of belly lead-colored at bases, may be tipped with white or fulvous, but never white at bases—family Cricetidae . . . 15a.

14b. Hairs on belly white to bases; never lead color, tipped with white —family Zapodidae—Jumping mice . . . 28a.

15a(14a). Tail flattened laterally; five clawed toes on front foot. Muskrat—*Ondatra zibethica*, page 132.

15b. Tail round; four clawed toes on front foot . . . 16a.

16a(15b). Total length less than 250 mm. . . . 17a.

16b. Total length more than 250 mm. . . . 27a.

17a(16a). Length of tail less than one-third total length; ears nearly concealed in long fur . . . 18a.

17b. Length of tail more than one-third total length; ears prominent, not concealed in long fur . . . 24a.

18a(17a). Length of tail more than 25 mm. . . . 19a.

18b. Length of tail less than 25 mm. . . . 23a.

19a(18a). Broad reddish band down back contrasting with gray sides. Boreal redback vole—*Clethrionomys gapperi*, page 123.

19b. Back about same color as sides, dark brown or grizzled . . . 20a.

20a(19b). Nose yellowish on top . . . 21a.

20b. Nose not yellowish on top . . . 22a.

21a(20a). Length of tail more than 42 mm. Yellownose vole—*Microtus chrotorrhinus*, page 127.

21b. Length of tail less than 42mm. Heather vole—*Phenacomys intermedius*, page 121.

22a(20b). Length of tail more than 38 mm., no yellowish on underparts. Meadow vole—*Microtus pennsylvanicus*, page 124.

22b. Length of tail less than 38 mm., yellowish on underparts. Prairie vole—*Pedomys ochrogaster*, page 128.

23a(18b). Back uniform auburn; no longitudinal grooves on front of upper incisors. Pine vole—*Pitymys pinetorum*, page 130.

23b. Back grizzled slate gray or grayish brown; longitudinal grooves on front of upper incisors. Southern bog lemming—*Synaptomys cooperi*, page 120.

24a(17b). Tips of hairs on belly white; tail usually distinctly bicolored, white below darker above (all young animals of the genus *Peromyscus* are slate gray and are sometimes difficult to distinguish) no grooves on incisors . . . 25a.

24b. Tips of hairs on belly not white, but slaty yellowish; tail usually not distinctly bicolored; if bicolored, then grooves on upper incisors . . . 26a.

25a(24a). Length of tail usually less than 65 mm.; ear from notch usually 15 mm. or less; upper parts slate gray sometimes faintly washed with fulvous. Deer mouse (southern grassland form) or: length of tail more than 65 mm. (usually more than 70 mm.); ear from notch, usually 19 mm. or more; from northern half of area (northern woodland form). Deer mouse— *Peromyscus maniculatus*, page 113.

25b. Length of tail usually 65–70 mm.; ear from notch usually 16–18 mm.; from southern half of area. White-footed mouse— *Peromyscus leucopus*, page 117.

26a(24b). Tail clothed with short hair, scales do not show plainly; incisors grooved. Western harvest mouse—*Reithrodontomys megalotis*, page 112.

26b. Tail naked, scales show plainly; incisors not grooved. House mouse—*Mus musculus*, page 135.

27a(16b). Tail bicolor, clothed in short hairs; ear more than 25 mm. from notch. Eastern woodrat—*Neotoma magister*, page 119.

27b. Tail not bicolor, nearly naked; ear less than 25 mm. from notch. Norway rat—*Rattus norvegicus*, page 134.

28a(14b). Tail not tipped with white; general color of upper parts with an olive tinge. Meadow jumping mouse—*Zapus hudsonius*, page 136.

28b. Tail usually tipped with white; general color of upper parts bright fulvous especially on sides. Woodland jumping mouse—*Napaeozapus insignis*, page 138.

VI. Order LAGOMORPHA—family Leporidae—Hares and rabbits.

1a. Length of hind foot more than 115 mm. . . . . 2a.

1b. Length of hind foot less than 115 mm. . . . . 3a.

2a(1a). Bases of hairs of upper parts slate; tail not black above; entire animal except for ear tips white in winter. Snowshoe hare—*Lepus americanus*, page 142.

2b. Bases of hairs of upper parts white; tail black above; does not turn white in winter. European hare—*Lepus europaeus*, page 144.

3a(1b). Distinct rusty patch on nape; no dark patch between ears. Eastern cottontail—*Sylvilagus floridanus*, page 145.

3b. Small pale patch, or none, on nape; dark patch between ears. New England cottontail—*Sylvilagus transitionalis*, page 148.

VII. Order ARTIODACTYLA—family Cervidae—Deer, moose, elk.

1a. Nose not covered with hair all way around nostril; bare nose-pad borders inside lower edge of nostril; metatarsal gland present on hind leg; antler, if present, not palmate . . . 2a.

1b. Nose covered with hair all way around nostril; no metatarsal gland; antlers, if present, palmate . . . 3a.

2a(1a). A large yellow rump patch; tail short and colored same as rump; head and neck dark brown, contrasting with paler back; color around nose same as rest of face; bottom of each front hoof more than 25 mm. wide. Elk—*Cervus canadensis*, page 149.

2b. No large yellow rump patch; tail conspicuous, white beneath, fawn above; head and neck same general color as back; a band of dusky brown immediately above nose-pad and above this a band of whitish, contrasting with much darker face and forehead; bottom of each front hoof less than 25 mm. wide. Whitetail deer—*Odocoileus virginianus*, page 151.

3a(1b). General coloration dark brown; head and neck about same color as back; hoofs sharply pointed, length of each hoof on bottom more than twice width; snout overhangs mouth; no brow prong extending down over nose between eyes. Moose—*Alces alces*, page 153.

3b. Head and neck whitish, contrasting with darker back; hoofs broad and rounded; length on bottom less than twice width; snout does not overhang mouth; antlers with a palmate brow prong extending down over nose between eyes; small white rump patch. Woodland caribou—*Rangifer caribou*, page 155.

VIII. ORDER PERISSODACTYLA—family Equidae—Horse.

KEY TO SKULLS ONLY

(Fig. 25)

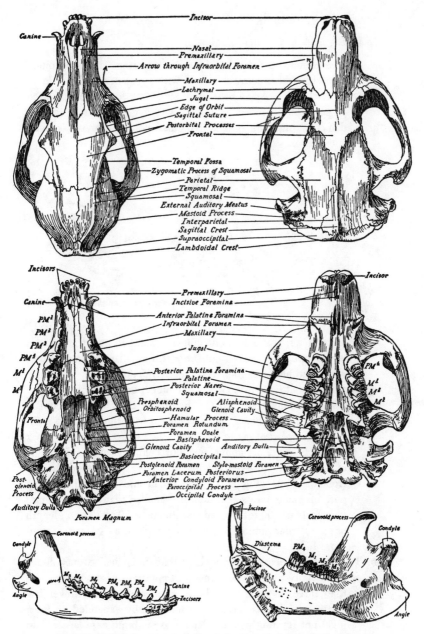

Fig. 25. Labeled parts of skulls of the gray fox and of the beaver.

KEY TO THE ORDERS

(Including man and domestic animals)

1*a*. Orbit not enclosed (Fig. 26) by solid bony ring formed by union of postorbital process of frontal with zygomatic arch . . . 2*a*.

1*b*. Orbit enclosed by solid bony ring (Fig. 28) formed by junction of postorbital process of frontal with zygomatic arch (except domestic pig, which has triangular pointed canines curved outward) . . . 7*a*.

 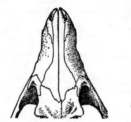 

Fig. 26. Open orbit of a wolf skull.   *Fig. 27. Rostrum of an opossum skull: expanded nasals.*   *Fig. 28. Closed orbit of a deer skull.*

2*a*(1*a*). Prominent sharp-pointed canines present in upper and lower jaws; uppers not curved outward (if triangular and curved outward, and has forty-four teeth, see 7*a*) . . . 3*a*.

2*b*. Canines absent, or if present, not prominent or noticeably different from adjoining teeth (in *Condylura* the third upper incisor is caniniform and should not be confused with the canine) . . . 5*a*.

3*a*(2*a*). Total number of teeth, fifty; twenty-six above and twenty-four below; five incisors above and four below on each side; angle of lower jaw inflected; nasals broadly expanded on face in front of orbits (Fig. 27), jugal broad and flattened, forming part of glenoid fossa; brain case smaller than rostrum; total length about 100 to 130 mm.; width about 60 to 70 mm.; length of mandibular ramus 80 to 110 mm. Opossum—order MARSUPI-ALIA, I.

3*b*. Total number of teeth never more than forty-two, twenty above and twenty-two below, sometimes minute; incisors never more than three on each side above or below; angle of lower jaw vertical (not inflected); nasals not broadly expanded on face; jugal not forming part of glenoid fossa; brain case larger than rostrum . . . 4*a*.

4a(3b). Premaxillaries separated in front by a distinct gap; upper incisors minute, not forming a continuous row between upper canines; total length of skull less than 25 mm.; canines not rounded, but with sharp-edged posterior borders, incisors never more than two on each side above. Bats—order CHIROPTERA, III.

4b. Premaxillaries fused (sutured) in front; upper incisors form a continuous row between canines; total length of skull more than 25 mm.; canines rounded or oval in cross section, incisors always three on each side of each jaw. Flesh eaters—order CARNIVORA, IV.

5a(2b). Total number of teeth never less than nine on each side of upper jaw (some teeth may not be visible without a hand lens); no great space (more than 2 mm.) between incisors and cheek teeth; zygomatic arches weak or absent; cheek teeth with sharply pointed cusps. Moles and shrews—order INSECTIVORA, II.

5b. Total number of teeth never more than eight on each side of upper jaw; a prominent space, diastema, between incisors and cheek teeth in upper (4 mm. or more) and lower jaws; incisors long, curved, chisel-like on ends and never more than two in lower jaw; zygomatic arches always present. Crowns of cheek teeth with flat grinding surfaces or with low rounded cusps . . . 6a.

6a(5b). Two incisors above (no small pair directly behind large pair); total number of teeth never more than twenty-two; bones of sides of face not porous or forming a delicate network. Rodents —order RODENTIA, VI.

6b. Four incisors above (two small ones directly behind large ones); total number of teeth twenty-eight; bones of side of face porous, forming a delicate network. Hares and rabbits—order LAGO-MORPHA, VII.

7a(1b). Upper incisors absent (except domestic pig, which has triangular canines curved outward, and forty-four teeth). Pigs, deer, and bison—order ARTIODACTYLA, IX.

7b. Upper incisors present, forming a continuous arc (if there are forty-four teeth and canine is triangular and curves outward, see 7a above) . . . 8a.

8a(7b). No diastema between incisors and cheek teeth; skull rounded, face short and nearly vertical; orbits face forward. Man—order PRIMATES, V.

8b. Long diastema (more than 60 mm.) between incisors and cheek teeth; blunt rounded canines sometimes present; face long and nearly horizontal; orbits face laterally. Horses—order PERIS-SODACTYLA, VIII.

KEY TO GENERA AND SPECIES BY ORDERS

I. Order MARSUPIALIA—family Didelphiidae. Opossum—*Didelphis marsupialis*, page 24.

II. Order INSECTIVORA—Moles and shrews.

1a. Total length more than 30 mm.; zygomatic arches present; teeth not dark chestnut brown—family Talpidae—Moles . . . 2a.

1b. Total length less than 30 mm.; no zygomatic arches; teeth often dark chestnut brown (some of unicuspids, single-pointed teeth in front of the broad cheek teeth, may be visible only from palatal view, minute)—family Soricidae—Shrews . . . 4a.

2a(1a). Total number of teeth, thirty-six; ten on each side of upper, eight on each side of lower jaw; width of skull more than 15 mm. Eastern mole—*Scalopus aquaticus*, page 26.

2b. Total number of teeth, forty-four (second upper incisor may be minute, sometimes lost in cleaning); eleven on each side of upper and lower jaws; width of skull less than 15 mm. . . . 3a.

3a(2b). Upper incisors curved downward and backward, not visible from dorsal view of cranium; bony palate terminates posterior to last molars. Hairytail mole—*Parascalops breweri*, page 28.

3b. Upper incisors project forward, easily seen from dorsal view of cranium; bony palate terminates anterior to last molars. Starnose mole—*Condylura cristata*, page 30.

4a(1b). Total number of teeth, thirty; nine on each side of upper, six on each side of lower jaw; only four unicuspids (Fig. 29h), fourth minute and wedged between third unicuspid and first large cheek tooth, visible only from palatal view; length of skull about 16.5 mm. Least shrew—*Cryptotis parva*, page 40.

4b. Total number of teeth, thirty-two (some of them minute); ten on each side of upper and six on each side of lower jaw . . . 5a.

5a(4b). Width of skull, 11 mm. or more. Shorttail shrew—*Blarina brevicauda*, page 42.

5b. Width of skull less than 11 mm. . . . 6a.

6a(5b). Three unicuspids in upper jaw plainly visible from side view, (Fig. 29d) third from front not (or barely) visible from outside view, much smaller than second or fourth and wedged between them; length of skull 15 to 16 mm.; length of mandibular ramus about 9.5 mm. Pigmy shrew—*Microsorex hoyi*, page 39.

6*b*. Four or five unicuspids in upper jaw plainly visible from side view (Fig. 29); length of skull 15–22.2 mm. . . . 7*a*.

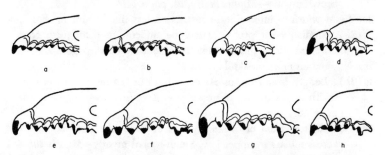

Fig. 29. Rostra of shrews, showing unicuspids: (a) *masked shrew* (Sorex cinereus), (b) *longtail shrew* (Sorex dispar), (c) *southeastern shrew* (Sorex longirostris), (d) *pigmy shrew* (Microsorex hoyi), (e) *smoky shrew* (Sorex fumeus), (f) *arctic shrew* (Sorex arcticus), (g) *northern water shrew* (Sorex palustris), (h) *least shrew* (Cryptotis parva).

7*a*(6*b*). Third unicuspid smaller than fourth (Fig. 29g). Northern water shrew—*Sorex palustris,* page 38.

7*b*. Third unicuspid not smaller than fourth . . . 8*a*.

8*a*(7*b*). Total length more than 17 mm. . . . 9*a*.

8*b*. Total length less than 17 mm. . . . 11*a*.

9*a*(8*a*). Width of cranium less than 8.4 mm. (Fig. 29*b*). Longtail shrew—*Sorex dispar,* page 38.

9*b*. Width of cranium more than 8.4 mm. . . . 10*a*.

10*a*(9*b*). Width of cranium usually less than 9.1 mm., range chiefly southeast (Fig. 29*e*). Smoky shrew—*Sorex fumeus,* page 34.

10*b*. Width of cranium usually more than 9.1 mm., range chiefly northern (if from an area north of the Great Lakes where the two overlap and the above measurement is 9.1, it may be impossible for the student to separate S. *arcticus* from S. *fumeus*) (Fig. 29*f*). Arctic shrew—*Sorex arcticus,* page 35.

11*a*(8*b*). Premaxillaries do not slope evenly backward and upward from incisors. (Fig. 29*c*) Southeastern shrew—*Sorex longirostris,* page 36.

11*b*. Premaxillaries slope evenly backward and upward from incisors (Fig. 29*a*). Masked shrew—*Sorex cinereus,* page 32.

III. Order CHIROPTERA—family Vespertilionidae—Bats.

1*a*. Total number of teeth, thirty-eight; nine on each side of upper and ten on each side of lower jaw; length of skull 14 to 15.5 mm.; width across upper canines less than 4.5 mm. . . . 2*a*.

1b. Total number of teeth less than thirty-eight . . . 5a.

2a(1a). Least width of interorbital constriction 4 mm. or more. Little brown myotis—*Myotis lucifugus,* page 44.

2b. Least width of interorbital constriction less than 4 mm. . . . 3a.

3a(2b). Median crest present (may be difficult to distinguish from *M. subulatus*). Indiana myotis—*Myotis sodalis,* page 45.

3b. No median crest on skull . . . 4a.

4a(3b). Length from front of canine to back of last molar greater than width across molars in upper jaw. Keen myotis—*Myotis keeni,* page 46.

4b. Length from front of canine to back of last molar less than width across molars in upper jaw. Small-footed myotis—*Myotis subulatus,* page 47.

5a(1b). Total number of teeth, thirty-six; eight on each side of upper and ten on each side of lower jaw; length of skull about 16.5 mm.; length of mandible about 12 mm.; width across upper canines more than 4.5 mm. Silver-haired bat—*Lasionycteris noctivagans,* page 48.

5b. Total number of teeth less than thirty-six . . . 6a.

6a(5b). Total number of teeth thirty-four; eight on each side of upper and nine on each side of lower jaw; length of skull about 12.5 mm. Eastern pipistrel—*Pipistrellus subflavus,* page 49.

6b. Total number of teeth less than thirty-four . . . 7a.

7a(6b). Total number of teeth, thirty-two; seven on each side of upper and nine on each side of lower jaw; first upper premolar sometimes minute and lies at inside angle between canine and first large premolar, may not be visible without lens . . . 8a.

7b. Total number of teeth thirty. Evening bat—*Nycticeius humeralis,* page 52.

8a(7a). Two incisors and four cheek teeth (without canine) on each side of upper jaw; first premolar not minute; length of skull about 19 mm.; length of mandibular ramus about 15 mm. Big brown bat—*Eptesicus fuscus,* page 50.

8b. One incisor and five cheek teeth on each side of upper jaw; first upper premolar minute (Fig. 30); length of skull 12.5 to 19 mm. . . . 9a.

9a(8b). Length less than 15.5 mm. Red bat—*Lasiurus borealis,* page 53.

9b. Length more than 15.5 mm. Hoary bat—*Lasiurus cinereus,* page 55.

IV. Order CARNIVORA—Flesh eaters.

1*a*. Total number of teeth, thirty-four or more; eight or more on each side of upper jaw, nine or more on each side of lower jaw; last upper molar sometimes reduced, but always more than twice as large as outer incisor . . . 2*a*.

Fig. 30. Palatal view of the teeth of a bat (Lasiurus).   Fig. 31. Rostrum of a marten (Martes).   Fig. 32. Rostrum of a river otter (Lutra).

1*b*. Total number of teeth, thirty or less; eight or less on each side of upper jaw, seven on each side of lower jaw; last upper molar about size of or smaller than outer incisor—family Felidae—Cats . . . 20*a*.

2*a*(1*a*). Last upper molar with antero-posterior diameter about one and one half times the lateral diameter, distinctly larger than tooth in front of it—family Ursidae. Black bear—*Ursus americanus*, page 57.

2*b*. Last upper molar with antero-posterior diameter about equal to or less than lateral diameter; about same size (except *Mephitis* and *Spilogale*) or smaller than tooth in front of it . . . 3*a*.

3*a*(2*b*). Total number of teeth, forty; ten on each side of upper and lower jaws—family Procyonidae. Raccoon—*Procyon lotor*, page 58.

3*b*. Total number of teeth never forty, either more or less than that number . . . 4*a*.

4*a*(3*b*). Total number of teeth thirty-eight or less; never more than nine on each side of upper jaw—family Mustelidae—Weasels . . . 5*a*.

4*b*. Total number of teeth, forty-two, ten on each side of upper jaw, eleven on each side of lower—family Canidae—Dogs . . . 16*a*.

5*a*(4*a*). Bony palate terminates at or slightly anterior to plane of posterior borders of last upper molars; last upper molar squarish, distinctly larger than tooth in front of it . . . 6*a*.

5*b*. Bony palate extends posteriorly beyond plane of posterior borders of last upper molars; last upper molar not squarish, about same size or smaller than tooth in front of it . . . 7*a*.

6a(5a). Total length more than 60 mm. Striped skunk—*Mephitis mephitis,* page 74.

6b. Total length less than 60 mm. Spotted skunk—*Spilogale putorius,* page 73.

7a(5b). Five cheek teeth on each side of upper jaw, back of canines . . . 8a.

7b. Four cheek teeth on each side of upper jaw . . . 10a.

8a(7a). Greatest diameter of infraorbital foramen more than 6 mm.; greatest width of brain case across mastoids more than 58 mm.; audital bullae flattened; rostrum broader than long (Fig. 32). River otter—*Lutra canadensis,* page 70.

8b. Greatest diameter of infraorbital foramen less than 6 mm.; greatest width of brain case across mastoids less than 58 mm.; audital bullae rounded; rostrum longer than broad (Fig. 31) . . . 9a.

9a(8b). Total length less than 95 mm. Marten—*Martes americana,* page 60.

9b. Total length more than 95 mm. Fisher—*Martes pennanti,* page 62.

10a(7b). Total length more than 80 mm.; last upper molar triangular in shape. Badger—*Taxidea taxus,* page 71.

10b. Total length less than 80 mm.; last upper molar somewhat dumbbell-shaped . . . 11a.

11a(10b). Total length more than 55 mm. Mink—*Mustela vison,* page 68.

11b. Total length less than 55 mm. . . . 12a.

12a(11b). Greatest width, 23.5 mm. or more (male). Longtail weasel—*Mustela frenata,* page 65.

12b. Greatest width less than 23.5 mm. . . . 13a.

13a(12b). Greatest width more than 19 mm. . . . 14a.

13b. Greatest width less than 19 mm. . . . 15a.

14a(13a). Postorbital processes sharply pointed (female).[1] Longtail weasel—*Mustela frenata,* page 65.

14b. Postorbital processes bluntly pointed (male).[1] Shorttail weasel—*Mustela erminea,* page 63.

15a(13b). Total length more than 33 mm. (female). Shorttail weasel—*Mustela erminea,* page 63.

---

[1] If the sex is known, the above key should hold in most cases with adult specimens. It is sometimes difficult without close comparison to distinguish the skulls of male shorttail weasels (*erminea*) from those of females or those of young males of longtail weasels (*frenata*).

15*b*. Total length less than 33 mm. Least weasel—*Mustela rixosa*, page 66.

16*a*(4*b*). Parietal (temporal) ridges distinct (1 to 3 mm. high) and separated at suture between frontals and parietals by a space of 15 mm. or more in width, not forming a sagittal crest; upper incisors not lobed (Fig. 33); notch on lower border of mandible

Fig. 33. (a) *Red fox: lobed upper incisors;* (b) *gray fox: upper incisors without lobes.*

(Fig. 34); length of skull about 130 mm., length of mandibular ramus about 95 mm. Gray fox—*Urocyon cinereoargenteus*, page 79.

Fig. 34. (a) *Red fox: mandible without notch;* (b) *gray fox: mandible with notch on lower border.*

16*b*. Parietal ridges, if present, low and separated at suture between frontals and parietals by a space of less than 10 mm. in width, often coming together to form a sagittal crest; upper incisors lobed (Fig. 33); no notch on lower border of mandible (Fig. 34) . . . 17*a*.

17*a*(16*b*). Total length less than 160 mm.; dorsal surface of postorbital process slightly concave, forming a shallow pit. Red fox—*Vulpes fulva*, page 77.

17*b*. Total length greater than 160 mm.; dorsal surface of postorbital process convex, not forming shallow pit . . . 18*a*.

18*a*(17*b*). Total length more than 230 mm. (232–58 mm.).[2] Gray wolf—*Canis lupus*, page 82.

[2] Some dogs may fall in this size class. If they do, the width across the first upper molars (outside) will be more than 31 per cent and the width of the rostrum more than 18 per cent of greatest length of skull.

18b. Total length less than 230 mm. . . . 19a.

19a(18b). Width of rostrum (see footnote 2) less than 18 per cent of greatest length of skull; upper incisors always closely set and even. Coyote—*Canis latrans*, page 80.

19b. Width of rostrum more than 18 per cent of greatest length; upper incisors usually with spaces between them. Domestic dog—*Canis familiaris*.

20a(1b). Four cheek teeth, back of canines, on each side of upper jaw. Domestic cat—*Felis domestica*.

20b. Three cheek teeth on each side of upper jaw . . . 21a.

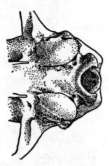
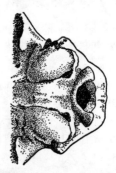

Fig. 35. *Basicranium of a lynx: separate foramina.*   Fig. 36. *Basicranium of a bobcat: confluent foramina.*

21a(20b). Length of upper carnassial (P⁴) more than 16.6 mm.; lower carnassial (M_1) more than 13.5 mm.; anterior condyloid foramen separate (Fig. 35). Lynx—*Lynx canadensis*, page 84.

21b. Length of upper carnassial (P⁴) less than 16.6 mm.; lower carnassial (M_1) less than 13.5 mm.; anterior condyloid foramen confluent with foramen lacerum posteriorus (Fig. 36). Bobcat—*Lynx rufus*, page 86.

V. Order PRIMATES—family Hominidae. Man—*Homo sapiens*.

VI. Order RODENTIA—Rodents.

1a. Zygomatic plate not horizontal, always broader than infraorbital foramen (Fig. 37a) . . . 2a.

1b. Zygomatic plate horizontal, narrower than and beneath infraorbital foramen (Fig. 37b) . . . 29a.

2a(1a). Total number of teeth, twenty or twenty-two . . . 3a.

2b. Total number of teeth sixteen or eighteen; upper incisors with or without longitudinal grooves on anterior faces; four or three

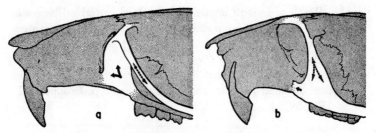

Fig. 37. Arrangement of zygomatic plate: (a) vertical plate, deer mouse (Peromyscus); (b) horizontal plate, jumping mouse (Zapus).

cheek teeth on each side of upper jaw—families Cricetidae and Muridae—Mice and rats . . . 15a.

3a(2a). Total number of teeth, twenty-two, five cheek teeth, first may be minute, on each side of upper jaw—family Sciuridae—Squirrels . . . 4a.

3b. Total number of teeth, twenty; four cheek teeth on each side of upper jaw . . . 11a.

4a(3a). Length of skull more than 70 mm.; width more than 40 mm.; flattened or concave between postorbital processes, which extend out along their posterior borders at right angles to longitudinal axis of skull. Woodchuck—*Marmota monax*, page 88.

4b. Length of skull less than 70 mm.; width less than 40 mm.; convex between postorbital processes, which extend backward and downward along side of brain case, incisors orange (pale in *Citellus*) on anterior surfaces . . . 5a.

5a(4b). Length of skull usually more than 60 mm.; width across interorbital constriction more than 16 mm. Eastern gray squirrel—*Sciurus carolinensis*, page 100.

5b. Length of skull less than 60 mm.; width across interorbital constriction less than 16 mm. . . . 6a.

6a(5b). Length of skull more than 42 mm. . . . 7a.

6b. Length of skull less than 42 mm. . . . 8a.

7a(6a). Length of skull less than 50 mm. Red squirrel—*Tamiasciurus hudsonicus*, page 98.

7b. Length of skull more than 50 mm. Franklin ground squirrel—*Citellus franklini*, page 93.

8a(6b). Total length of skull usually less than 33 mm. Least chipmunk—*Eutamias minimus*, page 94.

8b. Total length more than 33 mm. . . . 9a.

9a(8b). Width of frontals immediately back of postorbital processes more than 10 mm.; posterior border of zygomatic plate opposite M$^{1-2}$ (Fig. 38). Thirteen-lined ground squirrel—*Citellus tridecemlineatus,* page 90.

9b. Width of frontals immediately back of postorbital processes less than 10 mm.; posterior border of zygomatic plate opposite P^4 (Fig. 39).... 10a.

Fig. 38. *The relationships of the zygomatic arch and the molar teeth in the ground squirrel.*

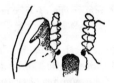

Fig. 39. *The relationships of the zygomatic arch and the molar teeth in the flying squirrel.*

10a(9b). Total length usually more than 36 mm.; width of skull more than 21.6 mm.; length of cheek tooth row more than 7 mm.; free points of postorbital processes more than 2 mm. long. Northern flying squirrel—*Glaucomys sabrinus,* page 106.

10b. Total length usually less than 36 mm.; width of skull less than 22 mm.; length of cheek tooth row less than 7 mm.; free points of postorbital processes less than 2 mm. long. Southern flying squirrel—*Glaucomys volans,* page 104.

Fig. 40. *Pocket gopher* (Geomys): *grooved upper incisors and external cheek pouches.*

Fig. 41. *Longitudinally grooved upper incisors of a lemming* (Synaptomys).

11a(3b). Face of each incisor with a deep longitudinal groove down center and a shallow groove near inner side (Fig. 40)—family

Geomyidae. Plains pocket gopher—*Geomys bursarius,* page 106.

11*b.* No grooves on incisors . . . 12*a.*

12*a*(11*b*). Length of skull more than 80 mm.; cheek teeth with flat grinding surfaces and transverse enamel loops separated by dentine—family Castoridae. Beaver—*Castor canadensis,* page 109.

12*b.* Length of skull less than 80 mm.; cheek teeth with low cusps and ridges, completely covered with enamel—family Sciuridae . . . 13*a.*

13*a*(12*b*). Length of skull more than 50 mm. Eastern fox squirrel— *Sciurus niger,* page 102.

13*b.* Length of skull less than 50 mm. . . . 14*a.*

14*a*(13*b*). Length of skull more than 42 mm.; length of upper cheek-tooth row more than 7 mm.; side of rostrum does not taper evenly from front base of zygomatic plate to anterior end of nasal. Red squirrel—*Tamiasciurus hudsonicus,* page 98.

14*b.* Length of skull less than 42 mm.; length of upper cheek-tooth row less than 7 mm.; side of rostrum tapers evenly from front base of zygomatic plate to anterior end of nasal. Eastern chipmunk—*Tamias striatus,* page 96.

15*a*(2*b*). Cheek teeth with folded enamel loops surrounding islands of dentine on flat grinding surfaces (Fig. 45) (also true of *Neotoma*); length of upper cheek-tooth row greater than length of anterior palatine foramina—subfamily Microtinae . . . 16*a.*

15*b.* Cheek teeth with low rounded cusps (except *Neotoma* and very old individuals where cusps are worn off); length of upper cheek-tooth row equal to or less than length of anterior palatine foramina . . . 23*a.*

16*a*(15*a*). Upper incisors with longitudinal grooves on anterior faces (Fig. 41). Southern bog lemming—*Synaptomys cooperi,* page 120.

16*b.* Upper incisors without longitudinal grooves on anterior faces (Fig. 42) . . . 17*a.*

17*a*(16*b*). Length of skull more than 50 mm. Muskrat—*Ondatra zibethica,* page 132.

17*b.* Length of skull less than 50 mm. . . . 18*a.*

18*a*(17*b*). Posterior border of palate straight without median projection, ends abruptly in a thin, bony shelf (Fig. 43), and connects with palatines only at the sides of narial cavity. Boreal redback vole—*Clethrionomys gapperi,* page 123.

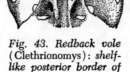

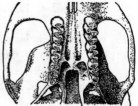

Fig. 42. Ungrooved upper incisors of a vole (Microtus).

Fig. 43. Redback vole (Clethrionomys): shelf-like posterior border of the palate.

Fig. 44. Vole (Microtus); central support of the posterior border of the palate.

18b. Posterior border of palate with median projection, does not end abruptly in thin bony shelf, connects with palatines at center as well as sides of narial cavity (Fig. 44) . . . 19a.

19a(18b). Least interorbital width usually more than 4 mm.; width of skull more than 58.5 per cent of length. Pine vole—*Pitymys pinetorum*, page 130.

19b. Least interorbital width usually less than 4 mm.; width of skull less than 58.5 per cent of length . . . 20a.

20a(19b). Audital bullae large, rounded, and much inflated, dorso-ventral diameter of bullae about 6 mm. or more; last upper molar with three or four re-entrant angles on outside (Figs. 45a and b) . . . 21a.

20b. Audital bullae somewhat flattened, slightly inflated, dorsoventral diameter of bullae usually less than 6 mm.; last upper molar with two re-entrant angles on outside (Figs. 45c and d) . . . 22a.

21a(20a). Last upper molar with three closed triangles; length of palatine foramina more than 5 mm. (Fig. 45a). Meadow vole—*Microtus pennsylvanicus*, page 124.

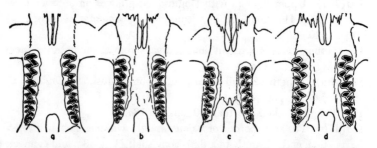

Fig. 45. Enamel patterns of the upper cheek teeth of microtines: (a) meadow vole (Microtus pennsylvanicus), (b) yellownose vole (Microtus chrotor-rhinus), (c) prairie vole (Pedomys), (d) heather vole (Phenacomys).

21*b*. Last upper molar with five closed triangles; length of palatine foramina less than 5 mm. (Fig. 45*b*). Yellownose vole—*Microtus chrotorrhinus,* page 127.

22*a*(20*b*). Length of upper tooth row less than 6 mm. (Fig. 45*c*). Prairie vole—*Pedomys ochrogaster,* page 128.

22*b*. Length of upper tooth row more than 6 mm. (Fig. 45*d*). Heather vole—*Phenacomys intermedius,* page 121.

23*a*(15*b*). Palate does not extend posteriorly beyond plane of last upper molars; incisors sometimes grooved; subfamily Cricetinae . . . 24*a*.

23*b*. Palate extends posteriorly beyond plane of last molars; incisors never grooved . . . 28*a*.

24*a*(23*a*). Total length more than 40 mm. Eastern woodrat—*Neotoma magister,* page 119.

24*b*. Total length less than 40 mm. . . . 25*a*.

25*a*(24*b*). Each upper incisor with deep longitudinal groove down center of face. Western harvest mouse—*Reithrodontomys megalotis,* page 112.

25*b*. No grooves on upper incisors . . . 26*a*.

26*a*(25*b*). Anterior border of zygomatic plate does not cover infraorbital foramen when viewed from the side (a space about 0.5 mm. or more in width shows in front of plate) (Fig. 47). Woodland deer mouse—*Peromyscus maniculatus gracilis,* page 116.

26*b*. Anterior border of zygomatic plate covers infraorbital foramen when viewed from the side (sometimes a very narrow part of the foramen shows along anterior border of plate) (Fig. 46) . . . 27*a*.

27*a*(26*b*). Length of skull more than 24.5 mm. (usually more than

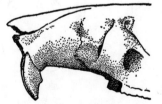

Fig. 46. The zygomatic plate and the infraorbital foramen, as seen from the side, in the white-footed mouse (Peromyscus leucopus).

Fig. 47. The zygomatic plate and the infraorbital foramen, as seen from the side, in the woodland and deer mouse (Peromyscus maniculatus gracilis).

25 mm.). White-footed mouse—*Peromyscus leucopus,* page 117.

27*b.* Length of skull usually less than 24.5 mm. Prairie deer mouse—*Peromyscus maniculatus bairdi,* page 114.

28*a*(23*b*). Length of skull more than 25 mm. Norway rat—*Rattus norvegicus,* page 134.

28*b.* Length of skull less than 25 mm. House mouse—*Mus musculus,* page 135.

29*a*(1*b*). Upper incisors not grooved—family Erethizontidae. Porcupine—*Erethizon dorsatum,* page 139.

29*b.* Upper incisors with longitudinal grooves on front faces—family Zapodidae—Jumping mice . . . 30*a.*

30*a*(29*b*). Four cheek teeth on each side of upper jaw. Meadow jumping mouse—*Zapus hudsonius,* page 136.

30*b.* Three cheek teeth on each side of upper jaw. Woodland jumping mouse—*Napaeozapus insignis,* page 138.

VII. Order LAGOMORPHA—family Leporidae—Hares and rabbits.

1*a.* Postorbital processes flared outward from brain case and not fused with frontals at posterior tips (Fig. 48*a*) (if fused, then skull more than 90 mm. in length); jugal noticeably broader at center than at either end—Hares . . . 2*a.*

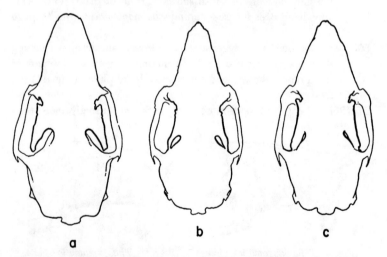

Fig. 48. *Top view of skulls of hares and rabbits:* (a) *snowshoe hare* (Lepus americanus), (b) *New England cottontail* (Sylvilagus transitionalis), (c) *eastern cottontail* (Sylvilagus floridanus).

1*b*. Postorbital processes continued back along brain case, where the
tips are usually fused with frontals (Figs. 48*b* and *c*); jugal
slightly, but not noticeably, broader in middle than at ends—
Cottontails . . . 3*a*.

2*a*(1*a*). Total length of skull more than 90 mm. European hare—
Lepus europaeus, page 144.

2*b*. Total length of skull less than 90 mm. (Snowshoe hare—*Lepus
americanus*, page 142.

3*a*(1*b*). Greatest diameter of auditory bulla more than 10 mm.; notch
at front of supraorbital process less than 5 mm. in antero-
posterior diameter (Fig. 48*c*). Eastern cottontail—*Sylvilagus
floridanus*, page 145.

3*b*. Greatest diameter of auditory bulla less than 10 mm.; notch at
front of supraorbital process more than 5 mm. in antero-posterior
diameter (Fig. 48*b*). New England cottontail—*Sylvilagus transitionalis*, page 148.

VIII. Order PERISSODACTYLA—family Equidae. Horse—*Equus caballus*

IX. Order ARTIODACTYLA—Pigs, deer, bison.

1*a*. Incisors present above and below; cheek teeth with low cusps;
orbit not surrounded by solid bony ring; no horns; forty-four
teeth—family Suidae. Pig—*Sus scrofa*.

1*b*. No incisors above; cheek teeth with crests and crescents of enamel
(for grinding); orbit enclosed by bony ring; horns present or
absent; less than forty-four teeth . . . 2*a*.

Fig. 49. *Cervidae: the lachrymal bone not connected with the
nasal.*

Fig. 50. *Bovidae: the lachrymal bone connected with the
nasal.*

2*a*(1*b*). Lachrymal bone does not connect with nasal (separated by
a vacuity 15 mm. or more in width (Fig. 49)—Family Cervidae
—Deer . . . 3*a*.

2*b*. Lachrymal bone connected with nasal (not separated by a vacuity 15 mm. or more in width) (Fig. 50)—Family Bovidae—Bison, cattle, sheep, and goats . . . 6*a*.

3*a*(2*a*). Length of nasals less than half length of distance from their anterior tips to the anterior tips of premaxillaries; length of skull more than 530 mm. Moose—*Alces alces,* page 153.

3*b*. Length of nasals about equal to or greater than the distance from the tips of the nasals to the anterior tips of the premaxillaries; length of skull less than 530 mm. . . . 4*a*.

4*a*(3*b*). Longitudinal, median bony partition (vomer) not attached to median suture of palatines; posterior narial cavity not separated (Fig. 51). Elk—*Cervus canadensis,* page 149.

4*b*. Longitudinal, median bony partition (vomer) attached to median suture of palatines for full length separating posterior narial cavity completely and supporting palate (Fig. 52) . . . 5*a*.

5*a*(4*b*). Width of audital bulla about one-half the length of the bony tube leading to the meatus; total length of skull more than 350 mm. Woodland caribou—*Rangifer caribou,* page 155.

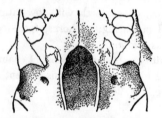 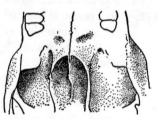

Fig. 51. Elk (Cervus): *posterior narial cavity not separated by the median vomer.*

Fig. 52. Deer (Odocoileus): *posterior narial cavity separated by the median vomer.*

5*b*. Width of audital bulla equal to length of bony tube leading to the meatus; total length of skull less than 350 mm. Whitetail deer—*Odocoileus virginianus,* page 151.

6*a*(2*b*). Length of cheek-tooth row less than 110 mm. . . . 7*a*.

6*b*. Length of cheek-tooth row more than 110 mm. . . . 8*a*.

7*a*(6*a*). Lachrymal bone distinctly concave, forming a deep pit directly in front of orbit. Domestic sheep—*Ovis aries.*

7*b*. Lachrymal bone only slightly concave, not forming pit directly in front of orbit. Domestic goat—*Capra.*

8*a*(6*b*). Branch of premaxillary does not extend to nasal (Fig. 53); frontal bone projects laterally, just back of orbit, beyond the zygomatic arch so that when viewed from directly above the arch is obscured; horns present in both sexes; occipital region projects back 30 mm. or more beyond posterior edges of horn cores, rounded without prominent boss. Bison—*Bison bison*, page 158.

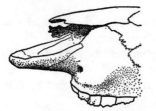 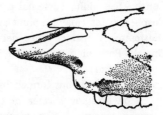

Fig. 53. *Bison: branch of the premaxillary bone not extended to the nasal.*

Fig. 54. *Cow: branch of the premaxillary bone extended to the nasal.*

8*b*. Branch of premaxillary extends to nasal (Fig. 54); frontal bone does not project laterally, just back of orbit, as far as zygomatic arch; when viewed from directly above, the arch is plainly in view; horns present or absent; if horns are present, occipital region does not project back more than 20 mm. beyond posterior edges of horn cores; a prominent boss is present. Domestic cow —*Bos taurus*.

GLOSSARY OF TERMS USED IN KEYS

Abdominal pouch – Fur-lined pouch on belly of female opossum, for carrying newborn young.

Angle of mandible – Posterior, lower part of lower jaw.

Anterior palatine foramina – Two elongate openings in palate just back of incisors.

Antler – Bony growth on head of deer, elk, moose, and caribou (erroneously called horn), shed annually.

Audital bulla – Inflated bony capsule at base of brain case, surrounding inner ear.

Bony palate – Roof of mouth, bordered by teeth except at back.

Calcar – Cartilaginous structure attached to inside of foot of bat, supports interfemoral membrane.

Canine – Tooth situated at suture between maxillary and premaxillary in upper jaw, at anterior outer corner of lower jaw; lower canine bites in front of upper.

Carnassial – Shearing tooth of carnivore, upper premolar 4 and lower molar 1.

Cheek teeth – Teeth set in the maxillary, back of canines when present, and those in lower jaw which oppose.

Claw – A pointed, curved, horny structure at the end of a toe.

Conch – See pinna (external ear).

Cusp – A point (may be blunt and rounded) on the crown of a tooth.

Diastema – A distinct space between two teeth.

Dorsal – Pertaining to the back or one of its parts (opposite of ventral).

Enamel loops – Loops formed by enamel ridges bordered by dentine, on grinding surface of tooth.

Foramen magnum – The opening at the back of the skull through which the spinal cord passes.

Forearm – In bats, the long wing bone between the elbow (near the body) and the wrist (near the short claw).

Frontal – One of two bones covering the anterior part of the brain case, above orbits.

Glenoid fossa – That part of cranium (depression) where lower jaw articulates.

Hoof – The horny covering which protects the end of the digit and supports the weight of the animal.

Horn – The horny sheath covering an outgrowth of bone from the skull, circular or oval in cross section and pointed at the extremity, not shed in mammals of the Great Lakes region.

Incisors – Teeth set in the front part of lower jaw and in premaxillaries of the upper jaw.

Infraorbital foramen – An opening through the zygomatic plate from the orbit to the side of the rostrum; for passage of nerves, blood vessels, or muscles.

Interfemoral membrane – The thin membrane in bats that extends from one leg to the other and encloses the tail.

Interorbital constriction – The narrowest part of the top of the skull, between the orbits.

Interorbital width – Smallest measurement at interorbital constriction.

Interparietal – An unpaired bone in the middle, at the extreme back and top of brain case.

Jugal – The connecting bone forming the middle part of the zygomatic arch (absent in shrews).

Keel – In bats, refers to the free flap of skin attached along the calcar.

Lachrymal – Small bone in the upper anterior part of the orbit, sometimes expanded on the face.

Lateral – Of or pertaining to the side.

Longitudinal – Extending along or pertaining to the antero-posterior (usually longest) axis of the body.

Mandible – Lower jaw.

Mandibular ramus – One side of the lower jaw.

Mane – (a) Pertaining to the long, coarse, black hair on the top of the tail of the gray fox; (b) the long hair on the top of the neck of the weasel and elk.

Mastoid – Lateral and ventral projection at base of brain case, back of audital bulla.

Meatus – An opening, here used as outward opening from ear capsule or bulla.

Metatarsal gland – A gland on the inside of the hind leg between foot and hock; position recognized by different hair pattern from remainder of leg.

Molar – One of the posterior cheek teeth, usually three-rooted and larger than premolars in front.

Nail – The horny plate on upper surface of the end of fingers and toes of man and some other animals; differs from claw and hoof only in shape and form.

Nape – The back part of the neck.

Nasal – Long (usually) paired bone at the front and top of the skull in front of the orbits; the roof of the rostrum.

Nose pad – The bare, thickened skin surrounding the nostrils.

Occipital – Pertaining to that part of the skull surrounding the foramen magnum.

Orbit – The bony socket for the eye.

Palatine – One of a pair of bones forming the posterior border of the palate and the sides of the posterior narial cavity.

Palmate – Flattened like a hand with spreading finger-like branches.

Parietal ridge – A bony ridge arising just back of the orbit and passing back over the brain case to converge posteriorly with its mate from the other side.

Pelage – The covering or coat of a mammal; wool, fur, hair.

Pinna – The fleshy external ear.

Posterior narial cavity – Large opening for nares at posterior border of palate.

Postorbital process – A process projecting laterally from the top of the skull just back of the orbits.

Premaxillaries – Anteriormost bones of the underside of the rostrum, forming the anterior part of the palate and carrying the upper incisors, when present.

Premolars – Teeth, usually simple two-rooted or single-rooted, between the molars and the canine.

Quill – The pointed, stiff, specialized hair of the porcupine.

Retractile – Capable of being drawn back, or in, as the claws of a cat.

Rostrum – That part of the skull in front of the orbits; snout.

Sagittal crest – A median, longitudinal ridge or crest on top of the brain case.

Tentacles – Finger-like, fleshy projections.

Total length of skull – Greatest length from front to back.

Tragus – Leaflike projection of skin near the bottom of the external opening of the ear; prominent in bats.

Tubercles (on foot) – Small fleshy pads on the soles of the feet.

Ventral – Pertaining to the underside, belly, of an animal.

Vomer – An unpaired bone at the anterior base of the brain case, sometimes divides the posterior narial cavity.

Width of skull – Greatest width, usually across the zygomatic arches.

Zygomatic arch – The bony arch bordering the outside of the orbit, usually curves outward.

Zygomatic plate – The flattened, expanded part of the maxillary in front of the orbit from which the anterior part of the zygomatic arch arises.

Dental Formulae of Mammals of the Great Lakes Region

The dental formula, as used below, has been divised so that the numbers of the different kinds of teeth in a mammal skull may be designated in condensed form. Mammals have "heterodont" teeth, different types of teeth for different functions. Those in front, set in the premaxillaries and the front of the lower jaw are single-rooted and are the incisors (I in the formula). Back of the incisors in some mammals are the canines (C). The upper canines emerge along the suture between the premaxillary and maxillary. The lower canines, in modern mammals, always bite in front of the uppers. These are single-rooted, and there are never more than four in one skull. Next in order are the premolars (P). These may be single- or double-rooted. The premolars are set in the front part of the maxillaries and in the lower jaw just back of the canines. The incisors, canines, and premolars are all replaced in most mammals. The molars (M) are not replaced. They are the teeth farthest back in both jaws. In the dental formula, the letters indicate the kinds of teeth, the numbers in the numerator indicate the number of teeth on each side above and those in the denominator, the number on each side below.

$$I\frac{5\text{-}5}{4\text{-}4}, \; C\frac{1\text{-}1}{1\text{-}1}, \; P\frac{3\text{-}3}{3\text{-}3}, \; M\frac{4\text{-}4}{4\text{-}4} = \frac{26}{24} = 50 \;\; \textit{Didelphis}$$

$$I\frac{3\text{-}3}{3\text{-}3}, \; C\frac{1\text{-}1}{1\text{-}1}, \; P\frac{4\text{-}4}{4\text{-}4}, \; M\frac{3\text{-}3}{3\text{-}3} = \frac{22}{22} = 44 \;\; \textit{Parascalops, Condylura, Sus}$$

$$I\frac{3\text{-}3}{3\text{-}3}, \; C\frac{1\text{-}1}{1\text{-}1}, \; P\frac{4\text{-}4}{4\text{-}4}, \; M\frac{2\text{-}2}{3\text{-}3} = \frac{20}{22} = 42 \;\; \textit{Ursus} \text{ (typical)}, \textit{Canis, Urocyon, Vulpes}$$

$$I\frac{3\text{-}3}{3\text{-}3}, \; C\frac{1\text{-}1}{1\text{-}1}, \; P\frac{4\text{-}4}{4\text{-}4}, \; M\frac{2\text{-}2}{2\text{-}2} = \frac{20}{20} = 40 \;\; \textit{Procyon}$$

$$I\frac{2\text{-}2}{3\text{-}3}, \; C\frac{1\text{-}1}{1\text{-}1}, \; P\frac{3\text{-}3}{3\text{-}3}, \; M\frac{3\text{-}3}{3\text{-}3} = \frac{18}{20} = 38 \;\; \textit{Myotis}$$

$$I\frac{3\text{-}3}{3\text{-}3}, \; C\frac{1\text{-}1}{1\text{-}1}, \; P\frac{4\text{-}4}{4\text{-}4}, \; M\frac{1\text{-}1}{2\text{-}2} = \frac{18}{20} = 38 \;\; \textit{Martes, Gulo}$$

$$I\frac{3\text{-}3}{2\text{-}2}, \; C\frac{1\text{-}1}{0\text{-}0}, \; P\frac{3\text{-}3}{3\text{-}3}, \; M\frac{3\text{-}3}{3\text{-}3} = \frac{20}{16} = 36 \;\; \textit{Scalopus}$$

$$I\frac{2\text{-}2}{3\text{-}3}, \; C\frac{1\text{-}1}{1\text{-}1}, \; P\frac{2\text{-}2}{3\text{-}3}, \; M\frac{3\text{-}3}{3\text{-}3} = \frac{16}{20} = 36 \;\; \textit{Lasionycteris}$$

$$I\frac{3\text{-}3}{3\text{-}3}, \; C\frac{1\text{-}1}{1\text{-}1}, \; P\frac{4\text{-}4}{3\text{-}3}, \; M\frac{1\text{-}1}{2\text{-}2} = \frac{18}{18} = 36 \;\; \textit{Lutra}$$

$$I\frac{2\text{-}2}{3\text{-}3}, \; C\frac{1\text{-}1}{1\text{-}1}, \; P\frac{2\text{-}2}{2\text{-}2}, \; M\frac{3\text{-}3}{3\text{-}3} = \frac{16}{18} = 34 \;\; \textit{Pipistrellus}$$

$$I\frac{3\text{-}3}{3\text{-}3}, \; C\frac{1\text{-}1}{1\text{-}1}, \; P\frac{3\text{-}3}{3\text{-}3}, \; M\frac{1\text{-}1}{2\text{-}2} = \frac{16}{18} = 34 \;\; \textit{Mustela, Spilogale, Mephitis, Taxidea}$$

$$I\frac{0\text{-}0}{3\text{-}3}, \; C\frac{1\text{-}1}{1\text{-}1}, \; P\frac{3\text{-}3}{3\text{-}3}, \; M\frac{3\text{-}3}{3\text{-}3} = \frac{14}{20} = 34 \;\; \textit{Cervus, Rangifer} \text{ (male)}$$

$$I\frac{3\text{-}3}{1\text{-}1}, \; C\frac{1\text{-}1}{1\text{-}1}, \; P\frac{3\text{-}3}{1\text{-}1}, \; M\frac{3\text{-}3}{3\text{-}3} = \frac{20}{12} = 32 \;\; \textit{Sorex, Microsorex, Blarina}$$

$$I\frac{2\text{-}2}{3\text{-}3}, \; C\frac{1\text{-}1}{1\text{-}1}, \; P\frac{1\text{-}1}{2\text{-}2}, \; M\frac{3\text{-}3}{3\text{-}3} = \frac{14}{18} = 32 \;\; \textit{Eptesicus}$$

$$I\frac{1\text{-}1}{3\text{-}3}, \; C\frac{1\text{-}1}{1\text{-}1}, \; P\frac{2\text{-}2}{2\text{-}2}, \; M\frac{3\text{-}3}{3\text{-}3} = \frac{14}{18} = 32 \;\; \textit{Lasiurus}$$

$$I\frac{2\text{-}2}{2\text{-}2}, \; C\frac{1\text{-}1}{1\text{-}1}, \; P\frac{2\text{-}2}{2\text{-}2}, \; M\frac{3\text{-}3}{3\text{-}3} = \frac{16}{16} = 32 \;\; \textit{Homo}$$

$$I\frac{0\text{-}0}{3\text{-}3}, \; C\frac{0\text{-}0}{1\text{-}1}, \; P\frac{3\text{-}3}{3\text{-}3}, \; M\frac{3\text{-}3}{3\text{-}3} = \frac{12}{20} = 32 \;\; \textit{Odocoileus, Alces, Rangifer} \text{ (female)}, \textit{Ovis, Capra, Bos, Bison}$$

$I\dfrac{3\text{-}3}{1\text{-}1}$, $C\dfrac{1\text{-}1}{1\text{-}1}$, $P\dfrac{2\text{-}2}{1\text{-}1}$, $M\dfrac{3\text{-}3}{3\text{-}3} = \dfrac{18}{12} = 30$ *Cryptotis*

$I\dfrac{1\text{-}1}{3\text{-}3}$, $C\dfrac{1\text{-}1}{1\text{-}1}$, $P\dfrac{1\text{-}1}{2\text{-}2}$, $M\dfrac{3\text{-}3}{3\text{-}3} = \dfrac{12}{18} = 30$ *Nycticeius*

$I\dfrac{3\text{-}3}{3\text{-}3}$, $C\dfrac{1\text{-}1}{1\text{-}1}$, $P\dfrac{3\text{-}3}{2\text{-}2}$, $M\dfrac{1\text{-}1}{1\text{-}1} = \dfrac{16}{14} = 30$ *Felis*

$I\dfrac{3\text{-}3}{3\text{-}3}$, $C\dfrac{1\text{-}1}{1\text{-}1}$, $P\dfrac{2\text{-}2}{2\text{-}2}$, $M\dfrac{1\text{-}1}{1\text{-}1} = \dfrac{14}{14} = 28$ *Lynx*

$I\dfrac{2\text{-}2}{1\text{-}1}$, $C\dfrac{0\text{-}0}{0\text{-}0}$, $P\dfrac{3\text{-}3}{2\text{-}2}$, $M\dfrac{3\text{-}3}{3\text{-}3} = \dfrac{16}{12} = 28$ *Lepus, Sylvilagus*

$I\dfrac{1\text{-}1}{1\text{-}1}$, $C\dfrac{0\text{-}0}{0\text{-}0}$, $P\dfrac{2\text{-}2}{1\text{-}1}$, $M\dfrac{3\text{-}3}{3\text{-}3} = \dfrac{12}{10} = 22$ *Marmota, Citellus, Eutamias, Sciurus carolinensis, Glaucomys, Tamiasciurus*

$I\dfrac{1\text{-}1}{1\text{-}1}$, $C\dfrac{0\text{-}0}{0\text{-}0}$, $P\dfrac{1\text{-}1}{1\text{-}1}$, $M\dfrac{3\text{-}3}{3\text{-}3} = \dfrac{10}{10} = 20$ *Tamias, Sciurus niger, Castor, Erethizon, Tamiasciurus, Geomys*

$I\dfrac{1\text{-}1}{1\text{-}1}$, $C\dfrac{0\text{-}0}{0\text{-}0}$, $P\dfrac{1\text{-}1}{0\text{-}0}$, $M\dfrac{3\text{-}3}{3\text{-}3} = \dfrac{10}{8} = 18$ *Zapus*

$I\dfrac{1\text{-}1}{1\text{-}1}$, $C\dfrac{0\text{-}0}{0\text{-}0}$, $P\dfrac{0\text{-}0}{0\text{-}0}$, $M\dfrac{3\text{-}3}{3\text{-}3} = \dfrac{8}{8} = 16$ *Reithrodontomys, Peromyscus, Neotoma, Synaptomys, Clethrionomys, Microtus, Pedomys, Phenacomys, Pitymys, Ondatra, Rattus, Mus, Napaeozapus*

TABLE III

SUMMARY OF MEASUREMENTS (IN MM.) AND LIFE HISTORY DATA

Species	Total Length	Tail Length	Hind Foot	Weight in Grams	Skull Length	Skull Width	No. of Teeth	Toes on Each Foot Front—Hind	Mammae	Gestation Period *	Litters per yr.	Young per Litter	Longevity (yrs.)	Home Range (acres)
Didelphis marsupialis	730–800	240–300	62–79	4–12†	116–127.5	60–70	50	5–5	11–17	13D	2	3–14	7+	11–40
Scalopus aquaticus	148–196	21–38	20–26	66–143	35.0–39.1	18.0–20.2	36	5–5	6	6W?	1+P	4–5	…	1/5
Parascalops breweri	150–170	23–36	18–20	40–64	31–33.8	13.9–15	44	5–5	8	4–6W	1?	4±	3–4	…
Condylura cristata	169–205	60–85	25–29	35–77	33.5–35.1	13.0–14.2	44	5–5	8	…	…	3–7	8	…
Sorex cinereus	80–109	33–46	10–13	3.5–5.5	16.0–17.4	7.4–8.4	32	5–5	6	…	…	4–10	1–2?	…
Sorex fumeus	110–125	45–48	13–15	6–11	18–18.6	8.7–9.0	32	5–5	6	…	2±	4–7	1+	…
Sorex arcticus	104–125	41–46	14–15	7–11	19.2–20.6	9.4–9.5	32	5–5	6	…	…	6±	1+	…
Sorex longirostris	78–90	27–33	10–11.5	3.5–5	14.1–15.9	7.0–7.8	32	5–5	6	…	1+P	4	1+P	…
Sorex dispar	113–130	52–62	14–15	5–6	17.3–18.2	7.9–8.1	32	5–5	6	…	2?	2+	1+	…
Sorex palustris	143–158	66–71	19–20	10–15.5	21.4–22.2	10.3–10.9	32	5–5	6	…	…	8±	…	…
Microsorex hoyi	78–103	30–34	8.5–11	2.3–4.0	15.0–16.5	6.1–7.4	32	5–5	…	…	…	7±	…	…
Cryptotis parva	69–84	13–17	9–11	4.0–6.5	16.2–17.1	7.6–8.3	30	5–5	…	…	…	3–5	1–2?	…
Blarina brevicauda	98–132	17–30	13–17	12–23	20.8–24.8	11.3–13.0	32	5–5	6	21D+	…	5–8	1–2?	½–1
Myotis lucifugus	80–95	31–45	8–11	6.0–9.5	14.1–15.4	8.5–9.6	38	5–5	2	…	1	1?	6+	…
Myotis sodalis	70–91	27–43.8	7–8.6	6–9	14.0–15.0	8.3–9.3	38	5–5	2	…	1	1	…	…
Myotis keeni	78–90	35–41	8–10	6–9	14.2–15.5	8.9–9.2	38	5–5	2	…	1	1	…	…
Myotis subulatus	73–82	30–35	6.6–7	5–8	13.2–14.2	8–9	38	5–5	2	…	1	1	…	…

Species														
Lasionycteris noctivagans	90–115	35–50	8–12	6–11	16.0–16.9	9.5–10.2	36	5–5	2	…	1	2	…	…
Pipistrellus subflavus	81–89	37–40	7.8–8.1	3.5–6	12.3–13.1	7.5–8.0	34	5–5	2	…	1	2	…	…
Eptesicus fuscus	96–117	34–49	10–14	11–17	18.1–20.6	11.5–13.4	32	5–5	2	…	1	1–2	…	…
Nycticeius humeralis	95	40	9	10	14.6	10.2	30	5–5	2	…	1	2	…	…
Lasiurus borealis	93–115	40–55	8–11	6.5–13.5	13.0–14.4	9.0–10.4	32	5–5	4	…	1	1–4	…	…
Lasiurus cinereus	130–149	60–61	10–13.4	26–31	17.0–18.2	11.8–12.8	32	5–5	4	…	1	2	…	…
Ursus americanus ‡	60–84	4	14.5	225–475†	257–291	150–176	42	5–5	6	29–30W	1	1–3	…	…
Procyon lotor	655–960	200–265	100–115	12–36†	110–115	69–74	40	5–5	6	63D±	1	3–7	…	…
Martes americana (♂)	610–630	200–208	90–95	2–4†	81–88	46–52.5	38	5–5	8	9–10M?	1	1–5	17	600–900
Martes americana (♀)	550–560	180–200	75–80	…	73.2–74.1	40–45.1	38	5–5	8	…	1	1–5	…	…
Martes pennanti (♂)	1000	380	125	4.5–10†	118.0–118.2	64.7–67.0	38	5–5	4	…	1	2–4	…	…
Martes pennanti (♀)	…	…	…	…	…	…	38	5–5	4	…	1	2–4	…	…
Mustela erminea (♂)	277–315	75–90	37–43	68–105	39–45.6	20.3–23.5	34	5–5	8	11.5M	1	2–4	…	…
Mustela erminea (♀)	242–245	42–70	28–33	45–74	35.6–37.5	17.1–17.9	34	5–5	8	9–11M	1	4–8	…	…
Mustela frenata (♂)	345–405	106–140	36–50	170–267	44.3–50.8	23.5–27.8	34	5–5	8	…	1	5–8	…	…
Mustela frenata (♀)	284–335	80–120	29–40	85–99	30.1–43.5	19.7–23.0	34	5–5	8	9±M	1	5–8	…	…
Mustela rixosa (♂)	189–205	30–37.5	21–22.8	40–50	31.5–32.8	15.8–17.5	34	5–5	…	…	2	4–6	…	…
Mustela rixosa (♀)	172–176	23–28	19–20.8	40–49	30.2–30.5	14.7–15.9	34	5–5	8	…	2	4–6	…	…
Mustela vison (♂)	520–620	180–210	56–68	567–964	61–69.3	33.5–39.8	34	5–5	8	7.5W	1	3–10	…	…
Mustela vison (♀)	420–520	128–180	54–60	665–850	58–59.6	31.8–32.3	34	5–5	8	…	1	3–10	…	…
Lutra canadensis	1000–1130	323–423	112–133	10–20†	99–115	66–78	36	5–5	4	11–12M	1	1–3	…	…
Taxidea taxus	720–775	98–154	87–150	13–25†	109–130	78–88	34	5–5	8	…	1	2–5	12	…
Spilogale putorius	400–550	181–223	44–51	450–1250	43.2–53.9	32.5–36	34	5–5	8	…	1	4–7	…	160+
Mephitis mephitis	509–665	180–233	53–75	4–10†	63–79.2	40–50.4	34	5–5	10–14	10W	1	2–10	…	…
Vulpes fulva	955–985	360–390	163–167	10–15†	135–158	68.8–78.6	42	5–4	8	7W+	1	4–9	…	…
Urocyon cinereoargenteus	988	372	142	8–13†	128.9	73.3	42	5–4	6	…	…	3–7	…	…
Canis latrans	1155–1320	275–395	180–220	23–50†	171–205	86–108	42	5–4	8	9W+	1	5–10	…	…
Canis lupus	1570–1650	420–480	270–290	70–100†	232–258	122–143	42	5–4	10	9W	1	3–14	…	…

*D = days; W = weeks; M = months. †Weight in pounds. ‡Body measurements in inches.

TABLE III (Continued)

SUMMARY OF MEASUREMENTS (IN MM.) AND LIFE HISTORY DATA

Species	Total Length	Tail Length	Hind Foot	Weight in Grams	Skull Length	Skull Width	No. of Teeth	Toes on Each Foot Front—Hind	Mammae	Gestation Period *	Litters per yr.	Young per Litter	Longevity (yrs.)	Home Range (acres)
Lynx canadensis	915	102	242	15–30†	126.5	82–88.9	28	5–4	6	2M	1	1–4?	10–15	....
Lynx rufus	755–890	130–140	165–185	15–30†	110–139.2	73.8–103.9	28	5–4	6		1	1–4	10–15	....
Marmota monax	530–645	105–150	74–92	5–10†	73–95	49–60.4	22	4–5	8	31–32D	1	2–6	4–5	40–160
Citellus tridecem-lineatus	215–294	64–98	30–38	82–207	37–41	20.7–24.6	22	4–5	10	28D	2+?	7–14	....	....
Citellus franklini	355–430	133–156	51–57	370–500	52–55	31–32	22	4–5	10–12		1	4–11	....	....
Eutamias minimus	185–222	80–100	28–35	42–53	31–33.3	16.2–18.8	22	4–5	8	1M?	2?	2–6	....	....
Tamias striatus	225–266	65–110	32–40	66–113	37.7–41.9	21–23.7	20	4–5	8	31D	1–2	2–8	3+	2±
Tamiasciurus hud-sonicus	283–345	98–148	40–57	120–250	42.9–48.7	24.1–28.2	20–22	4–5	8		1–2	4–7	10	8±
Sciurus carolinensis	405–510	193–250	60–75	340–680	59.4–63.9	31.8–35.6	22	4–5	8	44D	1–2	3–5	10–15	....
Sciurus niger	500–565	217–265	62–80	544–1360	62.4–70.0	35–40.1	20	4–5	8		1–2	2–5	10	10–40
Glaucomys volans	220–257	85–115	26–33	52–69	33.1–36.0	19.6–21.6	22	4–5	8	40D	1–2	2–6	5–13	4+
Glaucomys sabrinus	245–295	108–135	35.8–40	74–125	35.8–39.0	21.2–23.4	22	4–5	8		2	3–6?	....	....
Geomys bursarius	230–296	63–90	30–37	200–300	45–60	28–38	20	5–5	6		1	3–5	....	....
Castor canadensis	875–1020	230–260	160–180	30–60†	119–140	80–98	20	5–5	4	18W+	1	1–8	11+	8±
Reithrodontomys megalotis	120–152	51–70	14–17	8–15	19.9–22.2	10.2–11.1	16	4–5	6	23–24D		1–7	....	....
Peromyscus m. bairdi	119–156	47–69	16–20	10–24	22.2–24.8	11.1–12.9	16	4–5	6	21D+	4–6	1–7	1–2	.5–1
Peromyscus m. gracilis	155–205	69–107	18–23	12–31	24.3–27.8	12.4–13.9	16	4–5	6	21D+	4–6?	3–8	1–2	.5–2

Species														
Peromyscus leucopus	141–195	59–93	18–23	12–31	24.0–27.4	12.1–14.1	16	4–5	6	21D	4–5	2–6	1–2	.5–1.5
Neotoma magister	405–440	170–200	40–46	375–455	45–56	23.5–29	16	4–5	4	33D±	2–3	1–3	…	.3±
Synaptomys cooperi	99–132	15–23	16–19	14–39	24–27	14.6–16.6	16	4–5	8	…	…	2–6	…	…
Phenacomys inter- medius	130–150	31–38	19–20	30–40	23–26.5	12.8–15.5	16	4–5	8	…	2+	3–8	…	…
Clethrionomys gapperi	116–158	31–50	17–21	16–37	22.5–25.4	12.1–13.8	16	4–5	8	17–19D?	2+?	3–8	…	…
Microtus pennsylvani- cus	120–188	38–65	18–25	20–68	25.5–29.0	14–16	16	4–5	8	21D	10+?	1–9	1–3?	.1–1
Microtus chrotorrhinus	140–170	45–50	19–22	30–40	26.8–27.5	14.5–15.5	16	4–5	8	…	2+	3–4	…	…
Pedomys ochrogaster	118–155	29–39	18–21	22–35	25–29.7	13.8–16	16	4–5	6	21D?	8+?	3–6	1–3?	1±
Pitymys pinetorum	87–128	16–24	15.6–17	19–35	21.7–25.4	13.1–15.8	16	4–5	4	21D?	4+?	2–7	…	.25+
Ondatra zibethica	477–636	200–276	73–92	810–1580	61.2–69.0	36.9–43.7	16	5–5	6	22–30D	2–3	1–11	…	…
Rattus norvegicus	316–426	122–177	30–41	195–287	42.3–44.8	20.6–22.0	16	4–5	12	21–22D	12	6–22	12	…
Mus musculus	150–180	70–93	17–20	12–23	20.5–22.4	10.2–11.5	16	4–5	10	18–21D	10+?	3–11	…	.5–2
Zapus hudsonius	182–225	105–142	26–31	15–22.5	20.6–23.4	10.0–11.4	18	4–5	8	18–21D	2–3	4–8	1–2	1–2
Napaeozapus insignis	205–250	132–154	28–33	19–26.8	22.5–25.2	11.5–12.9	16	4–5	8	29D+	1–2?	1–6	…	…
Erethizon dorsatum	630–680	175–200	85–91	9.5–19†	93.5–110.8	62.5–78.9	20	4–5	4	7M	1	1	…	10
Lepus americanus	380–506	25–45	121–150	3–4†	74.9–85.2	37–42	28	5–4	8	36D?	1–2	1–7	…	…
Lepus europaeus	714–762	74–82	136–147	8–9†	92–105	45.2–50.2	28	5–4	6	30D?	…	2–8	12	…
Sylvilagus floridanus	400–485	39–70	80–110	2–4†	72–81.4	35.5–39.7	28	5–4	8	30D±	3–5	4–7	4–5	3–8
Sylvilagus trans- tionalis	370–450	35–50	85–105	2–3.5†	69–76	35–36	28	5–4	8	30D+	3+	4–6	4–5	2–6
Cervus canaden- sis (♂) ‡	84–108	5.5–6	25	550–800†	500–520	210–215	34	4–4	…	…	…	…	…	…
Cervus canaden- sis (♀) ‡	84–90	4.5–5	25	500†	415–437	185	34	4–4	4	8.5M	1	1	…	…
Odocoileus virgin- ianus ‡	72–78	6–11	20	150–300†	270–330	104–142	32	4–4	4	7M	1	1–2	…	…
Alces alces ‡	80–102	4–5	30–32	725–850†	540–588	210–230	32	4–4	4	8M	1	1–2	…	…
Rangifer caribou ‡	76	4	…	200–300†	395–450	180–188	32–34	4–4	4	29–30W	1	1–2	…	100

* D = days; W = weeks; M = months.   † Weight in pounds.   ‡ Body measurements in inches.

References

GENERAL WORKS

Anderson, Rudolph Martin.
    1947   Catalogue of Canadian Recent mammals. Bull. Nat. Mus. Canada, No. 102 (Biol. Ser., No. 31): vi + 238, 1 fig.

Anthony, Harold E.
    1925   The capture and preservation of small mammals for study. Amer. Mus. Nat. Hist., Guide Leaflet, No. 61: 1–53, 24 figs.

Barger, N. R.
    1951   Wisconsin mammals. Wisc. Conservation Dept., Publ. 351: 1–54, illus.

Beard, Daniel B., F. C. Lincoln, V. H. Cahalane, H. H. T. Jackson, and B. H. Thompson.
    1942   Fading trails. New York: The Macmillan Company. Pp. xv + 279, illus.

Bole, B. P., Jr., and P. N. Moulthrop.
    1942   The Ohio Recent mammal collection in the Cleveland Museum of Natural History. Sci. Publ. Cleveland Mus. Nat. Hist., vol. 5, no. 6: 83–181.

Burt, William H.
    1948   The mammals of Michigan. Ann Arbor: Univ. Mich. Press. Pp. xv + 288, 13 pls., 107 figs., 67 maps.
    1954   The subspecies category in mammals. Syst. Zool., 3: 99–104, 3 figs.

Burt, William H., and R. P. Grossenheider.
    1952 A field guide to the mammals. Boston: Houghton
    Mifflin Co. Pp. xxiv + 200, illus.
Cross, E. C., and J. R. Dymond.
    1929 The mammals of Ontario. Roy. Ont. Mus. Zool.,
    Handbook No. 1: 1–56, illus.
Department of Conservation, State of Michigan.
    1940 Tenth Biennial Report, 1939–1940. Lansing: Frank-
    lin DeKleine Co. Pp. 1–331, illus.
Dice, Lee R.
    1943 The biotic provinces of North America. Ann Arbor:
    Univ. Mich. Press. Pp. vii + 78, map.
Ellerman, J. R.
    1949 The families and genera of living rodents. London:
    British Museum (Natural History), 3: 1–210.
Gifford, Clay L., and Ralph Whitebread.
    1951 Mammal survey of south central Pennsylvania. Final
    Rept., Pittman-Robertson Project 38-R, Harrisburg: Penna.
    Game Comm. Pp. 1–75.
Grimm, W. C., and H. A. Roberts.
    1950 Mammal survey of southwestern Pennsylvania. Har-
    risburg: Penna. Game Comm. Pp. 1–99.
Grimm, W. C., and Ralph Whitebread.
    1952 Mammal survey of northeastern Pennsylvania. Final
    Rept., Pittman-Robertson Project 42-R, Harrisburg: Penna.
    Game Comm. Pp. 1–82, illus.
Gunderson, Harvey, and James R. Beer.
    1953 The mammals of Minnesota. Minneapolis: Univ.
    Minn. Press. Pp. 1–196, illus.
Hamilton, W. J.
    1939 American mammals. New York and London: Mc-
    Graw-Hill Book Co. Pp. xii + 432, illus.
    1943 The mammals of eastern United States. Ithaca: Com-
    stock Publishing Co., 2: 1–432, 184 figs.
Kennicott, Robert.
    1857 The quadrupeds of Illinois injurious and beneficial
    to the farmer. Rept. Comm. Patents, Agric., 1856: 52–110,
    pls. 5–14.
Lyon, M. W., Jr.
    1936 Mammals of Indiana. Amer. Midland Nat., 17:
    1–384, illus.

Miller, G. S., Jr., and R. Kellogg.
    1955 List of North American Recent mammals. U. S. Natl.
    Mus., Bull. 205: xii + 954.
Murie, Olaus.
    1954 A field guide to animal tracks. Boston: Houghton
    Mifflin Co. Pp. xxii + 374, illus.
Palmer, R. S.
    1954 The mammal guide. Garden City: Doubleday and
    Co. Pp. 1–384, illus.
Richmond, N. D., and H. R. Rosland.
    1949 Mammal survey of northwestern Pennsylvania. Penna.
    Game Comm. and U. S. Fish and Wildlife Service. Pp. 1–67.
Seton, Ernest T.
    1929 Lives of game animals. New York: Doubleday,
    Doran, and Co., Inc., Vols. 1–4, illus.
Simpson, George G.
    1945 The principles of classification and a classification of
    mammals. New York: Bull. Amer. Mus. Nat. Hist., 85:
    xvi + 350.
Zim, H. S., and D. F. Hoffmeister.
    1955 Mammals. New York: Simon and Schuster. Pp. 1–160,
    illus.

POPULATIONS, HOME RANGES, TERRITORIES

Allen, Durward L.
    1938 Ecological studies on the vertebrate fauna of a 500-
    acre farm in Kalamazoo County, Michigan. Ecol. Monog.,
    8: 347–436, 28 figs.
Blair, W. Frank.
    1940 A Study of prairie deer-mouse populations in south-
    ern Michigan. Amer. Midland Nat., 24: 273–305, 4 figs.
    1941a Techniques for the study of mammal populations.
    Journ. Mammalogy, 22: 148–57, 2 figs.
    1941b Some data on the home ranges and general life his-
    tory of the short-tailed shrew, red-backed vole, and wood-
    land jumping mouse in northern Michigan. Amer. Midland
    Nat., 25: 681–85.
Bole, Benjamin P.
    1939 The quadrat method of studying small mammal popu-
    lations, Sci. Publ. Cleveland Mus. Nat. Hist., 5: 15–77, 1 fig.

Burt, William H.
 1940 Territorial behavior and populations of some small mammals in southern Michigan. Misc. Publ. Mus. Zool. Univ. Mich., No. 45: 1–58, 2 pls., 8 figs.

Dice, Lee R.
 1938 Some census methods for mammals. Journ. Wildlife Management, 2: 119–30.

Elton, Charles.
 1942 Voles, mice and lemmings; problems in population dynamics. Oxford: Clarendon Press. Pp. 1–496, 22 figs., front.

Errington, Paul L.
 1941 Versatility in feeding and population maintenance of the muskrat. Journ. Wildlife Management, 5: 68–89.

Graham, Samuel A.
 1929 The larch sawfly as an indicator of mouse abundance. Journ. Mammalogy, 10: 189–96.

Hamilton, William J.
 1937a The biology of microtine cycles. Journ. Agric. Research, 54: 779–90, 2 figs.
 1937b Activity and home range of the field mouse, *Microtus pennsylvanicus pennsylvanicus* (Ord). Ecology, 18: 255–63, 2 figs.

Haugen, Arnold O.
 1942 Home range of the cottontail rabbit. Ecology, 23: 354–67, 4 figs.

Lay, D. W.
 1942 Ecology of the opossum in eastern Texas. Journ. Mammalogy, 23: 147–59.

Lincoln, Frederick C.
 1930 Calculating waterfowl abundance on the basis of banding returns. U. S. Dept. Agric., Circular, No. 118: 1–4, 1 fig.

Linduska, Joseph P.
 1942 Winter rodent populations in field-shocked corn. Journ. Wildlife Management, 6: 353–63, 7 figs.

Mohr, Carl O.
 1943 A comparison of North American small mammal censuses. Amer. Midland Nat., 29: 545–87, 1 fig.

MOLES AND SHREWS

Blossom, Philip M.
    1932   A pair of long-tailed shrews (Sorex cinereus cinereus) in captivity. Journ. Mammalogy, 13: 136–43.

Eadie, W. R.
    1939   A contribution to the biology of Parascalops breweri. Journ. Mammalogy, 20: 150–73.

Hamilton, William J.
    1929   Breeding habits of the short-tailed shrew, Blarina brevicauda. Journ. Mammalogy, 10: 125–34, 3 pls., 2 figs.
    1930   The food of the Soricidae. Ibid., 11: 26–39, 2 figs.
    1931   Habits of the star-nosed mole, Condylura cristata. Ibid., 12: 345–55.
    1940   The biology of the smoky shrew (Sorex fumeus fumeus Miller). Zoologica, 25: 473–92.
    1944   The biology of the little short-tailed shrew, Cryptotis parva. Journ Mammalogy, 25: 1–7, 1 pl.

Hatt, Robert T.
    1938   Feeding habits of the least shrew. Journ. Mammalogy 19: 247–48.

Hisaw, Frederick L.
    1923   Observations on the burrowing habits of moles (Scalopus aquaticus machrinoides). Journ. Mammalogy, 4: 79–88, 3 figs.

Jackson, Hartley H. T.
    1928   A taxonomic review of the American long-tailed shrews. North Amer. Fauna, No. 51: vi + 238, 13 pls., 24 figs.

Merriam, C. Hart.
    1895   Revision of the shrews of the American genera Blarina and Notiosorex. North Amer. Fauna, No. 10: 1–34, 3 pls., 2 figs.

Saunders, P. B.
    1929   Microsorex hoyi in captivity. Journ. Mammalogy, 10: 78–79.

Scott, Thomas G.
    1939   Number of fetuses in the Hoy pigmy shrew. Journ. Mammalogy, 20: 251.

Shull, A. Franklin.
    1907   Habits of the short-tailed shrew, Blarina brevicauda (Say). Amer. Nat., 41: 495–522, 5 figs.

West, James A.
>   1910   A study of the food of moles in Illinois. Bull. Ill. Lab.
>   Nat. Hist., 9: 14–22.

BATS

Allen, Glover M.
>   1939   Bats. Cambridge, Mass.: Harvard Univ. Press. Pp.
>   x + 368, 57 figs.

Griffin, Donald R.
>   1940   Notes on the life histories of New England cave bats.
>   Journ. Mammalogy, 21: 181–87.

Hamilton, William J.
>   1933a   The insect food of the big brown bat. Journ. Mam-
>   malogy, 14: 155–56.

Hitchcock, Harold B., and Keith Reynolds.
>   1942   Homing experiments with the little brown bat, *Myotis
>   lucifugus lucifugus* (Le Conte). Journ. Mammalogy, 23:
>   258–67, 2 figs.

Miller, Gerrit S., Jr.
>   1907   The families and genera of bats. U.S. Nat. Mus.
>   Bull., No. 57: xvii + 282, 14 pls., 49 figs.

CARNIVORES

Allen, Durward L.
>   1939   Winter habits of Michigan skunks. Journ. Wildlife
>   Management, 3: 212–28, 4 pls.

Crabb, W. D.
>   1948   The ecology and management of the prairie spotted
>   skunk in Iowa. Ecol. Monogr., 18: 201–32.

Hall, E. Raymond.
>   1936   Mustelid mammals from the Pleistocene of North
>   America with systematic notes on some Recent members of
>   the genera Mustela, Taxidea and Mephitis. Carnegie Inst.
>   Wash., Publ., No. 473: 41–119, 5 pls., 6 figs.
>   1951   American weasels. Univ. Kans. Publ. Mus. Nat. Hist.,
>   4: 1–466.

Hamilton, William J.
>   1933b   The weasels of New York, their Natural History and
>   economic status. Amer. Midland Nat., 14: 289–344, 4 pls.,
>   3 figs., 2 maps.

Hatt, Robert T.
　　1940　The least weasel in Michigan. Journ. Mammalogy, 21: 412–16, 1 map.
Hollister, Ned.
　　1913　A synopsis of the American minks. Proc. U. S. Nat. Mus., 44: 471–80.
Lagler, Karl F., and Burton T. Ostenson.
　　1942　Early spring food of the otter in Michigan. Journ. Wildlife Management, 6: 244–54, 3 figs.
Marshall, William H.
　　1936　A study of the winter activities of the mink. Journ. Mammalogy, 17: 382–92, 3 figs.
Murie, Adolph.
　　1936　Following fox trails. Misc. Publ. Mus. Zool. Univ. Mich., No. 32: 1–45, 7 figs., 6 pls.
　　1940　Ecology of the coyote in the Yellowstone. Fauna of the National Parks of the United States, Ser. No. 4: x + 206, front., 56 figs., 1 map.
Polderboer, Emmett B.
　　1942　Habits of the least weasel (*Mustella rixosa*) in northeastern Iowa. Journ. Mammalogy, 23: 145–47.
Stuewer, Frederick W.
　　1942　Studies of molting and priming of fur of the eastern raccoon. Journ. Mammalogy, 23: 399–404, 3 figs.
　　1943a　Reproduction of raccoons in Michigan. Journ. Wildlife Management, 7: 60–73, 1 pl., 5 figs.
　　1943b　Raccoons: their habits and management in Michigan. Ecol. Monogr., 13: 203–57, 55 figs.
Wood, N. A.
　　1922　The mammals of Washtenaw County, Michigan. Occ. Papers Mus. Zool. Univ. Mich., No. 123: 1–23.
Wright, P. L.
　　1948　Breeding habits of captive long-tailed weasels (*Mustela frenata*). Amer. Midland Nat., 39: 338–49.

RODENTS

Allen, Durward L.
　　1943　Michigan fox squirrel management. Lansing, Mich.: Dept. Conserv., Game Div. Publ., No. 100: 1–404, 212 figs. [Issued in Dec., 1944.]

Allen, Elsa G.

    1938 The habits and life history of the eastern chipmunk, Tamias striatus lysteri. Bull. N. Y. State Mus., No. 314: 1–122, 43 figs.

Bailey, Vernon.

    1924 Breeding, feeding and other life habits of meadow mice (*Microtus*). Journ. Agric. Research, 27: 523–35.

    1926 How beavers build their houses. Journ. Mammalogy, 7: 41–44, 9 pls.

Blair, William F.

    1942 Size of home range and notes on the life history of the woodland deer-mouse and eastern chipmunk in northern Michigan. Journ. Mammalogy, 23: 27–36.

Bradt, Glenn W.

    1938 A study of beaver colonies in Michigan. Journ. Mammalogy, 19: 139–62, 1 fig.

    1939 Breeding habits of beaver. *Ibid.*, 20: 486–89, 1 fig.

Cook, David B.

    1940 Beaver-trout relations. Journ. Mammalogy, 21: 397–401.

Hall, E. Raymond, and E. Lendell Cockrum.

    1953 A synopsis of the North American microtine rodents. Univ. Kans. Publ. Mus. Nat. Hist., 5 (No. 27): 373–498, illus.

Hamilton, William J.

    1934 The life history of the rufescent woodchuck, *Marmota monax rufescens* Howell. Ann. Carnegie Mus., 23: 85–178, pls. XV–XIX, 9 text figs.

    1935 Habits of jumping mice. Amer. Midland Nat., 16: 187–200, 1 pl., 2 figs.

    1936 Rats and their control. Cornell Extension Bull., No. 353: 1–32, 11 figs.

    1938 Life history notes on the northern pine mouse. Journ. Mammalogy, 19: 163–70, 1 fig.

Hatt, Robert T.

    1929 The red squirrel: its life history and habits, with special reference to the Adirondacks of New York and the Harvard Forest. Roosevelt Wildlife Annals, 2 (No. 1): 1–146, 52 figs.

    1930 The biology of the voles of New York. Roosevelt Wildlife Bull., 5 (no. 4): 513–623, 1 pl., 30 figs.

Hooper, Emmet T.
> 1942 Geographic variation in the eastern chipmunk, *Tamias striatus,* in Michigan. Occ. Papers Mus. Zool. Univ. Mich., No. 461: 1–5.

Howell, A. Brazier.
> 1927 Revision of the American lemming mice. North Amer. Fauna, No. 50: 1–38, 2 pls., 11 figs.

Howell, Arthur H.
> 1915 Revision of the American marmots. North Amer. Fauna, No. 37: 1–80, 15 pls., 3 figs.
> 1918 Revision of the American flying squirrels. *Ibid.,* No. 44: 1–64, 7 pls., 4 figs.
> 1929 Revision of the American chipmunks (genera Tamias and Eutamias). *Ibid.,* No. 52: 1–157, 10 pls., 9 figs.
> 1938 Revision of the North American ground squirrels, with a classification of the North American Sciuridae. *Ibid.,* No. 56: 1–256, 32 pls., 20 text figs.

Johnson, Charles E.
> 1925 The muskrat in New York: its natural history and economies. Roosevelt Wildlife Bull., 3 (no. 2): 199–320, 1 pl., 40 figs., 3 maps.
> 1927 The beaver in the Adirondacks. *Ibid.* (no. 4): 495–641, figs. 87–127, maps 4–6.

Johnson, George E.
> 1928 Hibernation of the thirteen-lined ground squirrel, Citellus tridecemlineatus (Mitchill). Journ. Exper. Zool., 50: 15–30.

Lantz, David E.
> 1907 An economic study of field mice (Genus *Microtus*). Dept. Agric., Biol. Surv. Bull., No. 31: 1–64, 8 pls., 3 figs.

Morgan, Lewis H.
> 1868 The American beaver and his works. Philadelphia: Lippincott. Pp. 1–330, illus.

Osgood, Wilfred H.
> 1909 Revision of the mice of the American genus Peromyscus. North Amer. Fauna, No. 28: 1–285, 8 pls., 12 figs.

Quimby, Don C.
> 1951 The life history and ecology of the jumping mouse, *Zapus hudsonius.* Ecol. Monogr., 21: 61–95.

Ruhl, Harry D., and Parish S. Lovejoy.
    1930 Beaver plantings in Michigan. Mich. Acad. Sci., Arts, and Letters, 11: 465–69.

Sheldon, Carolyn.
    1934 Studies on the life histories of Zapus and Napaeozapus in Nova Scotia. Journ. Mammalogy, 15: 290–300.

Silver, James.
    1937 The house rat. U. S. Dept. Agric., Circular, No. 423; 1–18, 15 figs.

Silver, James, and Winney E. Crouch.
    1942 Rat proofing buildings and premises. U. S. Dept. Int., Conservation Bull., No. 19: 1–26, 23 figs.

Silver, James, and Francis E. Garlough.
    1941 Rat control. U. S. Dept. Int., Conservation Bull., No. 8: 1–27, 10 figs.

Sollberger, Dwight E.
    1943 Notes on the breeding habits of the eastern flying squirrel (*Glaucomys volans volans*). Journ. Mammalogy, 24: 163–73, 1 pl.

Stegeman, LeRoy C.
    1930 Notes on Synaptomys cooperi cooperi in Washtenaw County, Michigan. Journ. Mammalogy, 11: 460–66, 2 figs.

Struthers, Parke H.
    1928 Breeding habits of the Canadian porcupine (Erethizon dorsatum). Journ. Mammalogy, 9: 300–308, 2 pls.

Svihla, Arthur.
    1930 Breeding habits and young of the red-backed mouse, Evotomys. Mich. Acad. Sci., Arts, and Letters, 11: 485–90.

Wade, Otis.
    1927 Breeding habits and early life of the thirteen-striped ground squirrel, Citellus tridecemlineatus (Mitchill). Journ. Mammalogy, 8: 269–76, 1 pl.
    1930 The behavior of certain spermophiles with special reference to aestivation and hibernation. *Ibid.*, 11: 160–88, 1 pl.

Warren, Edward R.
    1927 The beaver, its works and its ways. Baltimore: Williams and Wilkins. Pp. 1–177.

HARES AND RABBITS

Grange, Wallace B.
>   1932a   Observations on the snowshoe hare, Lepus americanus phaeonotus Allen. Journ. Mammalogy, 13: 1–19, 2 pls.
>   1932b   The pelages and color changes of the snowshoe hare, Lepus americanus phaeonotus Allen. *Ibid.*, 13: 99–116, 3 pls.

Hall, E. Raymond.
>   1951   A synopsis of the North American Lagomorpha. Univ. Kansas Publ., Mus. Nat. Hist., 5 (no. 10): 119–202.

Haugen, Arnold O.
>   1942   Life history studies of the cottontail rabbit in southwestern Michigan. Amer. Midland Nat., 28: 204–44.
>   1943   Management studies of the cottontail rabbit in southwestern Michigan. Journ. Wildlife Management, 7: 102–19, 2 pls., 3 figs.

Hickie, Paul.
>   1940   Cottontails in Michigan. Lansing, Mich.: Mich. Dept. Conser., Game Division. Pp. 1–109, illus.

Lyon, Marcus W., Jr.
>   1904   Classification of the hares and their allies. Smithsonian Misc. Coll., 45 (no. 1456): 321–447, pls. 74–110.

Nelson, Edward W.
>   1909   The rabbits of North America. North Amer. Fauna, No. 29: 1–314, 13 pls., 19 figs.

Soper, J. D.
>   1921   Notes on the snowshoe rabbit. Journ. Mammalogy, 2: 101–8, 1 fig.

MOOSE

Murie, Adolph.
>   1934   The moose of Isle Royale. Misc. Publ. Mus. Zool. Univ. Mich., No. 25: 1–44, 6 pls.

Peterson, R. L.
>   1955   North American moose. Toronto, Univ. Toronto Press. Pp. xi + 280, 66 figs.

Index

Aardvark, 183

Adaptation, aerial, 9, 11
  ambulatory, 10
  aquatic, 9, 12
  arboreal, 9, 11
  cursorial, 10
  digitigrade, 10
  feet, 10
  fossorial, 9, 11
  graviportal, 11
  limbs, 10
  plantigrade, 10
  semiaquatic, 12
  teeth, 12
  terrestrial, 9
  unguligrade, 10

Adaptive radiation, 9
  feet, 13
  limbs, 13
  teeth, 13

Agouti, 183

Alces, 220
  alces, 153, 154, 196, 214, 225

Allen, D. L., 21

Amphibian, 61, 70

Anomaluridae, 182

Anteater, 12, 15, 179, 183
  banded, 180

Antelope, 184

Antilocapridae, 184

Ape, 18

Aplodontiidae, 182

Arachnid, 43

Armadillo, 15, 183

Arthropod, 35

Artiodactyl, 18

Artiodactyla, 149, 184, 187, 196, 199, 213

Aye-aye, 180

Badger, 11, 71, 72, 181, 191, 204

Balaenidae, 182

Balaenopteridae, 182

Bandicoot, 180

Bat, 11, 43, 186, 189, 199, 201 (*see also* Myotis and Pipistrel)
  big brown, 50, 51, 52, 189, 202

Bat (*continued*)
  crestnose, 181
  disk-thumbed, 181
  evening, 52, 53, 190, 202
  fish-eating, 181
  freetail, 181
  fruit-eating, 181
  funnel-eared, 181
  hoary, 55, 190, 202
  horseshoenose, 181
  large-lipped, 181
  large-winged, 181
  leafnose, 181
  longtail, 181
  mustache-lipped, 181
  plainnose, 44, 181
  red, 53, 54, 190, 202
  sac-winged, 181
  silver-haired, 48, 49, 190, 202
  straw-colored, 181
  teeth, 203
  valvenose, 181
  vampire, 181
Bathyergidae, 182
Bear, 8, 56, 181
  black, 5, 57, 190, 203
Beaver, 5, 6, 8, 9, 12, 17, 18, 109, 110, 182, 194, 209
  giant, 4
  mountain, 182
  skull, 197
Becker, H. R., 53
Beetle, June, 92, 105
Bird, 61, 67, 69, 74, 81, 83, 86, 93, 103, 105
Bison, 5, 149, 158, 199, 213, 214
  skull, 215
Bison bison, 158, 215, 220
Blarina, 38, 40, 117, 220
Blarina brevicauda, 42, 43, 189, 200, 222
Blossom, P. M., 33
Bobcat, 5, 8, 85, 86, 192, 206
  basicranium, 206
Bos, 220
  taurus, 215
Bounty, 7
Bovidae, 184, 214
  skull, 213

Bradt, G. W., 111
Bradypodidae, 183

Caenolestidae, 180
Callithricidae, 180
Camel, 184
Camelidae, 184
Canidae, 76, 182, 192, 203
Canis, 78, 220
  familaris, 206
  latrans, 80, 81, 192, 206, 223
  lupus, 82, 83, 192, 205, 223
Capra, 214, 220
Capybara, 183
Caribou, 149
  woodland, 155, 156, 196, 214
Carnivora, 56, 84, 181, 187, 190, 199, 202
  references, 231
Castor canadensis, 109, 110, 194, 209, 224
Castoridae, 109, 182, 194, 209
Cat, 10, 12, 84, 182, 192, 203, 206
Cattle, 184, 214
Caviidae, 183
Cavy, 183
Cebidae, 180
Census, methods, 19, 20
Centipede, 43
Cercopithecidae, 180
Cervidae, 149, 184, 196, 213
  skull, 213
Cervus, 220
  canadensis, 149, 150, 196, 214, 225
  narial cavity, 214
Cetacea, 182
Chevrotain, 184
Chimpanzee, 181
Chinchilla, 183
Chinchillidae, 183
Chipmunk, 8, 18, 78
  eastern, 96, 97, 193, 209
  least, 94, 95, 193, 207
Chiroptera, 43, 181, 186, 189, 199, 201
Chrysochloridae, 180
Citellus, 221
  franklini, 93, 193, 207, 224

tridecemlineatus, 90, 91, 193, 208, 224
Civet, 182
Classification, mammals of the world, 179
Clethrionomys, 221
  gapperi, 123, 194, 209, 225
  palate, 210
Coati, 181
Collecting mammals, 161–165
  bats, 163
  chipmunks, 164
  equipment, 160
  mice, 164
  moles, 163
  pocket gophers, 163
  rabbits, 165
  shrews, 164
  squirrels, 164, 165
  woodchucks, 165
Condylura, 198, 220
  cristata, 30, 187, 200, 222
Conversion table, coins, 168
  inches to millimeters, 162
Cottontail, 5, 21
  eastern, 145, 146, 196, 213
    skull, 212
  New England, 148, 196, 213
    skull, 212
Cougar, 5, 16, 157
Cow, 14, 149, 187, 215
  sea, 183
  skull, 215
Coyote, 6, 7, 80, 81, 192, 206
Coypu, 183
Crabb, W. D., 74
Crayfish, 70
Cricetidae, 111, 182, 194, 207
Cricetinae, 111, 211
Cricket, 42
Cryptotis, 220
  parva, 40, 41, 189, 200, 222
Ctenodactylidae, 183
Cuniculidae, 183
Cynocephalidae, 181

Dassie, 183
Dasypodidae, 183
Dasyproctidae, 183

Dasyuridae, 180
Daubentoniidae, 180
Deer, 6, 8, 9, 10, 14, 20, 83, 149, 184, 187, 196, 199, 213
  narial cavity, 214
  skull, 198
  whitetail, 19, 151, 196, 214
Delphinidae, 182
Dental formulae, 219
Dermoptera, 181
Desmodontidae, 181
Didelphiidae, 24, 180, 187, 200
Didelphis, 219
  marsupialis, 24, 25, 187, 200, 222
Dinomyidae, 183
Dipodidae, 183
Diptera, 52
Disease, 19, 134
Distribution, 3
Dog, 10, 12, 18, 182, 192, 203, 205, 206
Dolphin, fresh-water, 182
  river, 182
Dormouse, 182
  spiny, 183
Dugong, 183
Dugongidae, 183

Eadie, W. R., 29
Earthworm, 28, 29
Echidna, 179
Economic importance, 6
Edentate, 183
Elephant, 4, 11, 14, 183
  sea, 182
Elephantidae, 183
Elk, 3, 5, 9, 19, 149, 150, 196, 214
  narial cavity, 214
Ellerman, J. R., 179
Emballonuridae, 181
Epipubic bones, 24
Eptesicus, 55, 220
  fuscus, 50, 52, 189, 202, 223
Equidae, 184, 196, 213
Equus caballus, 213
Erethizon, 221
  dorsatum, 139, 140, 192, 212, 225
Erethizontidae, 139, 183, 192, 212
Erinaceidae, 180

Eschrichtidae, 182
Eutamias, 221
    minimus, 94, 193, 207, 224
Eutheria, 22, 26, 180

Faunal, changes, 4
    position, 3
    relationships, 3
Felidae, 84, 182, 192, 203
Felis, 221
    concolor, 157
    domestica, 206
Fish, 61, 69, 70, 83, 133
Fisher, 4, 62, 191, 204
Flying squirrel (*see* Squirrel)
Fox, 182
    cross, 78
    flying, 181
    gray, 79, 192, 205
        mandible, 205
        skull, 197
        teeth, 205
    red, 77, 147, 192, 205
        mandible, 205
        teeth, 205
    silver, 78
Frog, 42, 69, 133
Furipteridae, 181

Galago, 180
Geiger counter, 17
Geomyidae, 106, 182, 194, 209
Geomys, 221
    bursarius, 106, 107, 194, 209, 224
    teeth, 208
Giraffe, 184
Giraffidae, 184
Glaucomys, 91, 221
    sabrinus, 106, 107, 193, 208, 224
    volans, 104, 193, 208, 224
Gliridae, 182
Glossary of terms, 215
Goat, 149, 184, 187, 214
Gopher, 90
    plains pocket, 106, 107, 194, 209
    pocket, 182, 208
Gorilla, 181
Grasshopper, 42
Ground squirrel (*see* Squirrel)

Gulo, 220
    luscus, 156

Habitats, 165
Hamilton, W. J., Jr., 19, 31, 35, 43, 52, 126
Hamster, 182
Hare, 141, 183, 187, 195, 199, 212
    European, 3, 144, 145, 196, 213
    references, 236
    skull, 212
    snowshoe, 5, 19, 85, 142, 143, 195, 213
Hawk, 127
Hedgehog, 180
Heteromyidae, 182
Hippopotamidae, 184
Hippopotamus, 184
Hipposideridae, 181
Home range, 15
    permanent, 16
    references, 228
    seasonal, 16
    semipermanent, 16
Hominidae, 181, 206
Homo, 220
    sapiens, 206
Homoiothermal, 22
Horse, 10, 14, 149, 184, 187, 196, 200, 213
Hutia, 183
Hyaenidae, 182
Hydrochoeridae, 183
Hyena, 182
Hymenoptera, 52
Hyracoidea, 183
Hyrax, 183
Hystricidae, 183
Hystricomorph, 139

Indriidae, 180
Iniidae, 182
Insectivora, 26, 180, 186, 187, 199, 200

Jackson, H. H. T., 35
Jerboa, 183

Kangaroo, 180
Kellogg, R., 102

Kennicott, R., 130
Key, to skins, 186
    to skulls, 196
Kinkajou, 181
Koala, 180
Kogiidae, 182

Lagler, K. F., 70
Lagomorpha, 141, 183, 187, 195,
    199, 212
Lasionycteris, 220
    noctivagans, 48, 49, 190, 202, 223
Lasiurus, 51, 220
    borealis, 53, 54, 55, 190, 202, 223
    cinereus, 55, 190, 202, 223
Lay, D. W., 25
Lemming, southern bog, 120, 121,
    195, 209
    teeth, 208
Lemur, 180
    flying, 181
    slow, 180
    woolly, 180
Lemuridae, 180
Leporidae, 141, 183, 195, 212
Lepus, 221
    americanus, 142, 143, 195, 213,
        225
        americanus, 144
        phaeonotus, 144
    europaeus, 144, 145, 146, 196,
        213, 225
    skull, 212
Lincoln, F. C., 20
Lion, mountain, 157
    sea, 18, 182
Llama, 184
Lophiomyidae, 182
Lorisidae, 180
Lutra, 62, 220
    canadensis, 70, 71, 191, 204, 223
Lynx, 5, 84, 85, 182, 192, 206
    basicranium, 206
Lynx, 221
    canadensis, 84, 85, 192, 206, 224
    rufus, 85, 86, 192, 206, 224

Macropodidae, 180
Macroscelididae, 180

Man, 14, 17, 18, 23, 181, 199, 206
Manatee, 22, 183
Marking mammals, 17
Marmoset, 180
Marmota, 221
    monax, 88, 89, 192, 207, 224
        monax, 90
        rufescens, 90
Marsupialia, 24, 180, 186, 187, 198,
    200
Marsupium, 23
Marten, 4, 11, 60, 61, 191, 204
Martes, 220
    americana, 60, 61, 191, 204, 223
    pennanti, 62, 191, 204, 223
Mastodon, 4, 14
Megadermatidae, 181
Mephitis, 203, 220
    mephitis, 74, 75, 191, 204, 223
        hudsonica, 76
        nigra, 76
Metacone, 12
Metatheria, 23, 180
Mice, 9, 17, 18, 23, 207
Microsorex, 32, 220
    hoyi, 39, 40, 188, 200, 222
        hoyi, 40
        intervectus, 40
        thompsoni, 40
Microtinae, 111, 209
Microtus, 221
    chrotorrhinus, 127, 194, 211, 225
        teeth, 210
        palate, 210
    pennsylvanicus, 124, 125, 194,
        210, 225
        teeth, 210
Miller, G. S., Jr., 102
Millepede, 43
Mink, 68, 69, 133, 181, 191, 204
Mole, 9, 11, 17, 78, 180, 186, 187,
    199, 200
    eastern, 5, 26, 27, 188, 200
    front foot, 187
    golden, 180
    hairytail, 28, 29, 188, 200
    marsupial, 180
    references, 230
    starnose, 30, 31, 187, 200

Mollusk, 43
Molosidae, 181
Mongoose, 182
Monkey, 18, 180
Monodontidae, 182
Monotremata, 22, 23, 179
Moose, 5, 8, 9, 149, 153, 154, 196, 214
  references, 236
Mouse, 16 (*See also* Vole)
  deer, 113, 114, 195
  hamster-like, 182
  house, 3, 7, 135, 195, 212
  jumping, 182, 194, 212
  meadow jumping, 136, 137, 195, 212
  pocket, 182
  prairie deer, 5, 114, 212
  western harvest, 112, 113, 195, 211
  white-footed, 117, 118, 195, 212
  woodland deer, 116, 211
  woodland jumping, 138, 195, 212
Muridae, 133, 182, 207
Mus, 221
  musculus, 135, 195, 212, 225
Musk oxen, 4
Muskrat, 12, 17, 18, 69, 132, 194, 209
Mussel, 133
Mustela, 60, 191, 220
  erminea, 63, 66, 191, 204, 223
  frenata, 64, 65, 191, 204, 223
  rixosa, 66, 67, 191, 205, 223
  vison, 68, 191, 204, 223
    mink, 70
    vison, 70
Mustelidae, 60, 181, 190, 203
Myotis, 49, 50, 52, 220
  keeni, 44, 46, 47, 189, 202, 222
  lucifugus, 44–47, 189, 202, 222
  sodalis, 44–46, 189, 202, 222
  subulatus, 47, 48, 190, 202, 222
Myotis, Indiana, 45, 46, 189, 202
  Keen, 46, 47, 189, 202
  little brown, 44, 45, 189, 202
  small-footed, 47, 48, 190, 202
Myrmecophagidae, 183

Mystacinidae, 181
Myzopodidae, 181

Napaeozapus, 221
  insignis, 138, 195, 212, 225
Narwhal, 182
Natalidae, 181
Neotoma, 209, 221
  magister, 119, 195, 211, 225
Noctilionidae, 181
Notoryctidae, 180
Nycteridae, 181
Nycticeius, 51, 221
  humeralis, 52, 53, 190, 202, 223

Ochotonidae, 183
Octodontidae, 183
Odobaenidae, 182
Odocoileus, 220
  narial cavity, 214
  virginianus, 151, 196, 214, 225
Ondatra, 221
  zibethica, 132, 194, 209, 225
Opossum, 5, 10, 24, 180, 186, 187, 198, 200
  skull, 198
Ornithorhynchidae, 179
Orycteropodidae, 183
Ostenson, B. T., 70
Otariidae, 182
Otter, 8
  river, 5, 12, 70, 71, 191, 204
Ovis, 220
  aries, 214
Owl, 127, 147

Paca, 183
Pacarana, 183
Pangolin, 183
Paracone, 12
Parascalops, 220
  breweri, 28, 29, 188, 200, 222
Peccary, 4, 184
Pedetidae, 183
Pedomys, 221
  ochrogaster, 42, 128, 194, 211, 225
  teeth, 210
Peramelidae, 180

Perissodactyla, 149, 184, 187, 196, 200, 213
Peromyscus, 221
　leucopus, 113, 117, 118, 195, 212, 225
　　zygomatic plate, 211
　maniculatus, 113, 114, 195
　　bairdi, 113, 114, 212, 224
　　gracilis, 113, 116, 211, 224
　　　zygomatic plate, 211
　　maniculatus, 117
　zygomatic plate, 207
Phalangeridae, 180
Phascolomiidae, 180
Pheasant, 78
Phenacomys, 221
　intermedius, 121, 122, 194, 211, 225
　teeth, 210
Phocidae, 182
Pholidota, 183
Phyllostomidae, 181
Physeteridae, 182
Pig, 14, 149, 184, 187, 199, 213
　guinea, 183
Pika, 141, 183
Pinnipedia, 182
Pipistrel, eastern, 49, 50, 190, 202
Pipistrellus, 220
　subflavus, 49, 50, 190, 202, 223
Pitymys, 90, 221
　pinetorum, 130, 131, 194, 210, 225
Platanistidae, 182
Platypus, duck-billed, 179
Polderboer, E. B., 68
Pongidae, 181
Populations, 18
　cycles, 18
　fluctuations, 18
　references, 228
Porcupine, 5, 8, 139, 140, 183, 192, 212
Porpoise, 182
Potamogalidae, 180
Predation, 19
Preparation of specimens, 165
　filling out skin, 172
　formalin, 166

label, 166, 167
measurements, 167
pinning, 175
recording the data, 166
skinning a large mammal, 177
skinning a small mammal, 169
skins and skulls, 166
skull and skeleton, 177
tying label, 175
Primates, 180, 199, 206
Proboscidea, 183
Procaviidae, 183
Procyon, 220
　lotor, 58, 59, 190, 203, 223
Procyonidae, 58, 181, 190, 203
Pronghorn, 184
Protocone, 12
Prototheria, 23, 179
Pteropidae, 181

Rabbit, 10, 14, 17, 18, 61, 78, 141, 183, 187, 195, 199, 212
　references, 236
Raccoon, 8, 58, 59, 181, 190, 203
Rangifer, 220
　caribou, 155, 156, 196, 214, 225
Rat, 23, 207
　bamboo, 182
　blind mole, 183
　cane, 182
　dassie, 183
　hamster-like, 182
　kangaroo, 182
　maned, 182
　mole, 182
　Norway, 3, 7, 134, 135, 195, 212
Rattus, 221
　norvegicus, 134, 135, 195, 212, 225
References, 226
　carnivores, 231
　general works, 226
　hares, 236
　home ranges, 228
　moles, 230
　moose, 236
　populations, 228
　rabbits, 236

References (continued)
  rodents, 232
  shrews, 230
  territories, 228
Reithrodontomys, 186, 221
  megalotis, 112, 113, 195, 211, 224
Reptile, 61
Rhinoceros, 184
Rhinocerotidae, 184
Rhinolophidae, 181
Rhinopomatidae, 181
Rhizomyidae, 182
Ringtail, 181
Rodentia, 87, 182, 187, 192, 199, 206
  references, 232

Saunders, P. B., 39
Scalopus, 220
  aquaticus, 26, 27, 188, 200, 222
  front foot, 187
Sciuridae, 88, 182, 192, 207, 209
Sciurus carolinensis, 100, 101, 193,
        207, 221, 224
    hypophaeus, 102
    leucotis, 102
    pennsylvanicus, 102
  niger, 102, 103, 193, 209, 224
Scott, T. G., 40
Seal, 18, 182
  eared, 182
  hair, 182
Seleviniidae, 183
Sheep, 149, 184, 187, 214
Shrew, 9, 10, 12, 16, 61, 78, 180,
        186, 187, 199, 200
  African water, 180
  Arctic, 35, 36, 188, 201
  jumping, 180
  least, 40, 41, 189, 200
  longtail, 37, 38, 188, 201
  masked, 32, 33, 35, 188, 201
  northern water, 38, 39, 188, 201
  pigmy, 32, 35, 39, 40, 188, 200
  references, 230
  shorttail, 42, 43, 189, 200
  smoky, 34, 188, 201
  southeastern, 36, 37, 188, 201
  tree, 180
Shull, A. F., 43

Simpson, G. G., 179
Sirenia, 183
Skunk, 8, 181, 190
  spotted, 73, 192, 204
  striped, 74, 75, 191, 204
Sloth, 15
  tree, 22, 183
Snail, 70, 83
Solenodon, 180
Solenodontidae, 180
Sorex, 220
  arcticus, 35, 36, 188, 201, 222
  cinereus, 32, 33, 38, 39, 188, 201,
      222
    cinereus, 34
    lesueuri, 34
  dispar, 37, 38, 188, 201, 222
  fumeus, 34, 38, 188, 201, 222
  longirostris, 36, 37, 188, 201, 222
  palustris, 34, 38, 39, 188, 201, 222
  hind foot, 187
Soricidae, 32, 180, 187, 200
Spalacidae, 183
Spilogale, 75, 203, 220
  putorius, 73, 192, 204, 223
Springhaas, 183
Squirrel, 11, 18, 61, 78, 88, 182, 192,
      207
  black, 100
  eastern fox, 102, 103, 193, 209
  eastern gray, 100, 101, 193, 207
  flying, 8
    zygomatic arch, 208
  fox, 5
  Franklin ground, 93, 193, 207
  gray, 5
  ground, zygomatic arch, 208
  northern flying, 106, 107, 193, 208
  red, 17, 98, 99, 193, 207, 209
  southern flying, 104, 193, 208
  spinytail, 182
  striped ground, 5
  thirteen-lined ground, 90, 91, 193,
      208
  tree, 8, 17
Suidae, 184, 213
Sus, 220
  scrofa, 213
Svihla, A., 124

Sylvilagus, 221
  floridanus, 145, 146, 196, 213, 225
    skull, 212
  transitionalis, 146, 148, 196, 213,
    225
    skull, 212
Synaptomys, 221
  cooperi, 120, 121, 195, 209, 225
  teeth, 208

Tachyglossidae, 179
Talpidae, 26, 180, 187, 200
Tamias, 221
  striatus, 96, 97, 193, 209, 224
    griseus, 98
    lysteri, 98
    peninsulae, 98
    rufescens, 98
Tamiasciurus, 221
  hudsonicus, 98, 99, 193, 207, 209,
    224
    hudsonicus, 100
    loquax, 100
    minnesota, 100
    regalis, 100
Tapir, 14, 184
Tapiridae, 184
Tarsier, 180
Tarsiidae, 180
Taxidea, 220
  taxus, 71, 72, 191, 204, 223
Tayassuidae, 184
Teeth, bat, 203
  brachy-lophodont, 14
  brachy-selenodont, 14
  bunodont, 14
  buno-lophodont, 14
  buno-selenodont, 14
  fox, 205
  heterodont, 23
  hypso-lophodont, 14
  lophodont, 14
  myrmecophagous, 15
  sectorial, 12
  selenodont, 14
  shrew, 201
  tritubercular, 12
  tuberculo-sectorial, 12
Tenrec, 180

Tenrecidae, 180
Territoriality, 17
Territory, 15
  references, 228
Theria, 23, 180
Thryonomyidae, 182
Thyropteridae, 181
Tragulidae, 184
Trichechidae, 183
Tubulidentata, 183
Tuco tuco, 183
Tularemia, 147
Tupaiidae, 180
Turtle, 133

Unicuspid, 201
Urocyon, 78, 220
  cinereoargenteus, 79, 192, 205,
    223
Ursidae, 56, 181, 190, 203
Ursus, 220
  americanus, 57, 190, 203, 223

Vanished species, 156
Vertebrae, 22
Vespertilionidae, 44, 181, 189, 201
Viscacha, 183
Viverridae, 182
Viviparity, 22
Vole, 19
  boreal redback, 123, 194, 209
  heather, 121, 122, 194, 211
  meadow, 7, 9, 19, 124, 125, 194,
    210
  pine, 90, 120, 130, 131, 194, 210
  prairie, 42, 128, 129, 194, 211
  yellownose, 127, 194, 211
Vulpes, 220
  fulva, 77, 192, 205, 223

Walrus, 182
Weasel, 12, 181, 190, 203
  least, 66, 67, 191, 205
  longtail, 65, 191, 204
  shorttail, 63, 191, 204
Whale, 9, 12
  baleen, 182
  beaked, 182
  finback, 182

Whale (*continued*)
  gray, 182
  humpback, 182
  pigmy sperm, 182
  sperm, 182
  white, 182
Wolf, 7, 16
  gray, 5, 82, 83, 192, 205
  skull, 198
Wolverine, 5, 156
Wombat, 180
Wood, N. A., 59
Woodchuck, 5, 88, 89, 192, 207

Woodrat, eastern, 119, 195, 211

Xenarthra, 183

Zapodidae, 136, 182, 194, 212
Zapus, 221
  hudsonius, 136, 137, 195, 212, 225
    americanus, 138
    breviceps, 138
    hudsonius, 138
    ontarioensis, 138
  zygomatic arch, 207
Ziphiidae, 182